DIGITAL TRANSFORMATION AND SOCIETY

Digital Transformation: Accelerating Organizational Intelligence

Print ISSN: 2811-0552
Online ISSN: 2811-0560

Series Editor: Jay Liebowitz *(Rollins College, USA)*

According to a report released by Veritis in 2021 "the global digital transformation market size is anticipated to reach USD 1009.8 billion by 2025 from USD 469.8 billion in 2020. The demand for digital transformation services is expected to rise at a Compound Annual Growth Rate (CAGR) of around 16.5% over the forecast period from 2021 to 2025. The growing adoption of digital technologies, including Artificial Intelligence (AI), cloud computing, big data, the Internet of Things (IoT), and Machine Learning (ML), is driving the growth of the digital transformation market." To be competitive in today's fast-changing marketplace, organizations need to apply the "alphabet" of digital transformation.

The focus of the book series is unique and will cover the various perspectives on organizational digital transformation, namely business & management, technology, legal and ethics, and social aspects.

Published:

More information on this series can be found at https://www.worldscientific.com/series/dtaoi

Digital Transformation
Accelerating Organizational Intelligence
– Volume 7

DIGITAL TRANSFORMATION AND SOCIETY

Edited by

Jay Liebowitz
Rollins College, USA

World Scientific

NEW JERSEY · LONDON · SINGAPORE · BEIJING · SHANGHAI · HONG KONG · TAIPEI · CHENNAI · TOKYO

Published by

World Scientific Publishing Co. Pte. Ltd.

5 Toh Tuck Link, Singapore 596224

USA office: 27 Warren Street, Suite 401-402, Hackensack, NJ 07601

UK office: 57 Shelton Street, Covent Garden, London WC2H 9HE

Library of Congress Cataloging-in-Publication Data

Names: Liebowitz, Jay, 1957– editor.
Title: Digital transformation and society / editor, Jay Liebowitz, Rollins College, USA.
Description: New Jersey : World Scientific, [2025] | Series: Digital transformation:
    accelerating organizational intelligence, 2811-0552 ; volume 7 |
    Includes bibliographical references and index.
Identifiers: LCCN 2024023922 | ISBN 9789811295133 (hardcover) |
    ISBN 9789811295140 (ebook) | ISBN 9789811295157 (ebook other)
Subjects: LCSH: Information society. | Technological innovations--Social aspects. |
    Technological innovations--Economic aspects.
Classification: LCC HM851 .D5447 2025 | DDC 303.48/33--dc23/eng/20240624
LC record available at https://lccn.loc.gov/2024023922

British Library Cataloguing-in-Publication Data
A catalogue record for this book is available from the British Library.

For any available supplementary material, please visit
https://www.worldscientific.com/worldscibooks/10.1142/13899#t=suppl

Desk Editors: Kannan Krishnan/Catherine Domingo Ong

Typeset by Stallion Press
Email: enquiries@stallionpress.com

Preface

Digital transformation should be pervasive throughout organizations and society in general. People often say that Rx=Dx, that is, the right prescription is digital transformation. It has become such a "hot topic" that a new journal was created in 2022 titled *Digital Transformation and Society.* Professor Robin Qiu (Penn State), the Editor-in-Chief of this new journal, describes the importance of this area in his inaugural Editorial *Embracing the Imperative Digital Transformation*[1]: "Today, it is well-recognized that digital transformation has fundamentally changed how organizations and businesses operate and deliver value to end users and how we live, learn, and socialize" (Vol. 1, No. 1, 2022, p. 1).

Digital transformation has a number of definitions, but it really deals with the integration of technology, people, process, culture, and leadership to provide a foundational change in how an organization delivers value to its customers (see Pratt and Boulton's article in *CIO* magazine, August 9, 2023).[2] One of the first books in my *Digital Transformation: Accelerating Organizational Intelligence* (World Scientific Publishing) book series is edited by Dr. Frank Granito/Institute for Digital Transformation and is titled *Digital Transformation Demystified.*[3] As mentioned in their book, along with many industry reports, there is a relatively high failure rate of

---

[1] https://www.emerald.com/insight/content/doi/10.1108/DTS-09-2022-019/full/pdf.

[2] https://www.cio.com/article/230425/what-is-digital-transformation-a-necessary-disruption.html.

[3] https://www.institutefordigitaltransformation.org/digital-transformation-demystified/#about.

digital transformation efforts for a variety of reasons. One key reason is that many digital transformation efforts are large-scale efforts that are very challenging in their scope and purpose. Also, if we move beyond the business or organization as the unit of study or context, it becomes even more arduous if we are looking at a community or society in general. Thus, the launch of the *Digital Transformation and Society* journal, along with this new book that you will hopefully find engaging and insightful, makes perfect sense for helping organizations, communities, nations, and society to advance.[4]

I would like to thank all the contributors to this book who provided different valuable insights on digital transformation as related to a number of areas affecting society. I would also like to thank World Scientific Publishing for their assistance in making this book possible. My students and colleagues allow me to continually look at the "bleeding edge" and explore, in this case, how digital transformation should become part of the fabric of organizations, communities, and societies.

Certainly, I would be amiss if I didn't mention my family that lets me sneak away at times to do "book patrol".

I hope this book energizes you a bit to explore how digital transformation can play a part in your life.

Enjoy!

Jay Liebowitz
Winter Park, Florida

---

[4] For those interested in the Alphabet of Digital Transformation, I point you to two of my articles at https://pubsonline.informs.org/do/10.1287/LYTX.2020.04.02/full/ and https://pubsonline.informs.org/do/10.1287/LYTX.2020.05.01/full/.

About the Editor

Jay Liebowitz is the Professor of Business Innovation and Industry Transformation and Director of a new AI-EDGE Center in the Crummer Graduate School of Business at Rollins College, as of August 2024. He has recently served as the inaugural Executive-in-Residence for Public Service at Columbia University's Data Science Institute. He was previously a Visiting Professor at the Stillman School of Business and the MS-Business Analytics Capstone and Co-Program Director (External Relations) at Seton Hall University. He previously served as the Distinguished Chair of Applied Business and Finance at Harrisburg University of Science and Technology. Before HU, he was the Orkand Endowed Chair of Management and Technology in the Graduate School at the University of Maryland University College (UMUC). He served as a Full Professor in the Carey Business School at Johns Hopkins University. He was ranked one of the top 10 knowledge management researchers/practitioners out of 11,000 worldwide and was ranked #2 in KM Strategy worldwide according to the January 2010 *Journal of Knowledge Management.* At Johns Hopkins University, he was the founding Program Director for the Graduate Certificate in Competitive Intelligence and the Capstone Director of the MS-Information and

Telecommunications Systems for Business Program, where he engaged over 30 organizations in industry, government, and not-for-profits in capstone projects.

Prior to joining Hopkins, Dr. Liebowitz was the first Knowledge Management Officer at NASA Goddard Space Flight Center. Before NASA, Dr. Liebowitz was the Robert W. Deutsch Distinguished Professor of Information Systems at the University of Maryland-Baltimore County, Professor of Management Science at George Washington University, and Chair of Artificial Intelligence at the U.S. Army War College.

Dr. Liebowitz is the Founding Editor-in-Chief of *Expert Systems With Applications: An International Journal* (published by Elsevier; ranked as a top-tier journal; Thomson Impact Factor from June 2021 is 8.665). He is a Fulbright Scholar, IEEE-USA Federal Communications Commission Executive Fellow, and Computer Educator of the Year (International Association for Computer Information Systems). He has published over 45 books and a myriad of journal articles on knowledge management, analytics, financial literacy, intelligent systems, and IT management. Dr. Liebowitz served as the Editor-in-Chief of *Procedia Computer Science* (Elsevier). He is also the Series Book Editor of the *Data Analytics Applications* book series (Taylor & Francis), as well as the Series Book Editor of the new *Digital Transformation: Accelerating Organizational Intelligence* book series (World Scientific Publishing). In October 2011, the International Association for Computer Information Systems named the "Jay Liebowitz Outstanding Student Research Award" for the best student research paper at the IACIS Annual Conference. Dr. Liebowitz was the Fulbright Visiting Research Chair in Business at Queen's University for the Summer 2017 and a Fulbright Specialist at Dalarna University in Sweden in May 2019. He is in the top 2% of the top scientists in the world, according to a 2019 Stanford Study. As of 2021, he is the Visiting Distinguished Professor at the International School for Social and Business Studies in Slovenia. His recent books are *Data Analytics and AI* (Taylor & Francis, 2021), *The Business of Pandemics: The COVID-19 Story* (Taylor & Francis, 2021), *A Research Agenda for Knowledge Management and Analytics* (Elgar Publishers, 2021), *Online Learning Analytics* (Taylor & Francis, 2022), *Digital Transformation for the University of the Future* (World Scientific, 2022), *Cryptocurrency Concepts, Technology, and Applications* (Taylor & Francis, April 2023),

Pivoting Government Through Digital Transformation (Taylor & Francis, 2024), and *Developing the Intuitive Executive: Using Analytics and Intuition for Success* (Taylor & Francis, 2024). His forthcoming book, *Regulating Hate Speech Created by Generative AI,* will be published by Taylor & Francis in the Fall 2024. He has lectured and consulted worldwide.

List of Contributors

Suchit Ahuja
John Molson School of Business, Concordia University, Montreal, Quebec, Canada

Kathryn Brohman
Queens's University, Kingston, ON, Canada

Fareeda Cassumbhoy
Pico Group, Hong Kong

Soumitra Chowdhury
Linnaeus University, Växjö, Sweden

Robert M. Davison
City University of Hong Kong, Kowloon Tong, Hong Kong

David Eisenberg
Montclair State University, Montclair, New Jersey, USA

G. Scott Erickson
Ithaca College, Ithaca, New York, USA

Joel Flink
Uppsala University, Uppsala, Sweden

Andrew Herd
European Space Agency, Noordwijk, The Netherlands

Yayoi Hirose
Information Networking for Innovation and Design, Toyo University, Japan

Adriana Veríssimo Karam Koleski
Programa de Pós-Graduação em Engenharia, Gestão e Mídia do Conhecimento (EGC) – Universidade Federal de Santa Catarina (UFSC), Florianópolis, Brazil

Kemal Gökhan Nalbant
Department of Software Engineering, Faculty of Engineering and Architecture, Istanbul Beykent University, Istanbul, Türkiye

Roberto C. S. Pacheco
Programa de Pós-Graduação em Engenharia, Gestão e Mídia do Conhecimento (EGC) — Universidade Federal de Santa Catarina (UFSC), Florianópolis, Brazil

John Peng
Private Consultant and Business Advisor, Beijing, China

Larissa Mariany Freiberger Pereira
Programa de Pós-Graduação em Engenharia, Gestão e Mídia do Conhecimento (EGC) — Universidade Federal de Santa Catarina (UFSC), Florianópolis, Brazil

Helen N. Rothberg
Marist College, Poughkeepsie, New York, USA

Arman Sadreddin
John Molson School of Business, Concordia University, Montreal, Quebec, Canada

Vida Skudiene
ISM University of Management and Economics, Vilnius, Lithuania

Eric W. Stein
Penn State Great Valley, Malvern, Pennsylvania, USA

Louie H. M. Wong
Nagoya University of Commerce and Business, Nisshin, Japan

Eigirdas Zemaitis
ISM University of Management and Economics, Vilnius, Lithuania

Contents

Chapter 1

Digital Transformations and Innovation Management: A Review and Research Agenda

Vida Skudiene[*,†] **and Eigirdas Zemaitis**[‡]

ISM University of Management and Economics, Vilnius, Lithuania

[†]*vida.skudiene@ism.lt*

[‡]*eigzem@ism.lt*

1. Introduction

It is widely accepted that digitalization has enabled a notable transformation and led to the emergence of new competitive dynamics changing the relationships' nature among the innovation ecosystem players (Carayannis & Campel, 2009). Innovations driven by digital technologies are changing and disrupting traditional markets (Bogers *et al.*, 2022) consequently affecting the way companies operate. In the rapidly changing business and technology landscape, the integration of digital transformations with innovation management has become a crucial driver of success for organizations in various industries (Cennamo *et al.*, 2020). Scholastic research confirmed that when companies embrace digital transformations, they have the potential to enhance their capabilities for innovation (Solberg *et al.*, 2020; Cockburn *et al.*, 2018; Fountaine *et al.*, 2019),

[*]Corresponding author.

including organizational processes, business models, and, on a macro level, cross-functional and cross-industrial integration.

However, despite the evident value of digitalization, the World Economic Forum's findings reveal that only 21% of organizations have completed their transformation journey. An overwhelming 87% believe that digitalization will disrupt their business, while only 44% see digital transformation as having the potential to positively impact innovation management (Appio *et al.*, 2021). This highlights the complexity of the transition and challenges the efforts of managers across various industries to digitalize innovation management systems (Benner & Waldfogel, 2020; Correani *et al.*, 2020).

The growing interest and ongoing debates about Digital Transformation (DT) have, in turn, driven scholars to explore how DT affects innovation management. Still, only since 2017, the research into digital transformation impact on innovation management has started to grow exponentially. Interest about digital transformation role in shaping innovation processes has, in turn, driven scholars to explore this phenomenon. Despite the increasing number of studies, our understanding of innovation management and digital transformation interplay remains limited, lacking a clear perspective and an embarrassing framework to direct future research (Bogers *et al.*, 2022). One of the central challenges in creating such a framework is the conceptual vagueness surrounding the key constructs that would underpin it. Consequently, various constructs have been used, sometimes interchangeably, to describe different aspects of the relationship between digital technology development and innovation. This has led to confusion and, as recently pointed out, an inconclusive debate about the impact of digital transformation on innovation management (Appio *et al.*, 2021).

The purpose of this chapter is to provide a comprehensive review of recent research trends on digital transformation and innovation management intersection that would allow structuring the research in the field. The proposed review employs the multilevel approach which includes the three clusters of DT and innovation management relationship research. The first cluster represents the studies that are not restricted to the boundaries of a specific industry or company and investigates a holistic perspective of innovation ecosystem (Hanelt *et al.*, 2021). The second cluster embraces the research into company-level issues related to DT and innovation management processes and capabilities. The third cluster refers to the studies analyzing DT and innovation interplay at individual level.

This chapter also outlines a future research agenda to guide scholars and practitioners in navigating this dynamic field.

2. Digital Transformation and Innovation: Holistic Perspective

Innovation management studies generally associate digital technologies and digital transformation with new possibilities for innovation development. In this line, innovation within digital transformation context research can be within organizations, across companies' networks, and at innovation ecosystem level. Scholars not only look to organizational innovation and digitalization interplay restricting to the boundaries of specific firms but also highlight a holistic digital transformation capacity of innovation ecosystems. The latter approach considers the examination of the phenomenon as a network of heterogeneous actors and their collaboration (Jacobides *et al.*, 2018; Leten *et al.*, 2013; Steenkamp, 2019; Tores-Loredo *et al.*, 2022; Carayannis *et al.*, 2018; Fidanoski *et al.*, 2022; Hillibong *et al.*, 2021; Isckia *et al.*, 2018; Chae, 2019) or how digital transformation impacts innovation governance policy (Adner & Zemsky, 2005; Eisenmann *et al.*, 2006; Xu *et al.*, 2023; Guellec & Paunov, 2018). The following discussion relates to the aforementioned two areas of research.

2.1. *Holistic Collaboration Perspective*

Research has emphasized the importance of organizations collaborating with external partners, including government, industry, university, customers, suppliers, competitors, and society to create innovation ecosystems (Jacobides *et al.*, 2018) by exploring how the systems facilitate the exchange of knowledge and help develop innovations. Studies in this field also investigate how the collaborative arrangements between the players affect their abilities to co-innovate (Leten *et al.*, 2013). The researchers aimed to highlight the vital role of Intellectual Property model to manage innovation ecosystem, that is, how the IP model may be beneficial for the successful functioning of innovation ecosystem. The study confirmed that a virtual innovation ecosystem enables the partners to benefit from joint research. Future research, according to the authors, may explore the classification of ecosystems taking into consideration different governance structures.

The triple/quadruple/quintuple helix innovation models have been developed to illustrate the necessity of interdisciplinary collaboration and knowledge exchange among the actors of the ecosystem (Steenkamp, 2019; Tores-Loredo *et al.*, 2022; Carayannis *et al.*, 2018). Tores-Loredo *et al.* (2022) explored the issues of innovation accelerators' integration in the interrelations among the actors of the quadruple helix for digital transformation. Regarding the helix spiral models' studies, scholars take a holistic perspective explaining the phenomenon of collaboration between different system participants who apply digital transformation tools to foster efficient innovation policies (Fidanoski *et al.*, 2022).

The research of Hillibong *et al.* (2021) provides more information about innovation development using platform ecosystems elaborating on the dynamic nature of the digital environment quality. The findings of the research demonstrate that ecosystem actors' activities must mitigate glitches and obsolescence in order to maintain integrity.

The digital innovation and platform-based ecosystems' framework developed by Isckia *et al.* (2018) focuses on the platform owner's capability to manage the two subsystems to support interrelationships among the players (individuals, organizations, communities, etc.). Chae (2019) in a similar line developed a framework for studying the digital innovation ecosystem. The developed framework reflects the use of digital data as well as evolutionary community detection examination for an empirical analysis, using big data ecosystem of the digital innovation landscape. The findings of the study reveal the range of the components including organizations, technologies, applications, infrastructures, knowledge, and applications that have developed in the big data ecosystem. The main contribution of the research is related to the evolution of digital innovation manifested in the two mechanisms: variation and selective retention.

To sum up, the macroeconomic expansion of the digital transformation, commonly referred to as the revolution, signifies the emergence of a novel digital economy. Within this digital economy, the transformation of critical stakeholders, including the government, industry, academia, civil society, and natural environment, is evaluated based on their capacity to achieve and exceed a new set of challenging performance standards. The lack of research into the development of innovation ecosystems enabled by digital transformation indicates that this phenomenon is still in the emerging phase.

2.2. *Holistic Governance Perspective*

Another cluster of studies has explored different governance models within innovation ecosystems, including hierarchical, modular, and platform-centric structures, and their impact on innovation outcomes (Adner & Zemsky, 2005; Eisenmann *et al.*, 2006).

According to these studies, the innovation policy system for the governance of digital innovation activities should be considered as digital transformation and market expansion output (Xu *et al.*, 2023). The digital transformation, as researchers claim, has shifted the focus of digital innovation governance policy research from controlling negative impact policies to the ones that expand positive impacts on society. The digital transformation, based on Guellec and Paunov (2018) research findings, has brought changes in the economics of information and knowledge, impacting innovation dynamics and requiring changes in innovation policies.

It is evident that digital transformation created the need for innovation policies to address data access issues, promote open science and data sharing, and encourage collaboration among innovators. Consequently, there is a growing awareness of the significance of policies and regulations guaranteeing data accessibility by this accelerating the need for the scholastic research on policy governance frameworks reflecting a digital transformation era of technology socialization (Xu *et al.*, 2023).

The research into a holistic digital transformation capacity of innovation ecosystems shows the recent increase of studies in the fields of policy governance into innovation and digital transformation processes including digital innovation exchanges and collaboration. The key holistic dimensions for promoting digital transformation and innovation proposed by scholars are focused on the development of research into innovative big data governance. Meanwhile digital platforms and ecosystem research have strong potential for development.

3. Digital Transformation and Innovation: Organizational Perspective

Digital transformation symbolizes the transformational implications of digital technologies for companies, that is, how companies may need to transform their capabilities, processes, products, and business models to innovate, embrace the digital transformation context, and successfully function in the market. According to Skare *et al.* (2023), digital transformation is a process that profoundly affects various aspects of business activities, including access to finance, competition, input costs, labor shortages, and regulatory issues. Recent research in digital transformation and innovation has tried to unpack this revolution by conducting the studies in more specific topics. A stream of studies is devoted to the exploration of digital transformation impact on different organizational areas, such as new business models (Müller & Hundahl, 2018; Bhatti *et al.*, 2021; Haaker *et al.*, 2021; Ciasullo & Lim, 2022), new customer behaviors (Wang, 2021; Erevelles *et al.*, 2016; Rialti *et al.*, 2019; Jain *et al.*, 2021; Kamboj & Gupta, 2018; Yi Lo *et al.*, 2021; Chen *et al.*, 2020; Mazzucchelli *et al.*, 2021; Pera *et al.*, 2021), and digital transformation effects on performance (Ardito *et al.*, 2021; Siachou *et al.*, 2021; Salvi *et al.*, 2021; Cherbib *et al.*, 2021; Goglio *et al.*, 2022; Li *et al.*, 2023; Zhang *et al.*, 2023). The following discussion relates to the aforementioned three areas of research.

3.1. *New Business Models*

The range of research addresses the emergence of new business models and the necessity to pursue present business models' innovations. Bhatti *et al.* (2021) in their research on the antecedents and consequences of business model innovation in the IT sector explore the organizational flexibility (agility), cognitive abilities of the leaders (mindfulness), and dynamic capabilities (knowledge absorption) as factors that may foster company performance through intermediary role of innovation of business models. The main contribution of the scholars is the analysis of business model innovations' improvement possibilities in the IT sector.

In line with IT sector research, the study conducted by Müller and Hundahl (2018) shed light on IT-driven business model innovation by examining 343 Danish companies experience in using IT to innovate their business. The authors present the systematic review of the literature using Business Model Canvas aiming to find answer how IT drives business model innovation and identify the three innovation sources: customers, infrastructures, and supply chains. The main contribution of the research is the identification of primary sources of innovation. The authors suggest that firms need to evaluate IT building blocks when implementing

IT-driven business model innovation. Future research perspectives refer to the investigation of IT-driven model innovations across different company types and the constituent building blogs (customers, infrastructures, and supply chains) of relationships.

The context of emerging markets is challenging for the companies particularly when developing new business models. Several recent studies on business model innovation aim to investigate Internet-of-Things (IoT) applications for business model innovation. For example, Haaker *et al.* (2021) were interested in what vital part IoT technologies play to empower the remote management of performance and facilitate innovations in service business models. The researchers conducted a novel application of morphological analysis and proposed a generic business model for IoT applications in emerging markets.

Ciasullo and Lim (2022) in their study claim that digital transformation has advanced the development of business model innovations and highlight the beneficial role that play new technologies adoption allowing companies to succeed in a disruptive and ambiguous market. The authors also propose questions for the future investigation of the capabilities that are required to successfully embrace digitalization and business model innovation, as well as the antecedents, and consequences of business model innovations leading to growth in emerging markets.

3.2. *New Customer Behaviors*

Digital technology has changed the nature of innovation management by offering platforms for interconnectedness with digital technologies and social participants of the market (Wang, 2021). The evolving digital landscape has changed the role of customers and their relationship with companies due to information availability and greater transparency. Jain *et al.* (2021) in their study on co-creation, hyper-personalization, digital clienteling, and transformation examine the changed customer behavior and update the technology-based service adoption model. More specifically, the study focuses on customer innovativeness, customer involvement, and willingness to co-create impact on customer intention to adopt co-creatively developed services. This research provides the lacking information on how digital technology enables customers to engage into innovative service development. This study offers a comprehensive framework of customer co-creative service innovation with the digital transformation and extends service-dominant logic (Vargo & Lusch, 2010) of service innovation by applying technology supported communication.

The emergence of Big Data Analytics (BDA) transformed the way companies function and innovate. The studies on Big Data analytics and customer involvement into co-innovation of services and products (Erevelles *et al.*, 2016; Rialti *et al.*, 2019) have proven that organizations need to re-organize their resources to cope with new problems, exploit opportunities, and benefit from them. Researchers have noted that BDA capability can help companies in their pursuit of ambidexterity, that is, exploitative and explorative innovation development.

Kamboj and Gupta's (2018) research shed light on customer involvement in service innovation and co-creation in the hotel industry. The findings offer a guide to managers about the technology adoption value in customer involvement in the innovation development of the services. In the same line, Yi Lo *et al.*'s (2021) study explores digital service platform adoption to involve customers in the enhancement of perceived benefits via customers' involvement in the evaluation of APP platforms.

The phenomenon of customers' co-innovation and co-creation of value has been investigated by many researchers, however recently a lot of attention has been paid on the digital transformation context role and customer involvement in the innovation process. For example, Chen *et al.* (2020) investigated the adoption of cognitive computing technology to employ the unstructured data from users for co-innovation. Based on the developed dynamic capabilities and complexity theory framework, researchers conceptualize the co-innovation process, divide it into the three stages (idea generation, idea integration, and idea evaluation), and complement them by cognitive computing methodologies and technologies. The study expands marketing scholars and managers' understanding how unstructured data may be used to enhance the co-innovation process by engaging customers.

These days, substantial number of companies are engaging customers in new product and new services development via social media platforms. Consequently, researchers are mainly exploring what motivates customers to participate in co-innovation process. For example, Mazzucchelli *et al.* (2021) in their research investigated the antecedents of success, their interrelationship, and their role in favoring customer behavior.

A distinctive study by Pera *et al.* (2021) focuses on the reasons why customers stop cooperating with companies drawing on customers as the source of innovation and investigates why co-creation occurs and why online game communities stop contributing looking into individual incentives to innovate. The findings demonstrate that customer involvement in the innovation process increases up to a certain level and that incentives to contribute to innovation decrease as the competition in the crowd becomes more intensive. The researchers identify the main factors that demotivate customers to co-innovate, such as lack of support, planned obsolescence, fierce competition, content appropriation, stealing, toxic behavior, and exploitation.

3.3. *Digital Transformation Effects on Performance*

Several studies have tried to analyze the digital transformation effect on business innovation performance. For example, Ardito *et al.*'s (2021) paper presents one of the first efforts to explore strategic commitments toward digitalization and environmental sustainability as innovation performance antecedents. The innovation performance is measured via product and process perspectives by assessing the impact of digital and environmental factors. The findings confirmed a positive effect of digital and environmental aspects on both product and process innovativeness. The study advances the literature by relating innovation performance and strategic perspective focusing on SME's context.

An interesting study presented by Siachou *et al.* (2021) explores how companies might be transformed digitally. The scholars also explore the moderating effect of absorptive capacity and strategic interdependence. The proposed conceptual model integrates the absorptive capacity and strategic interdependence of digital transformation claiming that the link between digital transformation and alliance knowledge is essential however not an absolute condition in conventional organizations. The authors introduced new digital transformation antecedents and confirmed that conventional organizations can digitally transform by enhancing their learning potential.

In this vein, Salvi *et al.* (2021) also focus on the company's disclosure of digital transformation knowledge as vitally important for investors' decision-making. The authors suggest that online information of digitalization may positively increase company value and may be an important indicator for investors. The confirmed significant positive relationship between company value and information about digitalization provided on the company's website has proven that information about digitalization is vital for companies to enhance their value. The authors have demonstrated the importance of corporate websites' management and disclosure of company's digitalization by conducting a survey with 114 international firms.

Another study by Cherbib *et al.* (2021) focuses on digital technologies and learning within asymmetric alliances. Moreover, the scholars are investigating the role of collaboration between partners. The study offers insights into digital technologies and learning dynamic relationships within asymmetric alliances between partners from the UK, USA, Sweden, France, and Tunisia operating in different sectors. The research has proven that asymmetric alliances' partners can employ digital technologies to develop their learning abilities even in dynamic and rather sophisticated environments.

Similarly, Goglio *et al.* (2022) studied the digital transformation effect on innovation and productivity within South African micro and small companies. The results based on 711 manufacturing MSEs show that digital communication technologies positively impact company's innovation, and innovation conditional on the use of digital communication technologies has a positive effect on labor productivity in a developing country context.

Likewise, Li *et al.* (2023) explored the digital innovation's effect on innovation performance and proposed a game model for the two companies that invest in digital transformation. The scholars analyze the enterprise digitalization level index with Python tools for text analysis. According to the findings, a company's digitalization and regional digital industry innovation level can promote the company's innovation.

Zhang *et al.* (2023) examined the digital transformation impact on corporate performance with the mediating effect of business model innovation and moderating effect of innovation capability in manufacturing. The empirical research based on 255 Chinese manufacturing companies demonstrates that explorative and exploitative digital transformation positively affects company's performance. Additionally, the results showed the moderating role of innovation capability in the relationship between explorative and exploitative digital transformations and business model innovation. The mediating effect of business model innovation has been confirmed between explorative and exploitative digital transformations and corporate performance. The scholars develop a conceptual framework on the basis of ambidexterity theory using the two stages of digital transformation: exploitative and explorative.

The recent research tendencies into digital transformation and innovation management at organizational level perspective indicate the increase in scholars' interest in digital transformation effect on organizations' innovation performance. There is a consensus that increased attention to digital transformation aspects could lead to enhanced innovation performance. The studies focused on new customer behaviors that occurred due to digital transformation mainly exploring what motivates customers to participate in the co-innovation process either for new products or new services development via social media platforms.

Scholars who study business model innovation dynamics and conditions agree that digital transformation has advanced the development of business model innovations and highlight the beneficial role that new technologies' adoption plays allowing companies to succeed in a disruptive and ambiguous market.

4. Digital Transformation and Innovation Management: Individual-Level Perspective

In the context of the service-focused and knowledge-oriented economy, employees who are motivated to innovate by adopting digital transformations are of paramount importance (Oeij *et al.*, 2019; Corvello *et al.*, 2023). Based on the reviewed literature, studies at the individual level are viewed from three perspectives: how digital transformations shape human resource management seeking to motivate employees to get involved in digital innovation processes (Bansal *et al.*, 2023; DiRomualdo *et al.*, 2018; Fenech *et al.*, 2019), how employees engage and respond to digital innovations (Zhang *et al.*, 2021; Bäckström *et al.*, 2019; Edelman, 2020), and what are the characteristics of people and teams involved in digital innovation processes (Firk *et al.*, 2021; Henver & Gregor, 2022; Muler *et al.*, 2019; Steinhauser, 2021; Corvello *et al.*, 2023; Hanelt *et al.*, 2021). The following discussion relates to the aforementioned three areas of research.

4.1. *Human Resource DT and Innovation Management*

In general, researchers agree that human resource management (HRM) plays a vital role in motivating and helping employees to use digital tools to enhance their innovation capabilities (DiRomualdo *et al.*, 2018).

Prior studies either examine technologies referring to HR disruptions and HR digitalization (Minbaeva, 2021; Strohmeier, 2020), or HR transformation (Sankar, 2021). Answering the call for a conceptualized approach to this phenomenon, Bansal *et al.* (2023) proposed an integrated human resource digital transformation (HRDT) construct. Drawing on the interview data with 20 senior HR specialists working in multinational companies, the authors created a multidimensional HRDT framework integrating digital and individual factors. The study expands the HRDT dynamic capabilities perspective and proposes that companies "must constantly upgrade organizational capabilities, manifested in the innovation capability with enablers such as — digital infrastructure, architecture, and individual capability and creativity" (p. 1).

According to Bresciani *et al.*'s (2021) study, HRM is suffering from inevitable disruptions due to the necessity to adopt technological innovations and work designs to compete in the market. The scholars claim that the digitalization of workplaces causes a paradigm shift that demands leadership to change for sustainable corporate performance. Research also suggests that if organizations seek to enhance their innovation capabilities, they should value the contribution of human resources and accordingly harmonize HRM practices and company's strategy to enhance the learning capability leading to innovation.

Another recent study by Zhang and Chen (2023) explores the drivers, directions, and impacts of HRM transformation phenomenon and proposes the five factors (internal customer digital needs, industry digital innovation, competitor challenges, digital innovation governance, and digital era needs) that cause HRM digital transformation. The study points out that digital human resource management can offer creative initiatives and novel practices that can enhance innovation management in the organization.

Demir *et al.* (2023) in their survey examine the relationship between innovation, digital transformation, and human resources planning in hotels. The authors investigate the impact of digital transformation on innovations and HR planning additionally testing the mediating impact of innovation on the digital transformation and HR planning relationship. The collected data analysis from 462 human resources (HR) managers at four- and five-star hotels in Turkey indicated the DT impacts on innovations and HR planning.

Ulatowska *et al.* (2023) analyzed the digital innovations introduced in the HRM field in the modern business service sector organizations in

Finland and Poland. The findings provide comprehensive information on the implementation of digital innovations by HRM departments and illuminate the significance of technological development for HRM departments in the digital transformation era.

In summary, HRM digitalization-innovation management link research addresses diverse perspectives of the phenomenon paying more attention to human resource management digitalization rather than its impact on innovation management. The studies in general indicate human resource digitalization and innovation management interdependence importance. Further research is needed to highlight how digital transformation enables human resource specialists to enhance employees' motivation and engagement in innovation processes.

4.2. *Employee-Driven Innovation and Digital Transformation*

In the 58 publications' systematic review, Opland *et al.* (2022) claimed that employee-driven digital innovation research may be divided into two main streams: focused (1) "on the outcome of employee-driven digital innovation" and (2) "on the use of digital tools to support employee-driven innovation" (p. 255). The review shows that the research on the topic has taken so far the two main perspectives: how employee-driven innovations supported digital products', processes', and products' development and how employees employed digital tools to support innovation processes. According to the study findings, this area of research is still in maturing phase and more research is necessary to further develop greater comprehension of the phenomenon as well as create better explanatory frameworks.

An interesting study by Bäckström and Lindberg (2019) demonstrates that digitally enhanced employee-driven innovation using web-based digital platform emphasizes client satisfaction rather than employee engagement and discourages employees from utilizing the digital platform and engagement in the innovation process. The findings also show that managers play a vital role in reshaping the innovation discourse due to digitalization and facilitating employee involvement in digital innovation processes.

Several recent studies confirmed that in today's digital transformation era the highly innovative workforce has become imperative for companies to survive (Edelman, 2020; Gerards *et al.*, 2021; Van Zyl *et al.*, 2021).

The study in a global ICT company, which could be characterized by rapid innovations and extreme work demands sector, revealed that work engagement is positively related to employee-driven innovative work behavior (van Zyl *et al.*, 2021). It was proven that engaged employees are more inclined to generate, promote, and implement innovative ideas in the context of new ICT ecosystem (Edelman, 2020).

In recent years, scholars have been interested more in high-tech service organizations, such as IT sector employee innovative behavior. The consensus among the researchers is that in the digital transformation context, constant innovation is primarily driven by employee-driven innovative behavior (Zhang *et al.*, 2021). Information Technology sector employees' personal creative identity has been proven to have a significant influence on their innovative behavior (Uddin *et al.*, 2020) as well as entrepreneurial leadership impact on employee innovative behavior (Iqbal *et al.*, 2021).

To sum up, employee-driven innovation employing DT perspective research encompasses multifaced perspectives mainly referring to the two clusters: (1) how employee-driven innovations supported digital products', processes', and products' development (Edelman, 2020; Van Zyl *et al.*, 2021; Zhang *et al.*, 2021; Iqbal *et al.*, 2021) and (2) how employees employed digital tools to support innovation processes (Bäckström & Lindberg, 2019). Most of the studies examine how employees can be motivated to become digital transformers. However, more information is still required about those organizational elements that can enhance employees' usage of digital tools to develop their innovation capabilities considering digital transformation characteristics. Another cluster of the research is devoted to high-tech companies and offers limited studies considering employee-driven digital innovations in other business sectors. In general, the phenomenon of DT offers an opportunity to advance existing knowledge about how DT relates to employee-driven innovation processes in all business sectors.

4.3. *Individual Characteristics and Innovation in DT Context*

The rise of digitalization of innovation processes and digital transformation has inspired scholars to investigate what factors influence successful digital innovation management processes at the individual level, that is, the characteristics of the players — business owners, managers, entrepreneurs, external experts, leaders, etc. — involved in these processes. According to Corvello *et al.* (2023), personal dimension factors' role in digital innovation processes is least studied.

A business owners' characteristics' influence on digital innovation processes study by Corvello *et al.* (2023), based on the data from 550 patent holder companies' owners involved in digital innovation, confirmed that education, gender diversity, and minority status of the owners significantly impact digital innovation performance. In the digital transformation period, processes are typically less structured and affected by subjects with power stimuli (Bartoloni *et al.*, 2021) and owners have much more power to enable behaviors that promote innovation. This study's findings may assist in identifying strategies for a more effective digital transformation process in the companies.

Scuotto *et al.*'s (2021) study in the micro-foundational perspective on Small and Medium-sized Enterprises' (SMEs) growth in the digital transformation era demonstrates the individual digital capabilities relevant to SMEs' successful innovation performance. The qualitative research based on SMEs in 26 European countries findings proved that employees' digital capabilities and skills are of crucial importance in the digital transformation era and highlight the need for individual employee digital capabilities to respond to digital transformation changes in the market. Scuotto *et al.* (2023) later talk about the importance of "digital humanism", as an emphasis on human skills in the digital transformation era.

Facing the necessity to enhance digital innovation capacity, industrial companies' top management plays a vital role by recognizing digital innovation strategic value. In this line, the research of Firk *et al.* (2022) aimed to examine top management team characteristics and digital innovation in industrial firms' sector. The findings indicated that the top management team's (TMT) digital knowledge is related to future digital innovation and that "more integrative CEO and the presence of a Chief Digital Officer amplifies the positive impact of top management digital knowledge on digital innovation" (p. 13). This study undoubtedly contributes to the knowledge about TMT's competencies that are crucial for successful digital innovation management (Hanelt *et al.*, 2021).

In general, the research of digital transformation and innovation management interplay at the individual level demonstrates that employees and innovation teams are required to develop new abilities and skills to incorporate opportunities offered by digital transformation in the innovation process. In terms of HRM and innovation management, the studies emphasize the importance of the HR department's necessity to digitalize their functions to involve and motivate employees to utilize digitalization opportunities in innovation processes.

5. Future Research Agenda

Recently, innovation management has been greatly affected by digital transformation posing new developments in ecosystems and businesses. The phenomenon has captured the attention of researchers and managers across several disciplines changing the understanding of how companies must run business and manage innovation processes in the digital transformation era. Scholars agree that digital transformation in general changed the nature of innovation management itself (Nambisan *et al.*, 2020).

A stream of scholars investigated these changes' manifestation through different perspectives offering a rather fragmented research landscape (Cenamo *et al.*, 2020; Berger *et al.*, 2020). In this chapter, we tried to provide a general understanding of the main directions grouping the studies into the three areas of research: holistic, organizational, and individual.

Future research in these three avenues is related to the research questions presented in Table 1.

Table 1.   Future research agenda.

Cluster of Analysis	Theme	Future Research Questions
Holistic	Collaboration perspective	How does DT affect horizontal and vertical collaboration?
		How does DT push companies to create and join new collaboration alliances?
		Under what conditions does DT enable effective collaboration between different participants?
	Governance perspective	How does DT accelerate innovation policies aiming to promote open science?
		How can governance models within innovation ecosystems affect innovation outcomes?
		How can innovation governance take advantage of DT?

Table 1.   (*Continued*)

Cluster of Analysis	Theme	Future Research Questions
Organizational	New business models	Under what circumstances does DT advance the development of business model innovations?
		In which way can DT support organizations in developing new business models?
	New customer behaviors	How does DT change the customers' role across different industries?
		How does DT impact mechanisms used to capture value from innovation?
		What changes does DT entail for organizations regarding customer involvement in innovation process?
	Digital transformation effects on performance	How does DT pave the way to enhanced business innovation performance?
		What are innovation performance antecedents under the effect of DT?
		What aspects of DT could lead to enhanced innovation performance?
Individual perspective	Human resource DT and innovation management	How can DT enable human resource specialists to enhance employee motivation and engagement in innovation processes?
		What HRM novel practices lead to increased company's innovation in DT era?
		How do DT initiatives prompt change in HRM processes for innovation?
	Employee-driven innovation and digital transformation	How can employee-driven innovations accelerate DT?
		What is the most effective way to motivate employees to become digital transformers?
		How does DT relate to employee-driven innovation processes in different sectors?

(Continued)

Table 1.   (*Continued*)

Cluster of Analysis	Theme	Future Research Questions
	Individual characteristics and innovation in DT context	What is the personal dimension factors' role in digital innovation processes?
		How does DT shape employees as related to innovation processes, skills, and capabilities?
		How can digital technologies assist in enabling teams to be more innovative?

6. Conclusion

The themes that have been considered in this chapter are meant to highlight common recent trends in digital transformation and innovation management research. We do not claim that the presented themes are the only ones. Indeed, there may be several others that could represent the recent tendencies, however we hope that our systemized illustration of the clusters enables a better understanding of existing research clusters in the field of digitalization for innovation and would give ideas for future research in the digital transformation field.

References

Adner, R. & Zemsky, P. (2005). Disruptive technologies and the emergence of competition. *The RAND Journal of Economics*, *36*(2), 229–254.

Appio, F. P., Frattini, F., Petruzzelli, A. M., & Neirotti, P. (2021). Digital transformation and innovation management: A synthesis of existing research and agenda for future studies. *Journal of Product Innovation Management*, *38*(1), 4–20.

Ardito, L., Raby, S., Albino, V., & Bertoldi, B. (2021). The duality and environmental orientations in the context of SMEs: Implications for innovation performance. *Journal of Business Research*, *123*, 44–56.

Bäckström, I. & Lindberg, M. (2019). Varying involvement in digitally enhanced employee-driven innovation. *European Journal of Innovation Management*, *22*(3), 524–540.

Bansal, A., Panchal, T., Jabeen, F., Mangla, S. K., & Singh, G. (2023). A study of human resource digital transformation (HRDT): A phenomenon of innovation capability led by digital and individual factors. *Journal of Business Research, 157*, 113611, 1–17.

Bartoloni, S., Calo, E., Marinelli, L., Pascucci, F., Dezi, I., Carayannis, E., Revel, G. M., & Gregori, G. I. (2021). Towards designing society 5.0 solutions: The new quintuple helix — Design thinking approach to technology. *Technovation, 113*, 285–309.

Benner, M. J. & Waldfogel, J. (2020). Changing the channel: Digitalization and the rise of "middle tail" strategies. *Strategic Management Journal, 24*, 1–24.

Berger, S., Bitzer, M., Hackel, B., & Voit, C. (2020). Approaching digital transformation — Development of a multi-dimensional maturity model. *Approaching Digital Transformation. ECIS 2020 Proceedings.* AIS Electronic Library (AISeL).

Bhatti, S. H., Santoro, G., Khan, J., & Rizzato, F. (2021). Antecedents and consequences of business model innovation in the IT industry. *Journal of Business Research, 123*, 389–400.

Bogers, M. L. A. M., Garud, R., Thomas, L. D. W., Tuertscher, P., & Yoo, Y. (2022). Digital innovation: Transforming research and practice. *Innovation: Organization and Management, 24*(1), 4–12.

Bresciani, S., Ferraris, A., Romano, M., & Santoro, G. (2021). Digital leadership. In *Digital Transformation Management for Agile Organizations: A Compass to Sail a Digital World* (pp. 97–115). Emerald Publishing Limited, United Kingdom.

Carayannis, E. G. & Campel, D. F. J. (2009). "Mode 3" and "quadruple helix": Toward a 21st century fractal innovation ecosystem. *International Journal of Technology Management, 46*(3–4), 201–234.

Carayannis, E. G., Grigoroudis, E., Campbell, D. F., Meissner, D., & Stamati, D. (2018). The ecosystem as helix: An exploratory theory building study of regional competitive entrepreneurial ecosystems. *R&D Management, 48*(1), 148–162.

Cennamo, C. G. B. D., Di Minin, A., & Lanzolla, G. (2020). Managing digital transformation: Scope of transformation and modalities of value co-generation and delivery. *California Management Review, 62*(4), 5–16.

Chae, B. K. (2019). A general framework for studying the evolution of the digital innovation ecosystem: The case of big data. *Journal of Information Management, 45*, 83–94.

Chen, S., Kang J., Liu, S., & Sun, Y. (2020). Cognitive computing on unstructured data for customer co-innovation. *European Journal of Marketing, 54*(3), 570–593.

Cherbib, J., Chebbi, H., Yahiaoui, D., Thrassou, A., & Sakka, G. (2021). Digital technologies and learning within asymmetric alliances: The role of collaborative context. *Journal of Business Research, 124*, 214–226.

Ciasullo, M. C. & Lim, W. M. (2022). Digital transformation and business model innovation: Advantages, challenges and opportunities. *International Journal Quality and Innovation, 6*(1), 1–6.

Cockburn, I., Henderson, R., & Stern, S. (2018). The impact of artificial intelligence on innovation. *Working Paper* No. 24449, JEL No. L1. National Bureau of Economic Research.

Correani, A., De Massis, A., Frattini, F., Petruzzelli, A. M., & Natalicchio, A. (2020). Implementing a digital strategy: Learning from the experience of three digital transformation projects. *California Management Review, 62*(4), 37–56.

Corvello, V., Belas, J., Giglio, C, Iazzolino, G., & Troise, C. (2023). The impact of business owners' individual characteristics on patenting in the context of digital innovation. *Journal of Business Research, 155*, 113397.

Demir, M., Yasar, E., & Demir, S. S. (2023). Digital transformation and human resources planning: The mediating role of innovation. *Journal of Hospitality and Tourism Technology, 14*(1), 73–89.

DiRomualdo, A., El-Khoury, D., & Girimonte, F. (2018). HR in the digital age: How digital technology will change HR's organization structure, processes and roles. *Strategic HR Review, 25*(1), 147–159.

Edelman, D. (2020). The war for digital talent is already here. Retrieved from https://www.forbes.com/sites/mckinsey/2012/01/23/the-war-for-digital-talent-is-already-here/?sh=d9eb25262cbf.

Eisenmann, T., Parker, G., & Van Alstyne, M. W. (2006). Strategies for two-sided markets. *Harvard Business Review*, 1–11.

Erevelles, S., Fukawa, N., & Swayne, L. (2016). Big data consumer analytics and the transformation of marketing. *Journal of Business Research, 69*(2), 897–904.

Fenech, R., Baguant, P., & Ivanov, D. (2019). The changing role of human resource management in an era of digital transformation. *Journal of Management Information and Decision Sciences, 22*(2), 166–175.

Fidanoski, F., Simeonovski, K., Kaftandzieva, T., Ranga, M., Dana, L. P., Davidovic, M., Ziolo, M., & Sergi, B. S. (2022). The triple helix in developed countries: When knowledge meets innovation? *Heliyon, 8*(8), 33–47.

Firk, S., Gehrke, Y., Hanelt, A., & Wolff, M. (2022). Top management team characteristics and digital innovation: Exploring digital knowledge and TMT interfaces. *Long Range Planning, 55*(3), 37–56.

Fountaine, T., McCharty, B., & Saleh, T. (2019). Building the AI-powered organization. *Harvard Business Review*, (July–August), 63–73.

Gerards, R., van Wetten, S., & van Sambeek, C. (2021). New ways of working and intrapreneurial behaviour: The mediating role of transformational leadership and social interaction. *Review of Managerial Science, 15*(7), 2075–2110.

Goglio, C., Kraemer-Mbula, E., & Lorenz, E. (2022). The effects of digital transformation on innovation and productivity: Firm-level evidence of South African manufacturing micro and small enterprises. *Technological Forecasting and Social Change, 182*, 121785.

Guellec, D. C. & Paunov, F. (2018). Innovation policies in the digital age. *OECD Science, Technology and Industry Policy Papers*, No. 59. Paris: OECD Publishing.

Haaker, T., Ly, P. T. M., Nguyen-Thanh, P., Nguyen-Thanh, N., & Nguyen, H. T. H. (2021). Business model innovation through the application of the Internet-of-Things: A comparative analysis. *Journal of Business Research, 126*, 126–136.

Hanelt, A., Bohnsack, R., Marz, D., & Marante, C. A. (2021). A systematic review of the literature on digital transformation: Insights and implications for strategy and organizational change. *Journal of Management Studies, 58*(5), 1159–1197.

Henver, A. & Gregor, S. (2022). Envisioning entrepreneurship and digital innovation through a design science research lens: A matrix approach. *Information and Management, 59*(3), Article 103350.

Iqbal, A., Nazir, T., & Ahmad, M. S. (2021). Entrepreneurship leadership and employee innovative behavior: An examination through multiple theoretical lenses. *European Journal of Innovation Management, 27*.

Isckia, T., Reuver, M., & Lescop, D. (2018). Digital innovation and platform-based ecosystems': An evolutionary framework. In *Proceedings of the 10th International Conference on Management of Digital EcoSystems, MEDES*.

Jacobides, M. G., Cennamo, C., & Gawer, A. (2018). Towards a theory of ecosystems. *Strategic Management Journal, 39*(8). DOI: 10.1002/smj.2904.

Jain, G., Paul, J., & Shrivastava, A. (2021). Hyper-personalization, co-creation, digital clienteling and transformation. *Journal of Business Research, 124*, 12–23.

Kamboj, S. & Gupta, S. (2018). Use of smart phone apps in co-creative hotel service innovation: Evidence from India. *Current Issues in Tourism*. Routledge: Taylor & Francis Group.

Leten, B., Vanhaverbeke, W., Roijakkers, N., Clerix, A., & Van Helleputte, J. (2013). IP models to orchestrate innovation ecosystems. *California Management Review, 55*(4), 51–64.

Li, S., Gao, L., Han, C., Gupta, B., Alhalabi, W., & Almakdi, S. (2023). Exploring the effect of digital transformation on firm's innovation performance. *Journal of Innovation & Knowledge, 8*(1), 100317.

Mazzucchelli, A., Gurioli, M., Graziano, D., Quacquarelli, B., & Aouina-Mejri, C. (2021). How to fight against food waste in the digital era: Key factors for a successful food sharing platform. *Journal of Business Research, 124*, 47–58.

Minbaeva, D. (2021). Disrupted HR? *Human Resource Management Review, 31*(4), 1–20.

Muler, S. D., Paske, N., & Rodil, I. (2019). Managing ambidexterity in startups pursuing digital innovation. *Communications of the Association for Information Systems, 44*(1), 273–298.

Müller, S. & Hundahl, M. (2018). IT-driven business model innovation: Sources and ripple effects. *International Journal of E-Business Research* (IJEBR) (IGI Global), *14*(2), 14–38.

Nambisan, S., Wright, M., & Feldman, M. (2020). The digital transformation of innovation and entrepreneurship: Progress, challenges, and key themes. *Research Policy, 48*, 1–9.

Oeij, P. R. A., Dhondt, S., Rus, D., & Van Hootegem, G. (2019). The digital transformation requires workplace innovation: An introduction. *International Journal Technology Transfer and Commercialization, 16*(3), 199–207.

Opland, L. E., Pappas, I., Engesmo, J., & Jaccheri, L. (2022). Employee-driven digital innovation: A systematic review and research agenda. *Journal of Business Research, 143*, 255–271.

Pera, R., Menozzi, A., Abrate, G., & Baima, G. (2021). When cocreation turns into co-destruction, *Journal of Business Research, 128*(6), 222–232.

Rialti, R., Zollo, L., Ferraris, A., & Alon, I. (2019). Big data analytics capabilities and performance: Evidence from a moderated multi-mediation model. *Technological Forecasting and Social Change, 149*, Article 119781.

Salvi, A., Vitolla, F., Rubino, M., Giakoumelou, A., & Raimo, N. (2021). Online information on digitalization processes and its impact on firm value. *Journal of Business Research, 124*, 437–444.

Sankar, J. P. *et al.* (2021). Human resource digital transformation of IT sector in India. *Webology, 18*(1), 219–232.

Scuotto, V., Giudice, M., Papa, A., Tarba, S., Bresciani, S., & Warkentin, M. (2021). A self-tuning model for smart manufacturing SMEs: Effects on digital innovation. *Journal of Product Innovation Management, 124*, 222–241.

Scuotto, V., Tzanidis, T., Usai, A., & Quaglia, R. (2023). The digital humanism era triggered by individual creativity. *Journal of Business Research, 158* (March), 15–33.

Siachou, E., Vrontis, D., & Trichina, E. (2021). Can traditional organizations be digitally transformed by themselves? The moderating role of absorptive capacity and strategic interdependence. *Journal of Business Research, 124*, 408–421.

Solberg, E., Traavik, L. E. M., & Wong, S. I. (2020). Digital mindsets: Recognizing and leveraging individual beliefs for digital transformation. *California Management Review, 62*(4), 105–124.

Skare, M., Obesso, M. M., & Ribeiro-Navarrete, S. (2023). Digital transformation and European small and medium enterprises (SMEs): A comparative study using digital economy and society index data. *International Journal of Information Management, 68*, 102594.

Steenkamp, R. J. (2019). The quadruple helix model of innovation for Industry 4.0. *Acta Commercii, 19*(1), 1–10.

Steinhauser, S. (2021). Enabling the utilization of potentially disruptive digital innovations by incumbents: The impact of contextual, organizational, and individual factors in regulated contexts. *International Journal of Innovation Management, 25*(2), 2150015.

Strohmeier, S. (2020). Digital human resource management: A conceptual clarification. *German Journal of Human Resource Management, 34*(3), 345–365.

Uddin, A., Priyanka, H. P. R., & Mahmood, M. (2020). Does a creative identity encourage innovative behavior? Evidence from knowledge-intense IT service firms. *European Journal of Innovation Management, 23*(5), 877–894.

Ulatowska, R., Wainio, E., & Pierzchala, M. (2023). Digital transformation in HRM of the modern service sector in Finland and Poland. *Journal of Organizational Change Management, 36*(7), 1180–1192.

van Zyl, L. E., van Oort, A., Rispens, S., & Olckers, C. (2021). Work engagement and task performance within a global Dutch ICT — Consulting firm: The mediating role of innovative work behaviors. *Current Psychology, 40*, 4012–4023.

Vargo, S. L. & Lush R.F. (2010). From repeat patronage to value co-creation in service ecosystems: A transcending conceptualization of relationship. *Journal of Business Marketing and Management, 4*, 169–179

Wang, P. (2021). Connecting the parts with the whole: Toward the information ecology theory of digital innovation ecosystems. *MIS Quarterly, 45*(1), 397–422.

Xu, C., Zhu, S., Yang, B., Miao, B., & Duan, Y. (2023). A review of policy framework research on promoting sustainable transformation of digital innovation. *Sustainability, 15*(9), 7169.

Yi Lo, F., Yu, T. H. K., & Chen, H. H. (2021). Purchasing intention and behavior in the sharing economy: Mediating effects of APP assessments. *Journal of Business Research, 121*, 93–102.

Zhang, J. & Chen, Z. (2023). Exploring human resource management digital transformation in the digital age. *Journal of the Knowledge Economy, 1*, 1–17.

Zhang, Z., Zahid, Y., & Muhammad, Y. (2021). Nexus of digital organizational culture, capabilities, organizational readiness and innovation: Investigation of SMEs operating in the digital economy. *Sustainability, 13*(720), 1–15.

Zhang, Y., Ma, X., Pang, J., Xing, H., & Wang, J. (2023). The impact of digital transformation of manufacturing on corporate performance — The mediating effect of business model innovation and moderating effect of innovation capability. *Research of International Business and Finance, 64,* 101890.

Chapter 2

The Art of Digital Transformation

Robert M. Davison[*,†,‖], **Louie H. M. Wong**[‡,**],
Fareeda Cassumbhoy[†,††], **and John Peng**[§,‡‡]

†*City University of Hong Kong, Kowloon Tong, Hong Kong*

‡*Nagoya University of Commerce and Business, Nisshin, Japan*

§*Private Consultant and Business Advisor, Beijing, China*

‖*isrobert@cityu.edu.hk*

**louie_wong@gsm.nucba.ac.jp*

††*fareedac@icloud.com*

‡‡*jqpeng@yahoo.com*

1. Introduction

Over the last 20 years, organizations have been undergoing a process of digital transformation (DT), leveraging digital technologies to revamp their business models, structures, and cultures in order to enhance their competitiveness. Although DT is a widely used term, there is remarkably little agreement about exactly what it entails: it encompasses many different activities with no consistent definition or scope. In some

---

*Corresponding author.

organizations, DT may apply to a range of activities across the board, whereas in others the focus may be on a single set of processes in one unit. Much of the academic literature on DT has either focused on success cases at the organization level, checklists of critical success factors, or the development of models that forecast how DT initiatives may pan out, and even what an ideal evolutionary path may look like. These one-size-fits-all descriptions are dangerous because they ignore the essential uniqueness of each organization and its situation. Indeed, some organizations may be better advised not to attempt DT at all, for instance, if they and their employees are not ready for change. Meanwhile, the people who are charged with leading the DT initiative are largely ignored in the research literature. In this chapter, in order to engage with what we term "the art" of DT, we take the perspective of the one person best qualified to lead and practice this art: the Chief Digital Officer (CDO). We narrate the personal stories of two CDOs as they recount their very different journeys.

2. Literature Review

Organizations globally are considering how they can leverage new digital technologies in order to "renew and transform their business models" (Kohli & Melville, 2019), enhance their competitiveness (Nwankpa & Roumani, 2016), and so transform how they operate and compete. As they put their plans for DT into effect, they find that their business models are closely connected with digital technologies (Wimelius *et al.*, 2021) and that this renewal and transformation thus induce radical changes across the organization, including to operations, structures, the nature of work, products, services, and the culture of the organization itself. Additional pressure to engage in DT has come from exogenous shocks, such as the COVID-19 pandemic (Kraus *et al.*, 2022), human-induced crises such as the Russia–Ukraine war, and the ongoing emergence of new technologies, such as generative AI.

Although there is broad agreement about the necessity for DT in the organization, there is surprisingly little agreement about exactly what DT entails. Vial (2019, p. 121) defines DT as a process that "aims to improve an entity by triggering significant changes to its properties through combinations of information, computing, communication, and connectivity technologies" (Vial, 2019, p. 121). This definition is so broad and vague that it could apply to almost any kind of change. Wessel *et al.* (2021) explain with similar opacity that DT involves activities that "leverage digital technology in *(re)defining* an organization's value proposition ... and the emergence of a new organizational identity". However, despite reading many articles on DT, we have not found any other consistent definition that is widely adopted.

In order to undertake DT, it is broadly recognized that significant changes are required in such diverse areas as strategizing (Matt *et al.*, 2015), the design of work and organizational processes (Karimi & Walter, 2015), and value creation paths (Vial, 2019). DT endeavors often relate to the implementation of software applications related to social media, mobile, business analytics, cloud, and the internet of things (Sebastian *et al.*, 2017), as well as digital technologies and techniques (e.g., artificial intelligence, robotic process automation, and machine learning), which can significantly enhance the collection and processing of information (Vial, 2019). When these changes are made, there will be impacts on other parts of the organization, notably its structure and culture. For instance, some functional managers may find that they lose (some of) their independence, and some people may find that their old jobs simply do not exist anymore. Such existential changes inevitably lead to resistance.

2.1. *Factors Influencing DT Trajectory*

Considerable effort has been put into the development of what we term "maturity models" that purport to delineate the trajectories that organizations might (seek to) follow as their DT initiative unfolds and matures (e.g., Westerman *et al.*, 2012; Granito, 2022). A wide variety of factors have been identified that might influence digital maturity, though these suffer from what Larsen and Hovorka (2012) call factorial synonymy, i.e., the factors have different names but similar descriptions. We coalesce these various factors into a short list of five: *digital support, digital vision, digital culture, digital capability,* and *digital workforce,* which we briefly describe in the following. Each of these factors has the potential to influence how a DT initiative is implemented, and indeed how successful it will be. We follow this list of factors with a short review of resistance to DT and the negative impacts that DT may bring, before moving on to consider the role of the Chief Digital Officer (CDO).

1. *Digital Support*: Digital maturity is dependent on both the moral and the financial support of top management (Fitzgerald *et al.*, 2014). When the CEO and other C-Suite executives publicly support DT, they heighten the willingness of the remainder of the organization to implement technology and thus adhere to an overarching digital

vision (Vial, 2019; Weritz *et al.*, 2020). However, although necessary, this support is not sufficient: senior executives must propagate the implementation of digital technology in person.

2. *Digital Vision*: Westerman *et al.* (2011) indicate that digitally mature organizations have a strong and overarching digital vision. This digital vision must be developed, strengthened, and communicated as part of the process of driving digital transformation. Early communication with regard to a digital vision prompts change and reduces organizational resistance (Westerman *et al.*, 2012). It clarifies for employees which former assumptions will no longer be valid. In the longer term, the effect of the digital vision may not only be to counter activities that endanger an organization's digital journey but also to energizes personnel to generate transformative change (Westerman *et al.*, 2012). Thus, a digital vision supports the development of leadership capabilities, such as governance and engagement.

3. *Digital Culture*: Digital champions accept the legitimacy of three prerequisite requirements: to invest in digital capabilities, to recruit digital experts, and to develop a digital culture (BCG, 2018). These requirements seem appropriate given that an organization with a digitally averse culture is unlikely to see the successful adoption of digital technology. Moreover, since a digital vision cannot flourish within a digitally-averse culture, organizations need to consider how they can develop a culture that embraces the use of digital technologies.

4. *Digital Capability*: The development of digital capabilities allows for a more seamless digital journey. Digital capabilities concern three areas: customer experience, operational processes, and business models. For instance, data analytics capabilities permit the implementation of technology-enabled initiatives, such as optimized pricing. In addition, go-to-market capabilities, including digital marketing, create possibilities for personalization (BCG, 2018). Meanwhile, cloud capabilities induce collaboration, which enhances operational processes. Thus, digital capabilities positively impact the implementation of technology-enabled initiatives, which in turn enhances customer engagement and internal operations. In order to develop digital capability, organizations must map which capabilities they need to achieve a specific digital vision, consider how to embed these capabilities within a functional process, and focus on "capability-generating practices", such as digital assets and digital research and design (Gurbaxani & Dunkle, 2019). Organizations should then be able to develop digital capabilities to carry out technology-enabled initiatives.

Each organization may identify a different portfolio of digital capabilities that it requires in order to achieve specific strategic objectives.

5. *Digital Workforce*: The characteristics of an organization's workforce substantially influence the digital journey. Ensuring that the workforce is imbued with digital talent can increase an organization's ability to transform itself (Soule *et al.*, 2016). The ability to attract, train, and retain digital talent affects an organization's digital maturity (Kane *et al.*, 2017; PWC, 2016), but it is recognized that digital talent is a rare commodity. Acquiring or developing digital talent is essential for the organization that wishes to take advantage of technological advancements that can promote collaboration and innovation (Gurbaxani & Dunkle, 2019). Eden *et al.* (2019) argue that DT is only possible when the workforce has been transformed. Thus, it is essential to train existing employees to use digital technology (Mettler & Pinto, 2018), and those who resist may have to be laid off.

2.2. The Dark Side of DT

Even though DT is widely accepted as being essential for competition and even survival, the changes required are not always popular. Even when the CEO has signed off on a DT initiative and there is strong support from senior management, considerable resistance may be experienced from employees and managers at all levels (Wade, 2020; Davison *et al.*, 2023), and so the DT journey is rarely plain sailing.

Beyond resistance, DT initiatives can either damage the organization itself or simply fail when they are not integrated into the fabric of the organization. However, given the hype associated with DT, the strategic and tactical angles are sometimes utterly ignored. For instance, there may be neither an assessment of how DT will benefit (or harm) the organization nor an analysis of the extent to which the organization and its employees are ready to undergo DT (Liu *et al.*, 2023). Indeed, there may be no appreciation that a digital strategy is any different from a regular strategy, or that digital business processes are any different from regular business processes. Unfortunately, the concept of "digital" has been fetishized (Miconi, 2023) to the extent that it is seldom questioned and all things "digital" are assumed to be good. The absence of serious strategic thinking is significant because it may lead to a DT initiative proceeding haphazardly with little cohesive structure. This can result in a plethora of apparently attractive digital offerings that were created primarily to meet the demands of particular stakeholders (customers, suppliers, and managers) yet that are mutually incompatible, that require separate maintenance, and that do not fit into any overall strategic rationale (Liu *et al.*, 2023). The overall effect of this mixed-bag approach to DT will be profoundly negative.

2.3. *Responsibility for DT: The Chief Digital Officer*

When DT initiatives were first proposed, they were generally held to be the responsibility of the Chief Information Officer (CIO) or the Chief Technology Officer (CTO). However, in parallel with the emergence of DT, a new breed of senior executive has been invented to spearhead DT in the organization, viz.: the Chief Digital Officer (CDO) (Engesmo & Panteli, 2019; Kunisch *et al.*, 2020). While not all organizations choose to employ a CDO, a DT initiative is more likely to be successful when it is led by an individual who exhibits both strong digital leadership and a sophisticated digital mindset (Kane *et al.*, 2017; Vial, 2019; Weritz *et al.*, 2020). The CDO needs to be aware of the digital maturity indicators that we described above but not follow them blindly, instead carefully determining which path to DT will be most effective.

It is noteworthy that Vial (2019, p. 129) suggests that "the creation of a CDO position signals the strategic nature of digital transformation for the entire organization". Thus, the appointment of a single person who is charged with the entire DT program and who is a member of the organization's C-Suite, playing an active role in strategic planning, is more likely to lead to a successful DT outcome. Given the potential scope of DT, CDOs often have a multifaceted portfolio and are equipped with a multitude of skills. They have both business and technology knowledge and experience, and blend these with excellent soft skills that they deploy when communicating with the organization's many internal and external stakeholders (Singh & Hess, 2017). Metzler *et al.* (2021) argue that CDOs play a critical signaling role inside and beyond the organization, which suggests that they need to possess excellent connections and superlative communication skills.

Any DT initiative needs to be initiated by a CDO who has the power and positional authority both to initiate the process and to keep it going. Although internal discussions about DT may have been positive prior to initiation with high expectations of the consequences, as soon as changes are enacted and the familiar status quo is punctuated (Gersick, 1991) with new organizational routines (Pentland & Feldman, 2008) resistance from affected employees is likely to emerge. Wade (2020) suggests that this resistance is one of the major contributors to the failure of DT and the untimely demise of the CDO. Indeed, organizations in general experience extremely high levels of DT failure due to the complexity and comprehensiveness of the actions they attempt to undertake (Singh & Hess, 2017). It is thus critical that CDOs persist and persevere when facing this internal resistance. Such persistence is rendered considerably more comfortable when the CDO has the full support of the CEO and other members of the senior management team.

3. Two Cases: The CDOs' Stories

In order to illustrate the nature of the CDO's work at a personal level, we now present two short cases. Each case is written by a serving CDO who documents the nature of DT work in his or her organizational context. The first case is written by James Zhang, the CDO of iCS, a major Chinese software developer. The second case is written by Felicity Wong the CDO of HPG, a global brand management company.[1] Each case follows the following structure. First, the CDO provides a short personal introduction before describing the situation whereby she or she became appointed as CDO. This is followed by an overview of the DT process and the challenges experienced.

3.1. *Digital Transformation in iCS*

James Zhang is currently the executive vice president and chief digital officer of iCS. He has been working in the software and information technology service area for over 30 years in various capacities from business analyst, system analyst, and software development manager to IT service delivery management and IT service executive. He also has extensive global business experience working many years in the US and managing the global business for iCS for 15 years.

Since 2015, DT has become a major business growth driver. It started in the US and Europe and has quickly spread to China and other economies around the world. James experienced DT first hand while working in the US as the president of the global business of iCS. He introduced the DT concept and US experience to iCS's executive management and senior

---

[1]Note that James Zhang and iCS, Felicity Wong and HPG are all pseudonyms.

business leaders and he spoke about it in conferences and forums on behalf of iCS. James was appointed the CDO in 2019 to lead the DT initiative of iCS.

Since his appointment as CDO, iCS has experienced significant change and growth. The digital business has become the main growth driver. In 2022, iCS went public on the Shenzhen Stock Exchange. Its business scope has expanded from the traditional ITO and BPO focus into consulting and the full range of digital technology solutions and services covering cloud, renewable energy, digital infrastructure, AIoT, Industrial Internet, electric vehicles and autonomous driving, smart devices, Open Harmony OS, and Open Euler OS.

The initial challenges were multifold. The first was to work with internal teams to help them understand what DT means to iCS and its clients. The second was to develop a strategy that would clearly articulate the value of DT and align all the business units with a set of goals and actions. The third was to develop the service offerings and capabilities to deliver. A critical challenge was to work with the executive and senior leadership (i.e., C-suite) and persuade them to endorse the idea that digital business is the future. From an opportunities perspective, the Chinese government made the digital economy its top growth driver, which opened the door for a new round of investment in building the new digital infrastructure and developing new technology and applications. These government-led national digital initiatives brought about many new areas of opportunities, especially in consulting, cloud services, data services, industrial internet, as well as AI services.

At the time James was appointed CDO, DT was just starting to gain momentum in China. iCS needed clear directions on how to become a leader in this emerging market space. As CDO, James' key responsibilities included corporate digital strategy development and execution, digital branding, as well as building an innovation ecosystem. Some of James' key challenges included articulating a corporate DT strategy that will align all businesses for iCS's future growth; ensuring that iCS would be able to provide solutions and services to help clients achieve their own DT, and telling the market that iCS is a DT player.

Crafting a DT strategy was the first priority. James led a strategy team under the guidance of the corporate CEO and developed iCS's DT plan, Digital iCS, which detailed the purpose, goal, and key actions iCS would take as it became a digital service leader in the emerging DT space.

The strategy pivoted around two major fronts: internal DT and DT solution and service for clients. The strategy was first introduced to all the executives and then to the middle- and upper-level managers. As the senior management became aligned with the Digital iCS strategy, the appropriate level of digital capability could also be developed. iCS organized a new business unit in which it integrated consulting, cloud service, data service, AIoT, and relevant digital solutions. The new business unit was designed to support all (internal) business groups in their digital business development and service delivery efforts. In the meantime, iCS created the iCS Innovation Institute, headed by CDO, which was tasked with supporting the digital strategy execution, digital business development, digital iCS branding, and ecosystem development.

Apart from the strategic challenges, James also had to face tactical issues as CDO. For instance, in executing the digital strategy, he needed to obtain cooperation and collaboration from different businesses and functional areas in a number of key internal DT projects, such as process automation, data governance development, and management dashboard development. To encourage compliance with the digital strategy, he employed a "stick and carrot" approach. The stick was the strategic mandate from the CEO and executive team, while the carrot involved his leveraging his relationships with the particular decision-makers and/or key influencers.

During the course of the implementation of the digital strategy, a number of problems arose. Many of these were related to data and data management. For instance, data consolidation and integration was a key activity, where the IT team had to identify various data sources and owners in many databases, and the business teams had to provide clarification of data and their use cases. Both of these activities required the active engagement of knowledgeable people. The initial resistance was quite strong since by sharing their knowledge, the teams may expose their "secrets" and/or lose their privileges and power that accompany the data ownership. In putting their resistance into practice, they would claim that they have no time, no knowledge, or no authorization to do the work that was requested. Thus, although no one actually said "No, I refuse to do it", there were many "excuses" where the CDO had to leverage his carrot and stick strategy, alternatively cajoling them to cooperate and threatening them with the consequences of non-compliance.

iCS's Digital Innovation Service has been growing rapidly since the launch of the digital strategy, from less than 20% to almost 50% of all iCS businesses. In the meantime, iCS has successfully built five new sub-brands: Digital Consulting, Fintech, Industrial Internet, Digital Energy, and Cloud Service. Since the launch of the digital strategy in 2020, iCS has become the leader in digital services in China. iCS was listed as a 2022 Top 10 Digital Leadership Company, among the Top 20 Most Competitive Software and IT Service Companies of China, 2022 Top 100 Industrial Internet Company, and 2022 Best ESG Practice Employer.

The CDO position is one with a high impact. It is more strategic than operational, and from this perspective, the CDO position may not be permanent in many organizations. A CDO's challenges may come from many directions: organizationally, establishing the necessary authority recognized by business units takes time and significant effort. From the business perspective, the CDO has to be resourceful and a relationship builder in order to be effective in strategy execution. Personally, the position requires the CDO to be savvy about the latest technology and trends, strategic thinking, high-level selling, and brand marketing. CDO is also a highly rewarding position because of the positive impact a CDO may have on overall business transformation and growth. A CDO can fail if s/he fails to add real value to the front-line business.

Key lessons learned:

- Top-down support for DT initiatives is necessary but not sufficient. The most effective change driver is the market demand or delivered value.
- DT is about mindset change and innovation. The best way to change mindset is to showcase the results of innovation: seeing is believing, as the old saying goes.

Key takeaways:

- Be strategic — think ahead and structurally
- Be practical — stay closely with businesses and support any DT initiatives with business cases
- Be innovative — actively develop showcases to stimulate more innovation
- Be missionary — articulate and communicate the values DT brings
- Be artistic — develop and leverage alliances internally and externally.

3.2. *Digital Transformation in HPG*

Felicity is the Group Chief Digital Officer (CDO) of HPG, a global brand activation and event management company listed in Hong Kong. She joined HPG in April 2018 and is responsible for driving the DT activities for the entire Group.

Before joining, Felicity was the Chief Strategy Officer of HDS, a prominent independent online digital marketing and media agency group in China. She held that position for seven years and helped transform the company from a small, medium-sized local media agency to a full-service integrated digital agency with a global footprint. The company was listed on the Shanghai Stock Exchange in August 2017. Thus, she had substantial experience transforming a business by building new capabilities.

In January 2018, a chance meeting with an old friend led to a formal introduction to the current Chairman of HPG. This friend provided much valuable background information about HPG, explaining that the HPG Group has been experiencing fierce competition around the world. Every day, they are chasing numbers with eroding margins. Meanwhile, the management team is getting over-mature and stagnating with no signs of young successors emerging. Most employees (including managers and younger people) are very traditional in their way of thinking and not attuned to the new digital world. The situation described here provided to be an attractive lure for Felicity who wondered if she could turn a traditional below-the-line event management agency into a data-driven enterprise.

She first encountered the rather over-mature management team, who lived in the pre-digital era without any awareness of the need to change. Digital technologies and disruptions seemed irrelevant to them. Most of them seemed happy to rest on their laurels until retirement. Hence, anything to do with innovations was out of the question.

The "Go Digital" strategy was originated by the Chairman in 2016 yet failed as HPG fell into the trap of a "blind leading the blind" syndrome. They hired the wrong CIO who could only experiment with ideas but change nothing and left after several months of burning cash. He left behind a team of young "wannabes" who hoped to build an "Airbnb" version of HPG for events and exhibition usage but were bleeding around 100,000 USD per month on overhead for nearly 18 months.

During her first meeting with the Chairman, Felicity found that rather than being interviewed for a job, she was interviewing him to understand what he wanted to achieve. She found that he wanted to do everything quickly and thought it could be done overnight. When she accepted the position of CDO, she was tasked to interview senior management and key stakeholders within the Group, including Business Unit (BU) heads in China, Hong Kong, and Singapore. She identified the first strategic issue and challenge: "How do we transform this siloed company into a unified group?"

HPG had been running a decentralized management approach with only financial measures to control the BUs; everything else, including management, operational process, and offerings, depended on the BU head's jurisdiction. An internal turf war made it difficult to control, not least since all of the BUs were cannibalizing each others' services and were only able to differentiate themselves from each other via price cuts. Every BU offered exactly the same scope of services, including design and build for exhibitions and events, event operations and management, showroom designs, and experiential fittings for retail, B2B, theme parks, museums, and business domains like automotive, ICT, FMCG, etc.

The second issue and challenge was how to seek executive buy-in and alignment beyond getting support from the Chairman. When Felicity started out, she encountered considerable skepticism of the entire "Go Digital" initiative and the newly established Group Digital Office as an additional corporate function. She found it hard to explain strategic or tactical objectives given the complete lack of trust in people who work in the corporate office. The DT initiatives were perceived more as relating to change management than to the implementation of digital technologies.

The key problem was the very limited level of basic technology understanding and competence in the workforce. While there were previous IT systems, they were fragmented, ancient, patchy, and in a state of disintegration. No one at HPG had any appreciation of why centralization or integration should be necessary in a global business. Even the previous IT department employees were unqualified to understand and handle the new types of enterprise technology stack.

The second issue concerned the different degrees of acceptance and willingness to try out new technologies. Some of the most IT-savvy BU heads understood all too well that with the adoption of new technology, everything would be exposed to management surveillance, including all their unreported (and unknown) bad habits. Their entire operational process would then become truly transparent. This potential transparency proved to be a source of great fear and consequently resistance, with many excuses raised and difficulties experienced in rolling out the implementation. For instance, historically the accounting books were only submitted in a lump sum without transactional breakdowns; the rolling forecast was vague and non-systematic. The inaccuracy of data input left a giant loophole for problem debts and bad debts. Essential knowledge and even business transaction records were lost when employees left HPG without any governance arrangements to ensure correct information capturing and archiving.

HPG's DT journey was thus an evolutionary one, yet some critical activities had to be implemented simultaneously and immediately! Felicity reported how she and her team used a step-by-step approach to conquer the BUs one by one. The first step was to assess how much room was left for change while pre-committed legacy systems, e.g., the Epicor ERP system, were untangled. Replacing Epicor was an option, but it would require writing off over USD1 million worth of sunk cost if there was a switch to a more suitable ERP system. Felicity and her team identified some quick wins to gain confidence and trust. They quickly adopted Microsoft 365 with Teams and Microsoft Outlook for email communications. Felicity also hired a new Chief Technology Officer (CTO) from Microsoft and one of Microsoft's Global VPs further helped by deploying a Fast Tracker Team to help HPG handle the software migration. Due to a lack of capable talent in-house, this move allowed HPG to drive better activation and ease of access to the latest technologies and talents.

Felicity chose to adopt an incremental change approach, i.e., "crossing the river by feeling the stones". She helped employees across HPG to get a taste of the new technical reality by engaging in deep communication before commencement and mass rollout. She found that she had to learn how to communicate with key stakeholders and explain risk and reward patiently. As she put it, "communication is an art". Employees did not know what they were afraid of; hence, listening to and understanding their concerns and fears were critical in the process. For instance, issues like the transparency of pre-commit revenue forecast will affect year-end performance bonus if there is a failure to hit the forecast numbers. Her learning curve includes learning how to gauge their willingness to change across different levels, countries, and disciplines. She started by identifying the spectrum of digital readiness per BU and selecting pilot groups and pioneering individuals as trailblazers to showcase small wins to attract and lure the laggards to take up the first trial. Early in the game, she observed who were the most influential among the top management team (TMT), and once she established good results with the influencers, it was easier to put peer pressure on the TMT.

Notable success stories included the global implementation of Microsoft Office 365 just one month before the emergence of COVID-19, with the selection of solid technologies like Salesforce and cloud services that help save costs and enable business continuity during lockdown periods. The system allows cross-country communications and management to improve efficiency and transparency. New business intelligence dashboards were built with a single-source enterprise data warehouse that saves a lot of manual labor within accounting departments worldwide. To date, HPG is proud to be associated with significant companies like Cathay Pacific, AXA, AIA, PCCW Global, and Prudential as fellow finalists for the Digital Transformation Company of the Year, Best Chief Digital Officer, and Best Chief Technology Officer awards.

4. Discussion: Lessons for Practice and Theory

The two cases that we present in this chapter differ markedly given the very different circumstances of the two organizations involved. Thus, while iCS is a technologically mature organization that occupies a central place in the IT services industry in China, HPG started off as a much less technologically mature player that for a very long time had what we characterize as an uncommitted stance toward technology advancement, in addition being riven by internal disputes. Notwithstanding these differences, it is instructive to examine and compare the DT journeys of these two organizations and their respective CDOs.

In the case of iCS, the CDO, James, was a seasoned industry insider who had worked for the firm in multiple roles over many years. Thus, he was intimately familiar with both the industry and indeed the firm, being appointed to the CDO role as an insider. He had already developed broad and deep relationships with the senior management team in particular and thus might be assumed to occupy a privileged position. Nevertheless, he still encountered what might be considered unexpected barriers to DT. For instance, although iCS was selling DT services to its clients, it had a harder time persuading its own internal managers to get on board. For instance, there were significant fears relating to transparency and loss of authority over data. As CDO, he found that he needed to combine personal communicative persuasion with the implicit threats from the corporate mandate that supported his position. This carrot-and-stick approach is by no means new, but it proved effective: the resisting managers found out that their resistance would only be tolerated to some degree and that in the end they would be required to comply with the corporate mandate, willingly or unwillingly. This is of course not the end of the journey, but James' account explains how the DT process unfolded inexorably and iCS has come to be recognized as a major player in this market.

Meanwhile, at HPG, Felicity was likewise an industry veteran with a strong technology and marketing background, yet was an outsider to HPG and thus was parachuted into the CDO position. This latter approach appears to be far more common: CDOs are usually externally appointed. However, it is acknowledged to be risky as the incoming CDO has no existing relationships or friends who can provide support. Instead, the new CDO has a steep learning curve (to become familiar with the intricacies of the new organizational context) and relationship-building curve, to forge new alliances internally. When the organization itself is a laggard in terms of technology adoption, as was the case with HPG prior to Felicity's arrival, the situation gets more complex. As Felicity discovered, not only had her predecessors failed to introduce effective IT-based changes but they had allowed the development of a chaotic IT environment with multiple inappropriate and incompatible platforms and systems. Her task was thus first to rectify these technological problems yet at the same time gain the confidence of the employees, many of whom were deeply suspicious of her given that she threatened to upend their comfortable (but ineffective and fundamentally uncompetitive) working environment. Such a transformation would inevitably be painful for almost all internal stakeholders. Her eventual success is a testament to her persistence and persuasive skills: She removed ineffective personnel, hired new people who report to her, identified quick-fix technological solutions that cost little but created appreciable value for stakeholders, and above all listened to their needs before implementing changes. She discovered that communication (both listening and talking) skills are critical for the art of DT that a CDO must have in spades.

Both James and Felicity have succeeded in their CDO positions, overcoming challenges and setting out a new DT path for their respective organizations. Although there are differences in their experiences, what they have in common is the position of a universal CDO, a person who is charged with a multitude of responsibilities. These responsibilities were often not apparent when they were first appointed to the CDO position: Instead, the responsibilities emerged as the opportunities arose during the course of their tenure. Thus, while a CDO may initially be appointed in order to help push an organization into and along a DT journey, the exact course of that journey is utterly unpredictable. The CDO needs to be adaptable to the infinite variety of circumstances that may arise and to ensure that the DT journey continues, even in modified form. Such adaptability is not necessarily a skill that every senior manager has, especially when their experience is limited to a narrow functional area. As Felicity discovered in HPG, many senior managers were, in her words, over-mature (!): They had served in their current position for too long with few challenges and were simply resting on their laurels, waiting for their hard-earned retirement. People like this would not be effective CDOs. Felicity herself, on the other hand, had worked in different positions in multiple organizations, a background that perhaps prepared her well for her most recent appointment as CDO. Meanwhile, although James had worked in iCS for many years, he too had served in different positions and in different countries, a background that served him well in his CDO appointment.

5. Conclusion

The literature on DT has tended to focus on the organizational level and to highlight successes more than failures. By redirecting attention to the individual CDO who leads the DT initiative, we have highlighted that DT is not simply an organizational-level initiative. Instead, we need to identify the people who lead DT efforts. While CDOs have been discussed in the prior literature, we lack detailed personal accounts from CDOs in different markets, especially those outside North America and Europe. By examining the experiences of CDOs in two organizations situated in the Greater China space, we reveal new ideas about CDO competence and communicative skills that are also critical to DT success. Although James, the CDO of iCS, suggested that his position may be of shorter tenure and end when the DT journey is complete and the entire organization has been digitalized, Felicity, CDO of HPG, has a longer-term view and senses that the journey will never be complete: There will always be new opportunities to take advantage of that will require a firm but flexible hand at the helm of the DT initiative. Indeed, the emerging consensus is that while DT is certainly an important initiative for organizations to consider, beyond DT they must also consider Digital Resilience, i.e., ways to ensure that their longer-term survival can be assured in turbulent times.

References

BCG (2018). Digital maturity is paying off. Retrieved from http://image-src.bcg. com/Images/BCG-Digital-Maturity-Is-Paying-Off-June-2018_tcm9-195218.pdf.

Davison, R. M., Wong, L. H. M., & Peng, J. (2023). The art of digital transformation as crafted by a chief digital officer. *International Journal of Information Management, 69*, 102617, 1–9.

Eden, R., Burton-Jones, A., Casey, V., & Draheim, M. (2019). Digital transformation requires work transformation. *MIS Quarterly Executive, 18*(1), 1–17.

Engesmo, J. & Panteli, N. (2019). Chief digital officers as protagonists in digital transformation. In Pappas, I. O., Mikalef, P., Dwivedi, Y. K., Jaccheri, L., Krogstie, J., & Mäntymäki, M. (eds.), *I3E 2019: The 18th IFIP Conference on e-Business, e-Services and e-Society. Digital Transformation for a Sustainable Environment* (pp. 730–737). Trondheim, Norway: Springer.

Fitzgerald, M., Kruschwitz, N., Bonnet, D., & Welch, M. (2014). Embracing digital technology: A new strategic imperative. *MIT Sloan Management Review, 55*(2), 1–12.

Gersick, C. J. G. (1991). Revolutionary change theories: A multilevel exploration of the punctuated equilibrium paradigm. *Academy of Management Review, 16*(1), 10–36.

Granito, F. (2022). Digital transformation demystified. In Liebowitz, J. (ed.), *Digital Transformation: Accelerating Organizational Intelligence*. Singapore: World Scientific Publishing.

Gurbaxani, V. & Dunkle, D. (2019). Gearing up for successful digital transformation. *MIS Quarterly Executive, 18*(3), 209–220.

Kane, G. C., Palmer, D., Nguyen-Phillips, A., Kiron, D., & Buckley, N. (2017). Achieving digital maturity. *MIT Sloan Management Review, 59*(1), 1–29.

Karimi, J. & Walter, Z. (2015). The role of dynamic capabilities in responding to digital disruption: A factor-based study of the newspaper industry. *Journal of Management Information Systems, 32*(1), 39–81.

Kohli, R. & Melville, N. P. (2019). Digital innovation: A review and synthesis. *Information Systems Journal, 29*(1), 200–223.

Kraus, S., Durst, S., Ferreira, J. J., Veiga, P., Kailer, N., & Weinmann, A. (2022). Digital transformation in business and management research: An overview of the current status quo. *International Journal of Information Management, 63*, 102466.

Kunisch, S., Menz, M., & Langan, R. (2020). Chief digital officers: An exploratory analysis of their emergence, nature, and determinants. *Long Range Planning, 55*(2), 1–18.

Larsen, K. R. & Hovorka, D. S. (2012). Developing interfield nomological nets. In *45th HICSS*.

Liu, S., Cassumbhoy, F., Wong, L. H. M., & Davison, R. M. (2023). Spearheading digital transformation: The role of the chief digital officer. In *27th Pacific Asia Conference on Information Systems*, Nanchang, China, July 8–12.

Matt, C., Hess, T., & Benlian, A. (2015). Digital transformation strategies. *Business & Information Systems Engineering, 57*(5), 339–343.

Mettler, T. & Pinto, R. (2018). Evolutionary paths and influencing factors towards digital maturity: An analysis of the status quo in Swiss hospitals. *Technological Forecasting and Social Change, 133*, 104–117.

Metzler, D. R., Bankamp, S., Muntermann, J., & Palmer, M. (2021). The role of CDOs in signalling digital transformation endeavours: An analysis of firms' external communication tools. In *42nd ICIS*, Austin, TX (pp. 1–17).

Miconi, A. (2023). On digital fetishism: A critique of the big data paradigm. *Critical Sociology.* https://doi.org/10.1177/08969205231202.

Nwankpa, J. K. & Roumani, Y. (2016). IT capability and digital transformation: A firm performance perspective. In *Proceedings of the 37th International Conference on Information Systems* (pp. 1–16).

Pentland, B. T., & Feldman, M. S. (2008). Designing routines: On the folly of designing artifacts, while hoping for patterns of action. *Information and Organization, 18*(4), 235–250.

PWC (2016). Industry 4.0: Building the digital enterprise. Retrieved from https://www.pwc.com/gx/en/industries/industries-4.0/landing-page/industry-4.0-building-your-digital-enterprise-april-2016.pdf.

Sebastian, I. M., Ross, J. W., Beath, C., Mocker, M., Moloney, K. G., & Fonstad, N. O. (2017). How big old companies navigate digital transformation. *MIS Quarterly Executive, 16*(3), 197–213.

Singh, A. & Hess, T. (2017). How chief digital officers promote the digital transformation of their companies. *MIS Quarterly Executive, 16*(1), 1–17.

Soule, D. L., Puram, A., Westerman, G. F., & Bonnet, D. (2016). Becoming a digital organization: The journey to digital dexterity. https://papers.ssrn.com/sol3/papers.cfm?abstract_id=2697688.

Vial, G. (2019). Understanding digital transformation: A review and a research agenda. *Journal of Strategic Information Systems, 28*(2), 118–144.

Wade, M. (2020). From dazzling to departed — Why chief digital officers are doomed to fail. https://www.weforum.org/agenda/2020/02/chief-digital-officer-cdo-skills-tenure-fail/.

Weritz, P., Braojos, J., & Matute, J. (2020). Exploring the antecedents of digital transformation: Dynamic capabilities and digital culture aspects to achieve digital maturity. In *Proceedings of the 26th Americas Conference on Information Systems* (pp. 1–22).

Wessel, L., Baiyere, A., Ologeanu-Taddei, R., Cha, J., & Blegind-Jensen, T. (2021). Unpacking the difference between digital transformation and

IT-enabled organizational transformation. *Journal of the Association for Information Systems, 22*(1), 102–129.

Westerman, G., Calméjane, C., Bonnet, D., Ferraris, P., & McAfee, A. (2011). Digital transformation: A roadmap for billion-dollar organisations. *MIT Center for Digital Business and Cap Gemini Consulting, 1*, 1–68.

Westerman, G., Tannou, M., Bonnet, D., Ferraris, P., & McAfee, A. (2012). The digital advantage: How digital leaders outperform their peers in every industry. *MIT Sloan Management and Cap Gemini Consulting, 2*, 2–23.

Wimelius, H., Mathiassen, L., Holmström, J., & Keil, M. (2021). A paradoxical perspective on technology renewal in digital transformation. *Information Systems Journal, 31*(1), 198–225.

Chapter 3

Competitive Advantage from the AI Digital Transformation: Intangibles Still Matter

G. Scott Erickson[*,†,§] and Helen N. Rothberg[‡,¶]

†*Ithaca College, Ithaca, New York, USA*

‡*Marist College, Poughkeepsie, New York, USA*

§*gerickson@ithaca.edu*

¶*helen.rothberg@marist.edu*

1. Introduction

The progress of digital technology into business competitiveness has been marked over the last couple of decades. Traditional sources of competitive advantage such as labor and capital have diminished as each is readily available for a price (basic labor or key personnel) or by accessing capital markets. Newer sources of competitive advantage such as key scarce resources came into vogue through the resource-based theory of the firm (Wernerfelt, 1984) and remain so.

One potential key asset might be intangible resources. Intangibles are a group of assets one can't hold or touch unlike tangible or physical assets, but that can be applied by organizations to track performance, solve

---

*Corresponding author.

problems, and make decisions. Digital tools have helped the growth of intangibles as they provide new ways to collect, store, analyze, and apply these assets, and digital transformations have changed the terms of how to best manage intangibles for competitive advantage more than once during the past couple of decades.

The idea that intangible assets might be the critical source of competitive advantage in today's economy grew out of studies in areas such as knowledge management (KM) and intellectual capital (IC). Those disciplines posit that competitive advantage is obtained from the unique knowledge held in the heads of the organization's workforce, their knowledge. To the extent organizational knowledge can be shared between employees not only person-to-person but digitally, knowledge development has been enhanced by the digital connections now available to firms. But intangible assets are more than individual and organizational knowledge; they can also include the data and information available to entities, a capability also obviously enriched by the digital transformation to big data competencies over the past decade.

But the most recent addition to areas of interest concerning intangible assets is artificial intelligence. Intelligence is a defined and familiar concept in theory, and the techniques for analyzing data, information, and knowledge for intelligence insights are also generally recognized. What is new is the capability of systems to learn on their own from intangible inputs, the artificial intelligence (AI) systems we've all followed over the past years. While a lot of questions about AI exist, one important unanswered one is as follows: How does this digital transformation to AI platforms impact competitive advantage in organizations? Is it possible to gain some unique, sustainable advantage in the marketplace based on AI capabilities defining this latest digital transformation?

In this chapter, we look at these three digital transformations in sequence. By understanding how organizations found success in the first transformation, the advent of digital knowledge management systems, we can set a foundation and define some terms. By then looking at the second transformation, the growth of interest in big data and analytics, we can see the progression of the tools and better understand their capabilities that have led us to today. Finally, we'll examine the third transformation, to ubiquitous AI systems and how organizations might use available frameworks to guide thinking about how to strategically employ AI for competitive advantage.

2. Knowledge to Intelligence

Roughly 20 years ago we published a book, *From Knowledge to Intelligence* (Rothberg & Erickson, 2005), that was the first to consider knowledge management (KM) and competitive intelligence (CI) as related topics. Serendipitously, one of us came from a competitive intelligence background and the other from an intellectual property (verging on intellectual capital/knowledge management) background and found ourselves often talking about the same topics, even if from different perspectives.

The field of knowledge management is predicated on the idea that organizations are made up of individuals possessing knowledge or know-how in their heads (Bontis, 1998; Nonaka & Takeuchi, 1995). To the extent this knowledge is unique to the firm, it has the potential to be a source of competitive advantage over other firms not holding the knowledge (Teece, 1998). And if the organization can develop it further by recognizing new knowledge to add and better leveraging the knowledge base through sharing, competitive advantage can be enhanced. So everyone in production, for example, learns the most efficient way to execute the process. Everyone on the sales team understands the best way to present the offering and convince prospects to become customers. And so forth. When circumstances are stable, employees and managers can know the right way to do things.

Intelligence, on the other hand, especially competitive intelligence, is more about drawing insights from multiple intangible inputs, such as data, information, and knowledge. Moreover, it is meant to be actionable. So, based on circumstances and all accumulated understanding, a decision-maker determines the best strategic action to launch a particular new product. And they then see what works and what doesn't and continue to learn for the next set of perhaps novel circumstances. In a competitive intelligence framework, part of the puzzle is identifying and collecting the right set of inputs and then executing an analysis process to create actionable insights for the decision-maker.

Within this broad context, the KM side has a number of more detailed considerations and insights. Core ideas of the field include that knowledge can be explicit or tacit (Nonaka & Takeuchi, 1995). Explicit knowledge is codifiable, sharable, and just generally easier to manage. It's the type of knowledge that can be stored in IT systems and that winds up in procedure documents. It's also much more scalable, and the knowledge can be transferred across a large number of individuals and so have a more apparent impact on outcomes, such as sales, profitability, and innovation.

Tacit knowledge is more personal, harder to codify, harder to express, and thus harder to share. It's much more likely to be transferred one-on-one between individuals through mentoring or apprenticeships. Although it can be stored and shared in IT systems, it's more in the form of written case histories, post-mortems, and other more qualitative formats.

Consequently, for an organization looking for competitive advantage through KM, understanding the nature of the knowledge and employing the right systems to manage it are important (McEvily & Chakravarthy, 2002). Likewise, understanding other contextual variables such as absorptive capacity (ability to take in and use new knowledge), social capital (organizational culture, trust, and other aspects enabling willingness to share and learn), and similar situation-specific variables (Nahapiet & Ghoshal, 1998) is equally important.

Organizations able to identify valuable knowledge in their workers successfully motivate sharing and learning, and then applying the knowledge across the entity should see superior performance. Knowledge in the heads of individual workers is, pretty much by definition, unique to the firm, potentially valuable, and very hard for competitors to copy. Thus, defensible, sustainable competitive advantage.

With digital transformation, at this time in the early to mid-2000s, consultancies were driving the installation of massive KM IT solutions, looking to systematize and scale knowledge assets in organizations. Much of the valuable knowledge (chiefly explicit) in companies was being captured in IT systems. This meant the knowledge was now in a digital form, shared widely throughout the organization (and perhaps a wider network of partners) with multiple points of access. As a result, competitive intelligence (CI) efforts to gather knowledge (and information and data) from a target were considerably enhanced. A CI incursion could conceivably result in the loss of huge swaths of a knowledge catalog at one time.

Given that perspective, there is a balance between developing and sharing knowledge versus protecting it. Given offsetting risks, that means there is an optimal level of KM development. Before that optimal point, there are more advantages to be gained by continuing to leverage the knowledge. After that point, the risks of competitive incursions outweigh any additional benefits. This concept was the basis of the *From Knowledge to Intelligence* book, assessing the risks and optimal development points across industries.

Four scenarios were developed, representing extremes but allowing a visual, 2 × 2 matrix conceptualization. Each had a circumstance, labeled by its knowledge exposure:

- SPF 45: Cold War, high KM potential, high CI vulnerability
- SPF 30: Glass House, low KM potential, high CI vulnerability
- SPF 15: 800-pound Gorilla, high KM potential, low CI vulnerability
- SPF 5: Brilliance, low KM potential, low CI vulnerability.

The purpose of the scenarios was to provide a tool for strategic management of knowledge. If decision-makers understood their circumstances, they would know whether to aggressively develop knowledge for competitive advantage, take critical counterintelligence steps to protect knowledge, or perhaps choose less knowledge sharing given the risks involved with potential losses to competitors. At the time, much of the practitioner and scholarly world assumed more and more investment in identifying and leveraging knowledge was an unambiguously good thing.

From that foundation, a couple of the scenarios have fairly obvious reasoning. In a high KM/high CI world (Cold War), if a firm develops its knowledge and finds it contributes to competitive advantage and financial success (high KM), then one would figure a competitor would also be interested in it (high CI). At the other extreme, in a low KM/Low CI environment (Brilliance), if knowledge development doesn't lead to substantive advantage or is so individualized as to be hard to share (low KM), then competitors probably wouldn't go out of their way to acquire it (low CI).

The more complex situations are the middle scenarios. In a high KM but low CI environment, we suggested that additional factors such as market dominance (the 800-pound Gorilla) provided more protection from competitors employing the originating firm's knowledge effectively. In the low KM but high CI environment (Glass House), our explanation was that really valuable knowledge was scarce and so hard to develop. But when its presence was manifest, competitors would be all over the originator trying to uncover the details for themselves.

A second book, *Intelligence in Action* (Erickson & Rothberg, 2012), attached data to the framework. We measured KM development with a modified Tobin's q, essentially market capitalization to assets, with the difference taken as the intangible assets of the firm, essentially its knowledge assets and related intangibles. We assessed CI by the number of competitive intelligence professionals operating in the industry, taken from membership rolls of the Society of Competitive Intelligence Professionals (SCIP) and from attendee lists at major CI training conferences.

The data enabled us to classify industries by the four SPF types. Broadly, in the high/high cell contained industries, one would expect high knowledge-added environments, such as pharmaceuticals and software. Both of which, of course, are also notorious for heavy competitive intelligence activity. The low/low cell was also not a surprise, chiefly containing highly mature and/or regulated industries such as utilities or commodity manufacturing or industries dependent on single, brilliant individuals for guidance. In this case, little new, critical knowledge was being developed, and so CI efforts were unnecessary.

Once again, the other two SPF classifications were especially interesting. The high KM/low CI category was indeed populated by big consumer brands, the brand reputation and market leadership apparently providing some protection from CI. We also began to develop the idea that perhaps the nature of the knowledge assets might be different. Especially in the case of valuable brands, a lot of the knowledge was likely about customers and customer relationships, something that could be hard for a competitor to use effectively even if provided access. In the case of low KM/high CI, the most notable industry was financial services (actually numerous financial services industries, from banking to investing to insurance). Again, as we thought about it, it began to make sense. Financial services are awash in data: transactions, financial market results, etc. But data isn't knowledge. Knowledge insights might be pulled out of it, but the ability to do so is rare and highly personal. So the data could be captured by competitors, perhaps even duplicated with supplements from external sources, but the insights of key decision-makers could be the difference in successful strategies. Those thought processes or bases for decisions would be valuable but also very hard to uncover. The knowledge would not scale in the metrics, but aggressive competitive intelligence efforts to obtain it could be fruitful.

As before, the exercise in creating and exploring strategic knowledge management through this SPF framework engaged us for several years. We thought the concepts were solid and could provide guidance to practitioners and academics in thinking about when and where to pursue aggressive knowledge discovery and sharing. And it was from that foundation that we saw the second digital transformation take place — the explosion of interest in big data and analytics.

3. The DIKW Hierarchy

By the second decade of the 21st century, big data was a big topic. The second digital transformation enabled data collection from all sorts of sources, particularly those associated with firm operations or with the internet, including websites and browsing behavior, social networks, apps, e-tail transactions, and others. Where, previously, the expense of storing and processing the huge amounts of data being harvested might have been prohibitive, these new capabilities were enabled by decreasing costs. The affordability was particularly enhanced by the growth in cloud computing — the ability to rent storage and processing capacity from highly efficient third-party providers. These capabilities had the potential to massively impact competitive advantage and firm performance (Chen *et al.*, 2012; Manyika *et al.*, 2011).

Big data was often defined by the "3 V's": volume, velocity, and variety (McAfee & Brynjolfsson, 2012; Laney, 2001). Other versions had additional V's in their definitions, but the core three really captured what was different about the new environment. Volume referred simply to the massive amounts of data moving through systems and, again, the growing capabilities in handling those massive amounts. Velocity covered the speed of data collection and transfer, enabling real-time sharing rather than monthly, weekly, or even daily reports. And variety had to do with the increasing ability to handle not just basic structured data but inputs of all sorts, including text, images, video, and all types of unstructured data. As before, the declining costs of computing helped a lot as unstructured data typically requires much more storage space and can be resource-heavy when processed.

Analytics became another term often associated with big data. Analytics in this context typically meant one of two things. Initially, the arrival of big data and real-time reporting allows monitoring of activities, from operations to marketing to web behavior to social networking and all sorts of other aspects of the organization. Google Analytics, for example, provides instant metrics on website activity and performance through a monitored dashboard. Any out-of-the-ordinary results can be instantly investigated and addressed with a response, either through human or, more recently, artificial intelligence.

Alternatively, analytics can mean actual data analysis. Mining the data for new insights can involve advanced statistical techniques, including discovering correlations, clustering variables, or other tools designed to uncover relationships or differences. This approach obviously takes more insight and discovery than the monitoring function (though choosing the right action for a dashboard anomaly can involve some creativity) and is actually what most observers mean when referring to data analytics. Such processes are also aspects of what we commonly refer to as business intelligence, marketing intelligence, and so forth. But more on the topic of intelligence in a bit.

To really get deep into the weeds of capturing what big data and analytics mean in the KM world discussed previously, however, it helps once again to go back to some theory. Way back, one of the most useful concepts is the DIKW hierarchy first discussed by Ackoff (1989) and others decades ago, well before the growth of interest in knowledge management, big data, analytics, and intelligence.

DIKW, for data, information, knowledge, and wisdom, came out of information science and broke down the concepts (Rowley, 2007). Again, it is a hierarchy and so presented as a progression beginning with data and ending with wisdom. A simple explanation is that data is a collection of observations that become information when put into some sort of order. Knowledge refers to understanding what the information means while wisdom is drawing insights from the data/information/knowledge. One example that we've always thought represented the concepts well concerns traffic lights. Data are the specific light frequencies that result in a yellow light. Information would be that and other data put together to identify a traffic light at a particular location and direction has just turned yellow. Knowledge is the realization from a driver heading in that direction and location that their traffic light has turned yellow and they should take action. Wisdom is knowledge in context, so the driver draws together all available inputs such as speed, distance, time left to red, and such, and then decides whether they should continue or stop. Note that the last step includes a decision and action.

Consequently, when we started applying DIKW and the full range of intangible assets to strategic use of knowledge management and intelligence (Rothberg & Erickson, 2017), we saw a connection between wisdom and intelligence — indeed, our conclusion was that intelligence was a better term for how the hierarchy would apply to a more contemporary environment. A DIKI hierarchy, if you will. The hierarchy implies a progression, and maybe there is more value in intelligence than in data or information. Intelligence is certainly more rare and harder to use effectively and gain competitive advantage from. But big data has also pretty firmly established that there is value in data, information, and everything across the hierarchy. Data, information, knowledge, and intelligence can and should all be managed strategically. All have some potential to provide competitive advantage.

4. Cynefin Framework

A further interesting spin on an intangibles hierarchy perspective is key work from Snowden and others and a concept they refer to as the Cynefin framework (Snowden & Boone, 2007; Kurtz & Snowden, 2003). The framework has evolved over time but was envisioned by its creators as a tool to categorize decision-making environments and how better decisions can be made in each. The environments can be summarized as follows:

- *Simple*: orderly, connected, known knowns, a right answer exists, it needs to be uncovered.
- *Complicated*: orderly, connected with center, known unknowns, multiple right answers can be determined by experts.
- *Complex*: less orderly, disconnected, unknown unknowns, multiple possible answers, creativity required to identify a solution.
- *Chaotic*: disorderly, high turbulence, disconnected, unknowable, patterns not discernable, immediate decisions without full information needed.

The usefulness of the framework is having some sense of how to proceed with decisions in different identified environments. A manager realizing they are in a simple environment, where exploring information resources can help uncover an optimal, tested solution is quite different from one in a chaotic environment where decisions must be made more on intuition and a personal sense of what might work.

Continued work on the framework placed it more in the context of traditional KM theory and the DIKW hierarchy (Simard, 2014). With that perspective, it can be viewed as a hierarchy with the environment in part determined by the nature of intangible assets available and/or how to manage the intangibles to best effect. A revised, more hierarchical framework can be illustrated as follows:

- *Simple*: environment defined by data and information. Highly structured, easily communicated to both a centralized storage location and across individuals on the periphery. Patterns in the database are identifiable and applicable to decisions through known analytical tools. Data/information and knowledge on how to use them are easily sharable.
- *Complicated*: environment defined by explicit knowledge. Still structured and can be captured and stored centrally with KM IT systems and then shared back out to others on the periphery. Decision-makers can use knowledge systems as a tool, using what has already been done and already applied in similar situations to make the best decisions. Knowledge is analyzable and readily shared.
- *Complex*: environment defined by tacit knowledge. Less structured, knowledge is much more personal and less easily shared. When shared, often one-to-one, so less susceptible to capture by the center transferable individually on the periphery. Knowledge base is less organized but may hold anecdotes or case histories of what has worked in other situations, and creative solutions might apply those insights to a new situation.
- *Chaotic*: environment defined by intelligence. Unstructured, turbulent, knowledge as it is normally defined doesn't fully exist. Unique individuals come up with creative, intuitive solutions. These decision-making processes are almost impossible to share with others or for others to learn/copy. It's in these situations that irreplaceable stars rise to the top.

What this perspective provides is an understanding that as one goes up the stages, the intangibles get more complex, as the DIKW framework always suggested. But they are also more personalized and harder to communicate or share with others. As a result, the competencies required to apply intangibles are increasingly rare and harder to acquire. As opposed to copying data/information from a competitor, an organization would need to try to duplicate the decision-making processes and abilities of the competitor's superstar. The further up the hierarchy one goes, the more difficult the decision-making scenario and the more difficult it will be to gain competitive advantage based on intangibles.

This revised framework also provides a convincing explanation for what we saw in the SPF analysis. Some intangibles are easier to leverage and share internally and some (many the same) are more at risk of a competitor acquiring access to them (Erickson & Rothberg, 2018).

More specifically, in SPF 5 (Low KM/Low CI: Brilliance), the empirical study suggested heavy representation by old-line, commodity manufacturers, regulated industries like utilities, and creative industries, such as fashion. The data show low levels of knowledge development but these industries do tend to have considerable data/information. Decision-making based on such widely available intangibles is straightforward and similar across firms (Cynefin simple environment). Consequently, there is little knowledge unique to the firm, in that context, to be developed and little reason to invest in knowledge management. In the case of creative industries, valuable intangibles are likely to be highly tacit or even intelligent (Cynefin chaotic environment). A star creative director (e.g., Tom Ford) or a star innovator (e.g., Steve Jobs) has a unique, intuitive ability to make decisions, but the nature of their gift is almost impossible to teach to others, so KM investment also makes little sense. And in both contexts, competitive intelligence is also not useful as there is either no knowledge of value or it is almost impossible to transfer to the competitor.

In SPF 15 (High KM/Low CI: 800-pound gorilla), the empirical work slotted big brands of consumer goods and services industries into the category. Cynefin helps understand this context by suggesting an environment combining complicated and complex. In an age of big data, consumer-facing firms have the ability to collect huge amounts of data/information on customers (shopping patterns, loyalty apps, and social networks) which can turn into knowledge concerning their likes/dislikes and how to keep them engaged. Tacit knowledge and even intelligence will discern even further insights from studying other intangible inputs. But the data/information and knowledge are specific to the firm and not necessarily useful to a competitor even if it captured them. And, of course, the higher level of highly tacit knowledge or intelligence would be hard to transfer as well.

For SPF 30 (Low KM/High CI: Glass house), financial services firms were the most prominent representatives. Financial services are one of the most data/information-heavy sectors of a big data world, with data flowing from transactions, market results, financial reporting, and numerous other sources. Much of that is widely available, as is explicit knowledge to manage it. Competitive advantage comes more from tacit insights or intelligence. So there is an aspect of simple/complicated Cynefin environments in routine operations of all firms but a more complex Cynefin environment where decisions are made to differentiate firms. As a result, developing explicit knowledge is a lower priority and not as distinguishing a characteristic. Competitive advantage comes from individual insights on how to manage the substantial data/information/knowledge resources. To the extent these insights are incorporated into asset management, investing, or trading strategies, competitors have an interest in trying to uncover them — the tacit aspects are sharable even if some of the intelligence pieces might not be.

Finally, in SPF 45 (High KM/High CI: Cold War), innovative industries such as pharmaceuticals and information technology are heavily represented. Innovation will always require a variety of intangible inputs and a spark of creative insight (Eureka!) as the inventive idea comes into mind. But if that is the research part of the new product process, there is also the development part. Development is more about optimizing the creation and delivery of the innovation and is often much more about explicit knowledge that can be codified and captured in procedures (e.g., pharmaceutical manufacturing which must be documented for FDA approval). One could make the case that SPF 45 has elements of all the Cynefin environments, depending on the task or function facing the organization. Some data/information, explicit knowledge, or even tacit knowledge can be shared and leveraged, hence the metrics suggested high KM development. And those types of intangibles, of course, are of interest to competitors and can be effectively used by them if obtained. But SPF 45 firms also have highly tacit or intelligence applications that may allow even further competitive advantage but that are less easily copied by others.

Why is all this detail important? In strategizing how to obtain competitive advantage in an intangibles-driven world, the type of intangible and the circumstances of use make a difference. The conceptual background provides clear distinctions between data/information, explicit knowledge, tacit knowledge, and intelligence. In understanding the potential of artificial intelligence (AI) for competitive advantage, a settled, established definition of intelligence is useful, even if it may need adaptation for this new application. Further, the circumstances within which the different intangibles might be employed for competitive advantage also help. We have practical examples of how competitive advantage works or doesn't work with specific types of intangibles. Those examples are further extended by considering when to aggressively develop intangible assets, when not to, and when to take special care to protect value data, information, or knowledge from competitive intelligence efforts.

5. Artificial Intelligence

Consequently, we come to a discussion of the potential of AI for competitive advantage. In what might be considered the third major digital transformation to be discussed in this chapter, we can note the sudden ubiquity of AI in general and generative AI in particular.

Artificial intelligence has a number of capabilities, but the main idea is that it is a system capable of taking in sometimes massive amounts of inputs and analyzing them to make a recommendation or a decision (Brynjolfsson *et al.*, 2023; Chui *et al.*, 2023). Forms of it have been around for some time, including automated decision-making such as that used in manufacturing processes or to track web behavior. If a production machine is supposed to operate within given tolerances and then goes out of those tolerances, the intelligence system should be able to analyze what happened and make a correction. Or if visits to a website suddenly drop to nothing, the system would investigate and, again, self-correct if an obvious solution is found.

The more recent explosion of interest in AI has to do with the massive amounts of inputs that systems can process and make suggestions from. Again, the concept isn't that new. Recommendation engines for services such as retail (Amazon) and entertainment (Netflix and Spotify) have been scooping up data, information, and knowledge about users for years and then trying to recommend the best potential next product, video, or artist for each individual. What's changed, again, is the amount of inputs, going from a pretty huge level to one that's almost unimaginable. Generative AI systems have been fed big chunks of the entire Internet universe, not just an individual's interactions with a single firm. Based on those inputs, much more than any human could possibly take in and process, these newer AI systems are able to look for patterns, answers to previous questions, changes in circumstances, and numerous other variables, making individualized answers.

Those answers to previous questions, however, point to another important facet of these systems that actually gets to the "intelligence" part of the equation. Contemporary AI can learn. Famously, the consumer-facing AI platforms make mistakes ("AI hallucinations"). But that is how they learn and make better recommendations the next time, and the next, and the next. The better the system learns, the better the outputs will be in the future. There is a sense of trial-and-error that we can recognize from knowledge systems where successes and mistakes also lead to learning by humans. The same applies to AI systems.

So where do AI systems fit in terms of competitive advantage, given the discussion we've had throughout this chapter? The platforms are obviously an advancement in the gathering, processing, and use of intangible assets. Can that be harnessed for competitive advantage for a given firm? Perhaps. Consider some of the likely requirements.

5.1. *Unique Inputs*

As noted, AI systems have the ability to draw from a universe of data, information, explicit knowledge, tacit knowledge, and existing intelligence. That creates a data analysis and recommendation engine beyond the capability of most single firms. Harking back to the previous discussion, AI would be effective at drawing inputs from any of the Cynefin environments and providing recommendations based on more learning from intangibles than any current tools. AI can make sense of chaotic, hard-to-understand input scenarios in a way human or enhanced decision-making systems cannot. The organizations that apply a tool like that will be able to base decisions on a much bigger and more diverse set of intangible inputs while still making sense of them.

But does that grant competitive advantage? Not really, if the system is available to all. At some level, everyone using the same system (e.g., OpenAI) would get much the same recommendation, allowing for some random variation over time. All are looking at the same inputs and, if the sensemaking is done in the same manner, would receive much the same outputs.

Where competitive advantage would accrue would be from unique sets of inputs. That may be difficult to combine with open-access systems but could be done if differentiation from competitors is desired. Organizations holding large amounts of unique data/information can combine those assets with the AI systems existing data sources to provide context, arriving at more deeply analyzed solutions for their particular needs. Similarly, explicit knowledge holdings in IT systems and even tacit knowledge learnings might be stored as unstructured data, such as case histories. Starting from a different base could provide different, more tailored, and useful results.

This perspective fits what we know from the earlier discussion. Just organizing the data/information, the knowledge, or existing intelligence is a low-level activity in both the traditional DIKW view and in a Cynefin world. Complexity is added as higher-level judgments are made about what intangibles to include, how to make the database different, and how to create a more unique database capable of generating better suggestions.

5.2. *Directed Analysis*

Another lesson we are learning from public-facing AI systems is that the prompts matter. How one asks the platform a question is key to what recommendations come out. Better-framed questions will lead to better solutions.

Competitive advantage for individual firms related to AI would come from finding better questions that lead to the most useful recommendations. This is related to learning that is related to knowledge management. As noted above, individuals learn and turn that into knowledge. They learn from successes, and they learn from mistakes. As questions are posed, answers provided, and those answers acted upon, there will be successes and failures. The organizations learning most effectively and most quickly from those results will begin to differentiate themselves from competitors as AI systems are applied to key strategic and operational applications.

Again, going back to the theoretical foundation, knowing the right questions to ask is a higher-level intangible capability. Individuals learn from repeated interactions with the AI database what questions get the best answers. With repetition, this becomes unique learning/knowledge and can lead to singular insights/intelligence, again creating more likelihood of competitive advantage than a commoditized system.

5.3. *System Learning*

As just noted, AI platforms make recommendations for decisions. Some will work, some will not. Just as operators will learn to ask better questions, so the system will learn to make better recommendations. But how does that happen so the organization can ensure proper learning and benefit?

As also mentioned earlier, we know generative AI famously makes errors, from the highly publicized case of the law brief with multiple fabricated case precedents to students submitting imperfect assignments. These outcomes are actually part of the plan of AI. As also noted earlier, intelligence as we know it is actionable. It recommends actions (do this, change that, or submit this for your assignment). Intelligence grows as it learns, and it learns from whether the recommended actions are effective.

So, the example of a manufacturing process with a task that goes out of tolerance would have prompted a recommendation for an action to put it back in order. If it works, the system knows to recommend the same action next time. If not, the system knows to try something different. Similarly with autonomous cars. In these more complex, even chaotic environments, the AI system uses maps and route histories combined with sensors providing more immediate context of what is happening around the vehicle. As the car approaches a yellow light, the AI system driving the car would take action. It might be right, and it would learn to do something similar in similar conditions. If wrong, that would provide learning as well. The reason we don't yet have widely available autonomous vehicles is that the AI systems still haven't learned to make correct decisions at an acceptable level near 100%.

In the case of using AI in a competitive environment, to make strategic and operational decisions that are effective and lead to success, the system needs to know what success is and what isn't. When humans are making decisions, they learn — whether explicit knowledge about doing the job correctly, tacit knowledge about more complicated environments, or intelligence on how to make successful, intuitive decisions, they learn. With AI systems, there needs to be a feedback loop so the system knows it is being successful or not. It can then process success/failure along with context to learn to make a potentially better decision the next time.

An organization with an AI system learning more effectively and more quickly than competitors' platforms has the potential for competitive advantage. As with autonomous vehicles, this could be a long and complicated process but could lead to a unique, sustainable, deep competitive advantage.

Further, if one puts all the possibilities together: unique inputs, directed analysis, and system learning, the components can build upon each other to create a truly unique intangible capability — a capability almost impossible for a competitor to copy and also protectable from CI incursions as it has data/information differences, knowledge differences, and intelligence/learning differences. Some of that comes from the objective AI system but quite a bit of the direct that makes the platform unique and difficult to copy is the human element choosing the inputs, directing the analysis, and ensuring effective learning takes place. It is one thing for an AI system to transform data into recommendations and to learn from their outcomes. It is quite another for decision-makers to choose which actions to take in response to unique AI-generated insights. What is done with the intelligence generated by AI is where potential competitive differentiation resides.

6. Conclusion

This chapter has reviewed three digital transformations impacting organizations and competitive advantage over the last 20+ years. In each transformation, we've seen changes in the capabilities of digital systems that have changed how intangible assets are effectively employed. From the explosions in the size, speed, and variety of databases to how different types of knowledge can be identified and leveraged to how insights are created and acted on, each step has increased our understanding of how to use the new digital tools.

In the case of artificial intelligence, the newest systems have the ability to gather massive amounts of inputs, analyze them to make effective responses to specific prompts, and then learn from the results of the recommendation. Individuals and organizations are working with these new systems to determine how to best use them for their own purposes. But, of course, the readily available platforms that everyone can use become something of a commodity. They are important to employ just to keep up with competitors but not to grant any kind of unique advantage.

But based on what we know from the previous digital transformations, there are ways to add a unique element to tools for managing intangibles like data, knowledge, and intelligence. The more an organization can provide unique inputs, the more it can learn how to better direct the system in its recommendations, learning the best ways to prompt and guide decision-making. And the more it can learn from the success/failure of the recommendations, the more that organization can separate itself from competitors and gain some sense of unique, defensible competitive advantage from its intangible assets.

References

Ackoff, R. (1989). From data to wisdom. *Journal of Applied Systems Analysis*, *16*, 3–9.

Bontis, N. (1998). Intellectual capital: An exploratory study that develops measures and models. *Management Decision*, *36*(2), 63–76. https://doi.org/10.1108/00251749810204142.

Brynjolfsson, E., Li, D., & Raymond, L. R. (2023). Generative AI at work. *National Bureau of Economic Research Working Paper #33161*, (November). DOI: 10.3386/w31161.

Chen, H., Chiang, R. H., & Storey, V. C. (2012). Business intelligence and analytics: From big data to big impact. *MIS Quarterly*, *36*(4), 1165–1188. https://doi.org/10.2307/41703503.

Chui, M., Hazan, E., Roberts, R., Singla, A., & Smaje, K. (2023). The economic potential of generative AI. *McKinsey & Co.*

Erickson, G. S. & Rothberg, H. N. (2012). *Intelligence in Action: Strategically Managing Knowledge Assets*. London: Palgrave Macmillan.

Erickson, G. S. & Rothberg, H. N. (2018). Intangible dynamics: Knowledge assets in the context of big data and business intelligence. In Hawamdeh, S. & Chang, H-C. (eds.), *Analytics and Knowledge Management* (pp. 325–354). Boca Raton: CRC Press.

Kurtz, C. F. & Snowden, D. J. (2003). The new dynamics of strategy: Sensemaking in a complex-complicated world. *IBM Systems Journal*, *42*(3), 462–483. DOI: 10.1147/sj.423.0462.

Laney, D. (2001). 3D data management: Controlling data volume, velocity and variety. Retrieved from http://blogs.gartner.com/doug-laney/files/2012/01/ad949-3D-Data-Management-Controlling-Data-Volume-Velocity-and-Variety.pdf.

Manyika, J., Chui, M., Brown, B., Bughin, J., Dobbs, R., Roxburgh, C., & Hung Byers, A. (2011). *Big Data: The Next Frontier for Innovation, Competition and Productivity*. McKinsey Global Institute.

McAfee, A. & Brynjolfsson, E. (2012). Big data: The management revolution. *Harvard Business Review*, *90*(10), 60–66.

McEvily, S. & Chakravarthy, B. (2002). The persistence of knowledge-based advantage: An empirical test for product performance and technological knowledge. *Strategic Management Journal*, *23*(4), 285–305. https://doi.org/10.1002/smj.223.

Nahapiet, J. & Ghoshal, S. (1998). Social capital, intellectual capital, and the organizational advantage. *Academy of Management Review*, *23*(2), 242–266. https://doi.org/10.2307/259373.

Nonaka, I. & Takeuchi, H. (1995). *The Knowledge-Creating Company: How Japanese Companies Create the Dynamics of Innovation.* New York: Oxford University Press.

Rothberg, H. N. & Erickson, G. S. (2005). *From Knowledge to Intelligence: Creating Competitive Advantage in the Next Economy.* Woburn, MA: Elsevier Butterworth-Heinemann.

Rothberg, H. N. & Erickson, G. S. (2017). Big data systems: Knowledge transfer or intelligence insights. *Journal of Knowledge Management*, *21*(1), 92–112. https://doi.org/10.1108/JKM-07-2015-0300.

Rowley, J. (2007). The wisdom hierarchy: Representations of the DIKW hierarchy. *Journal of Information Science*, *33*(2), 163–180. https://doi.org/10.1177/0165551506070706.

Simard, A. (2014). Analytics in context: Modeling in a regulatory environment. In Rodriguez, E., & Richards, G. (eds.), *Proceedings of the International Conference on Analytics Driven Solutions 2014* (pp. 82–92).

Snowden, D. J. & Boone, M. E. (2007). A leader's framework for decision making. *Harvard Business Review*, *85*(11), 68.

Teece, D. J. (1998). Capturing value from knowledge assets: The new economy, markets for know-how, and intangible assets. *California Management Review*, *40*(3), 55–79. https://doi.org/10.2307/41165943.

Wernerfelt, B. (1984). The resource-based view of the firm. *Strategic Management Journal*, *5*(2), 171–180. https://doi.org/10.1002/smj.4250050207.

https://doi.org/10.1142/9789811295140_0004

Chapter 4

The Digital Transformation of Agriculture: Industry 4.0 Advances in Hydroponic Vertical Farms and Greenhouses

Eric W. Stein

The Pennsylvania State University, USA

Center of Excellence for Indoor Agriculture, USA

ews3@psu.edu

estein@ericwstein.com

1. Introduction

This chapter explores the profound impact digital technologies have had on farming by revolutionizing agricultural practices and fostering more sustainable and efficient food production. We look at the integration of cutting-edge technologies, data analytics, and smart systems to optimize resource utilization, enhance crop yields, and address the challenges of contemporary agriculture. We have narrowed the scope of this research to examine a relatively new type of farming; i.e., indoor farming, which includes modern greenhouses and vertical farms. Indoor farming was made possible by advances in LED lighting, irrigation methods (e.g., hydroponics), facility environmental controls (Stein, 2021), and advanced digital technologies aligned with Industry 4.0.

We begin with an examination of the meaning of digital transformation (DT) to frame a working definition of DT as it applies to agriculture. We then look at the parallel transformations of industry and agriculture based on the availability and application of evolving forms of information technology (IT), with particular attention paid to IoT, artificial intelligence (AI), machine learning (MI), big data (BD), robotics, and blockchain. We then take a deeper look at the characteristics of indoor farms, the value proposition they offer to owners, investors, and consumers, the principal components of costs associated with these ventures, and their impact on the environment. To better understand how digital technologies can be leveraged to save costs and raise the value proposition of crops produced via this means, we lay out the value chain of the typical indoor farm. Next, we outline the primary control systems that govern the production of crops indoors and discuss the role of building digital twins and how to align these systems with the digital technologies that have the most promise of impacting the business models of agriculture enterprises. To contextualize these concepts, we describe the application of Industry 4.0 technologies to strawberry production at an indoor farm start-up venture. We close with a discussion of some of the future challenges, opportunities, and impacts that will result from the digital transformation of agriculture.

2. Conceptual Development

2.1. *Digital Transformation*

Digital Transformation (DT) has emerged as a unifying and important descriptor of a range of activities related to organizational and IS research. It has been applied to the understanding of strategic IS issues (Bharadwaj *et al.*, 2013; Piccinini *et al.*, 2015b), to IS practice (e.g., Westerman *et al.*, 2011), and to a better understanding of the changes taking place in a variety of industries from automotive to healthcare (e.g., Piccinini *et al.*, 2015a; Agarwal *et al.*, 2010). On the other hand, some argue that DT has become an overused buzzword (Ossewaarde, 2019) that has been loosely defined. Vial (2019) reviewed 282 DT-related works and identified 23 different definitions of DT, which Owoseni (2023) attributes to the localization of social constructs. Another study by Gong and Ribiere (2021) aimed at constructing a unified definition of DT resulted in the identification of 134 definitions of DT based on a content analysis of 354 research articles (i.e., "Definition Collection Phase"). Subsequently, they analyzed each of these definitions and developed a draft definition of DT, which was then evaluated by experts in the field, resulting in a final unified definition of DT: "A fundamental change process, enabled by the innovative use of digital technologies accompanied by the strategic leverage of key resources and capabilities, aiming to radically improve an entity (e.g., an organization, a business network, an industry, or society) and redefine its value proposition for its stakeholders" (Gong & Ribiere, 2021, p. 12).

We agree with this definition with a few caveats. One issue is the implicit assumption that digital transformation is *inherently good* or beneficial. Indeed, from the perspective of the firm, it may be. On the other hand, like all transformations, the impact of DT may be differential depending on the stakeholder; i.e., there may be winners and losers. The other issue is one of omission. Digital transformations create opportunities by impacting the business model of the firm by lowering costs, raising quality (e.g., value), or both, i.e., DT can result in the creation of Blue Oceans (Kim & Mauborgne, 2015). Accordingly, we augment the general definition of DT as it applies to agriculture as follows:

Digital Transformation of Agriculture: A fundamental change process (with differential impacts on the firm's stakeholders) enabled by the innovative use of digital technologies, key resources and capabilities designed to radically improve an agricultural enterprise by redefining its value proposition and business model(s).

We use this definition to drive the analysis of the ongoing digital transformation taking place in agriculture. We examine the primary digital technologies being deployed, the changes taking place throughout the value chain, the opportunities for new business models, and the impacts on the stakeholders of agricultural firms.

2.2. *Digital Technologies*

Digital technologies have been defined in a variety of ways in terms of processes, technical artifacts, and impacts. Digital technologies have been framed as enablers of data collection, analysis, and decision-making (Gabriel & Gandorfer, 2023; Tey & Brindal, 2021). The Organization for Economic Co-operation and Development (OECD) defined digital technologies as, "ICTs (information communication technologies), including the Internet, mobile technologies and devices, as well as data analytics used to improve the generation, collection, exchange, aggregation, combination, analysis, access, searchability and presentation of digital content, including for the development of services and apps" (Mushi, 2022; OECD, 2014). Fitzgerald *et al.* (2014) identified digital technologies as social media, mobile, analytics, or embedded devices (Khin & Ho, 2019). Some of the more advanced digital technologies used to promote organizational innovation also include big data (BD), the Internet of Things (IoT), cloud computing (CC), augmented and virtual reality, artificial intelligence (AI), and cyber-physical systems (Urbinati *et al.*, 2018; Khin & Ho, 2019).

In the context of agriculture, Gabriel and Gandorfer (2023) identified 30 different digital technologies employed by Bavarian crop and livestock farmers. The technologies most cited included forecasting models, automated steering systems, farm management information systems (FMIS), digital maps, control systems, drones, telemetry, robotics, fleet management models, and remote sensors. Blockchain, big data, and machine learning (ML) models have also been identified as technologies enabling smart agricultural management (Hossain *et al.*, 2023; Mushi *et al.*, 2022; Protopop & Shanoyan, 2016; Liu & Liu, 2023). For the purposes of this analysis, we focus on the implementation of digital technologies in indoor agriculture most closely aligned with Industry 4.0 and Agriculture 4.0 as elaborated in the following.

2.3. *Industry 4.0 versus Agriculture 4.0*

Both industry and agriculture have been characterized as having gone through four periods of growth, development, and "revolution" (See Figure 1).

Prior to 1800, Agriculture 1.0 consisted of back-breaking manual labor facilitated by the use of crude tools and animals. Modern industrial development (Industry 1.0) began in the mid to late 18th century with the commercialization of steam engines and the water wheels, which offloaded much of the heavy work to machines. The transition to Industry 2.0 was facilitated by the invention of mass production methods, automobiles, and the commercialization of electricity. At about the same time, agriculture was transitioning to Ag 2.0 with the addition of tractors, fertilizers, and pesticides. These inventions heralded the dawn of the "green revolution", thus soundly rejecting the limits proposed by Malthus,[1] who argued that population would grow exponentially while food production

---

[1] *An Essay on the Principle of Population* published in 1798.

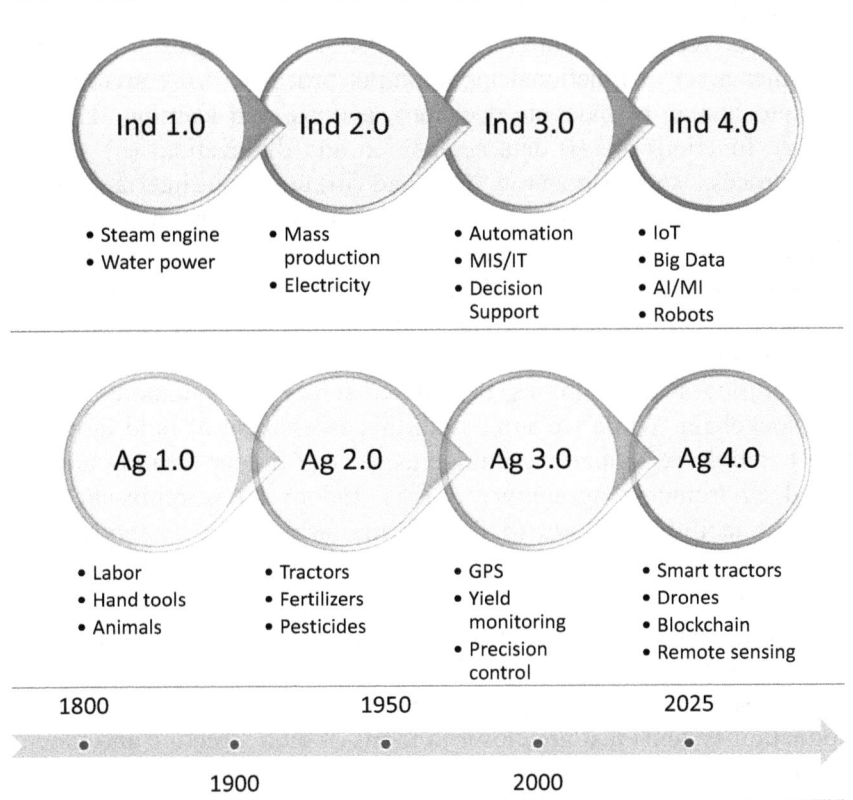

Figure 1. Evolution of industrial and agricultural technologies and practices.

Source: Inspired by Liu *et al.* (2021) and Aceto *et al.* (2019).

would grow arithmetically. Industry 3.0 was characterized by the application of automation, GPS, and information technologies to manufacturing and other industries from the 1960s to the 1990s, which ultimately led to Agriculture 3.0 and the period of "precision agriculture".

The current period denoted as Industry 4.0 (e.g., 2010 to the present) saw the maturation of several data analytic technologies (e.g., artificial intelligence and machine learning), the ubiquity of large heterogeneous databases (e.g., "big data"), and the emergence of IoT as an integrative architecture for data acquisition, connectivity, analytics, and applications. Other transformative technologies of Industry 4.0 include cloud computing, blockchain, robotics, open-source software, and improvements in human–computer interaction (Aceto *et al.*, 2019). Manufacturing especially has benefited from the IT assets that Industry 4.0 offers. Of course, Industry 4.0 represents more than just a list of technologies or capabilities but rather a set of functional input–output processes for converting raw data into human or machine decisions, actions, and learning. The three primary functions are (i) data acquisition and digitization, (ii) a hub to store, process, and analyze raw data, and (iii) an output interface to issue commands, make decisions, send results to other systems and so on. See Figure 2. It should be noted that the arrows represent networks and channels of communication (e.g., LAN, WAN, wireless, wired, and cloud).

According to Liu (2021), field farming has embraced several technologies aligned with Agriculture 4.0, especially well-suited to traditional field farming such as drones, distributed sensors, autonomous vehicles, and blockchain. While we agree with this assessment of field farming, it does not fully recognize the unique aspects of indoor farming and controlled environment agriculture (CEA). Indoor farms represent small-footprint facilities relative to field farms (which can be thousands of acres) with high levels of environmental control. We would argue that indoor farming has more in common with manufacturing than field farms, prompting Japanese researchers (e.g., Kozai *et al.*, 2016) to conceptualize indoor farms as "plant factories". In other words, indoor farms (e.g., greenhouses and indoor vertical hydroponic farms) represent localized production systems that are closer in terms of their structure and function to manufacturing systems and thus will utilize digital technologies better suited to Industry 4.0 than Agriculture 4.0. For the purposes of this analysis, we focus on the application of five Industry 4.0 digital technologies to indoor farming: the Internet of Things (IoT), artificial intelligence models (e.g., neural nets, machine learning algorithms), robotics, big data (BD), and blockchain.

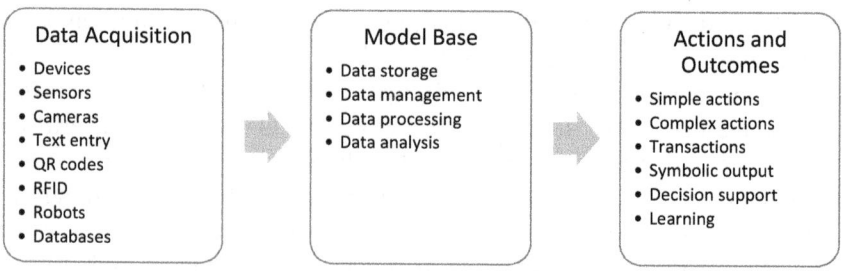

Figure 2.   A general input–output model of Industry 4.0.

2.4. *Industry 4.0: Architecture*

2.4.1. *IoT*

The Internet of Things (IoT) represents a comprehensive architecture (see Figure 3) that includes (i) raw data generated by industrial sensors on the edge that can send and receive data via a network, (ii) network connections and protocols that enable the transfer and processing of raw data at a central hub, (iii) an IoT platform that performs several functions including but not limited to device management, data management, integration, analytics, application development, and security, and (iv) an application layer, which may include alerts, displays, dashboards, and integration with other enterprise-level applications and databases (see Sorri *et al.*, 2022 for a comprehensive examination of definitions of IoT).

This robust architecture has been a driver of the production of smart consumer goods like dishwashers and dryers as well as motivating innovation in consumer, commercial, and industrial contexts. Since indoor farming is closer to an industrial model, we focus on the defining characteristics of industrial IoT, which is referred to as Industrial Internet of Things (IIoT). Five key parameters characterize IIoT as distinct from consumer or commercial applications: interoperability, scalability, adaptability, reliability, and security (e.g., Amjad *et al.*, 2021; Mirani *et al.*, 2022). (1) Interoperability requires that devices from disparate manufacturers function together. (2) Can the architecture scale as the enterprise grows and accumulates more data? (3) Can sub-components adapt to changes in the work environment over time? (4) Is the system reliable and within tolerances mandated for the industry? This is critical when it comes to production, food safety, and logistics of indoor farms. (5) Is the system secure? We illustrate how these parameters are addressed in indoor farms later in this chapter.

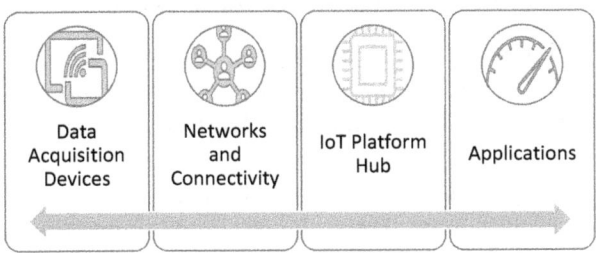

Figure 3.   Components of IoT architecture.

2.5. *Industry 4.0: Data Acquisition*

2.5.1. *Big Data*

Industry 4.0 is characterized by the advent of inexpensive, network-capable sensors and devices, which created new opportunities as well as challenges. Since they were cheap, companies could now afford to purchase tens, hundreds, and even thousands of sensors to collect simple numeric data as well as media-rich (Trevino *et al.*, 2000) data, such as images. The problem is how to store, process, and manage such a variety of real-time data inputs since traditional databases (e.g., SQL) were not designed for these types of problems. The industry needed a solution to the problem of what is now referred to as "big data".

Big data differs from traditional data in four important ways: volume, variety, velocity, and veracity (see, for example, Favaretto *et al.*, 2020; Yaseen & Obaid, 2020). (1) Big data sets are typically orders of magnitude greater than traditional data sets, e.g., BD may be measured in petabytes (1000s of terabytes) or even larger quantities. (2) Big data databases contain large quantities of unstructured and heterogeneous data, i.e., text, numbers, images, audio, and video, unlike traditional databases which contain structured text and numeric data. Consequently, BD databases require dynamic schema rather than fixed relational schema. (3) Unlike traditional databases that are relatively static, BD databases must accommodate and process new data in real time. (4) The quality requirements for BD are oftentimes much greater than in traditional settings. Big data sets may require robust validation processes that are capable of detecting errors in real time.

2.6. *Industry 4.0: Models*

2.6.1. *Artificial Intelligence and Machine Learning*

Artificial intelligence (AI) technologies represent a research agenda[2] that began in the 1950s, whose goal was to replicate human capabilities, such as reasoning, pattern recognition, learning, processing visual data

---

[2]Although Alan Turing speculated on the possibility of AI in a seminal paper written in 1950, it wasn't until 1956 at the Dartmouth Conference that research began in earnest, initiated by John McCarthy, Marvin Minsky, and others.

into concepts and ideas, speaking, writing, and understanding natural language, and imitating human movement, touch, and even smell. The immense computational complexities of solving any one of these problems frustrated any attempts to integrate them into a walking, talking, immensely smart human-like figure as popularized in movies like *Star Wars* and its derivatives. Instead, groups of researchers tackled subareas including search technologies, knowledge representation, visual processing, natural language processing (NLP), neural networks, robotics, machine learning, and other areas. Industry 4.0 thus represents the application of the fruits of over sixty years of work by thousands of researchers. One of the most promising developments in AI has been the advent of machine learning (ML). Machine learning is a method of training a computer to build a model of a specific domain of knowledge or problem space based on the acquisition of thousands or millions of like cases (Janiesch *et al.*, 2021). For example, to train a computer to recognize magnesium (Mg) deficiency in plants, the system would be fed numerous images of Mg-deficient plants so that it could easily recognize that state when presented with real-time visual data. Machine learning is enabled by a variety of mathematical methods including machine learning algorithms, neural networks, and recurrent neural nets (Janiesch *et al.*, 2021).

2.6.2. *Blockchain*

I have included blockchain under the model section of our framework because blockchain provides a means to accurately track transactions over time using encryption models. Blockchain is a type of centralized or decentralized database (e.g., ledger) for timestamping, storing, and validating data about assets exchanged between one or more parties (Di Pierro, 2017; Xu *et al.*, 2019; Khan & Salah, 2018). For example, blockchain can process exchanges of tangible assets (e.g., products, houses, land, and crops) or intangible assets (e.g., copyrights, patents, trademarks, and election votes). For businesses, this might mean tracking a product through its value chain from raw materials through production to packaging and shipment to consumers. What makes blockchain unique is the computational resources dedicated to validating each transaction. Every time new information is added, it is appended to existing blocks of data about the asset. A set of blocks (or blockchain) must together validate the transaction by solving for a "hash", which is a hexadecimal number associated with an equation used to encrypt the data. All blocks within the chain must arrive at the same hash number, otherwise the transaction is not validated. Some of the benefits of blockchain are immutability of records, transparency, and improved tracking from cradle to grave of the asset (Bettin-Díaz, 2018). It has been applied to a variety of contexts including supply chains in food production (Bettin-Díaz, 2018; Antonucci, 2019).

2.7. *Industry 4.0: Actions and Outcomes*

2.7.1. *Robotics*

Robots represent the deployment of artificial intelligence capabilities in physical form (unlike most AI which exists only as lines of code that enable symbol manipulation). Robots can perform several functions, from gathering and processing visual data, to manipulating physical objects in the real world, to making real-time decisions to navigating in three dimensions. Robots may be programmed to learn and act on their own or with input from human operators. For an overview of the application of robots in agriculture, the reader is referred to Vijay and Ponnusamy (2023), Wang *et al.* (2022), and Botta *et al.* (2022), among others.

2.8. *Toward a General Framework for Digital Transformation*

It is clear from the preceding sections that there must be alignment between the goals of Industry 4.0 as represented in Figures 2 and 3 and the digital technologies that facilitate those goals. We offer a high-level illustration of the alignment of the processes of digital transformation with advanced digital technologies in Figure 4. We use this model to analyze the ways modern indoor farms are adapting their business processes to achieve Industry 4.0 transformation in search of new business models. In the following section, we flesh out the unique characteristics of indoor farms, how they differ from traditional field farming methods, and why they are aligned with Industry 4.0 innovations.

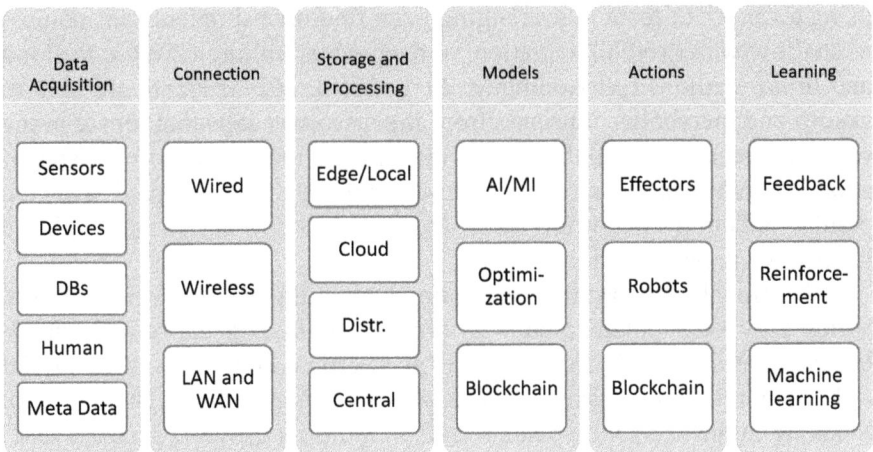

Figure 4. Digital transformation as a function of process and technology.

3. Indoor Farm Systems

3.1. *Indoor Farming Defined*

Indoor farming is a method of growing vegetables and other plants that require light under controlled environmental conditions, which was enabled in the past 25 years by advances in LED lighting and other technologies.[3] These farm systems are variously referred to as indoor farms, vertical farms, vfarms, zfarms, greenhouses, controlled environment agriculture (CEA), and plant factories (Stein, 2020, 2021; Thomaier, 2014; Kozai *et al.*, 2016). We focus on the characteristics of controlled environment indoor vertical farms (aka "plant factories") and greenhouses, which are the primary means enabling large-scale production of leafy greens and other vegetables that require natural or artificial light.

Indoor farms typically use hydroponic (water-based) methods to grow plants. Seeds are germinated in inert materials such as stone wool or peat, which are then irrigated with nutrient-rich water. Water is administered

---

[3] The one exception to this assertion is mushroom production, which requires only ambient lighting. The latter have been grown indoors in compost under controlled conditions without light for more than 100 years.

using a variety of techniques ranging from fine-mist sprayers (aeroponics) to shallow water (NFT) irrigation, to deep water culture (DWC), to flood and drain methods (Al-Kodmany, 2018; Stein, 2021). Plants are able to absorb and metabolize nutrients from the dissolved salts that ionize in the water. Alternatively, smaller farms may utilize the nutrient-rich water of adjacent fish farms (i.e., aquaponic systems) that are coupled with the plant production system (Al-Kodmany, 2018; Stein, 2021), although the latter have their limitations.

In greenhouse production facilities, lighting comes from the sun, which may be supplemented with artificial light, especially in northern latitudes (Stein, 2021). Plant factories and vertical farms use only artificial lighting but maximize growing area using stacking methods (Stein, 2021). Stacking in the horizontal plane results in multitier growing systems starting at ground level, which may attain heights of up to 25 feet. An alternative is to use vertical drip irrigation grow systems. This design is characterized by cylindrical multisite growing towers starting at ground level. In these systems, plants grow "sideways" toward artificial lights that are positioned at a right angle (Stein, 2021).

Indoor farming and controlled environment agriculture (CEA) methods share the characteristic of offering high levels of environmental control and monitoring (Stein, 2021), i.e., grower control of the interior climate, including light intensity, wavelength, and photoperiod, wind velocity, temperature, and humidity. The root zones of the plants in solution are also managed to obtain optimal levels of nutrients, PH, and dissolved oxygen (Al-Kodmany, 2018; Stein, 2021; Pennisi *et al.*, 2020; Gnauer *et al.*, 2019; Benke & Tomkins, 2017). Pesticides and herbicides are drastically reduced (Stein, 2021). Advanced farms make extensive use of sensors, IoT, robotics, automation, and control systems designed to optimize yields and minimize labor (Stein, 2021). CEA farms have the ability to produce plants with certain desired morphologies and nutritional profiles based on high levels of control (Stein, 2021). Sharathkumar *et al.* (2020) suggest that CEA enables environmental modification of plants on par with genetic manipulation.

The principal sustainable benefits of indoor farming methods are a significant reduction in the use of water, the reduction or elimination of pesticides, and mitigation of the effects of excess fertilizer run-off (Stein, 2021). The reduction in the use of energy, however, is not a characteristic of indoor farms. The ability to control the production environment results in several economic benefits: a stable supply chain, price stability, long-term contracts with distributors and retail markets, and high yields per square foot (Stein, 2021). Reduced pesticide use puts produce grown using CEA on par with organics, which command premium pricing (Stein, 2021). Indoor farms designed correctly can reduce labor costs and may be located closer to urban centers. The distribution of the means of production provides resilience to climate change, flooding, droughts, and other climate-related disruptions (Stein, 2021). The public sector envisions a role for indoor farms to ameliorate food deserts and unemployment and as a means to re-purpose abandoned buildings and lots (Stein, 2021; Thomaier *et al.*, 2014; Chance *et al.*, 2018; Despommier, 2010; Eigenbrod & Gruda, 2014).

3.2. *Indoor Farm Value Chain*

Indoor farms encompass a set of operations similar to regular farms with a few exceptions. The value chain (Porter, 1985) of a typical indoor farm is illustrated in Figure 5.

The value chain begins with the acquisition of raw materials from the farm's supply chain, e.g., seed, substrate, nutrients, and water conditioners. Once raw inputs are assembled, production begins with germination in climate-controlled areas. When the plants are 1–2 weeks old, they are transferred to seedling holding areas and after that to an area for maturation. Typical production times are 1–2 weeks for microgreens and 4–6 weeks for full-sized heads of lettuce. When mature, the plants are harvested live or the farm can cut the product for packaging. Live plants are usually packaged in plastic containers or boxes while cut plants are typically bagged. Plants waiting for shipment must be maintained at a temperature of 40 degrees or below (but above freezing) per the USDA

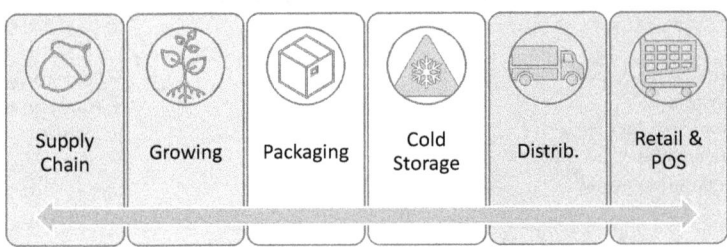

Figure 5.   Indoor farm value chain.

and refrigerated trucks must be maintained at similar temperatures. Once the product arrives at its destination, it is unloaded and stacked on shelves in consumer markets or warehouse holding areas for commercial customers. At each stage of the value chain, costs accumulate (see Figure 6).

Direct production costs include the costs of labor, energy (e.g., electric and gas), raw materials, and distribution. Research (e.g., Kozai *et al.*, 2016; Stein, 2021) has shown that labor and energy can account for nearly 80% of the cost to grow plants and only about 20% is from materials and distribution. Production labor activities include seeding, transfers, plant care, harvesting, and packaging. Working in conjunction with line personnel are horticultural specialists who analyze plant health, manage production flow, and troubleshoot problems as they occur. The primary energy costs for indoor farms are electricity for pumps, lighting, and HVAC, which may include other sources of energy, such as natural gas, propane, solar, and geothermal. Energy costs per plant for lighting, which can be significant, vary by the type of cultivar and planting density. Raw material

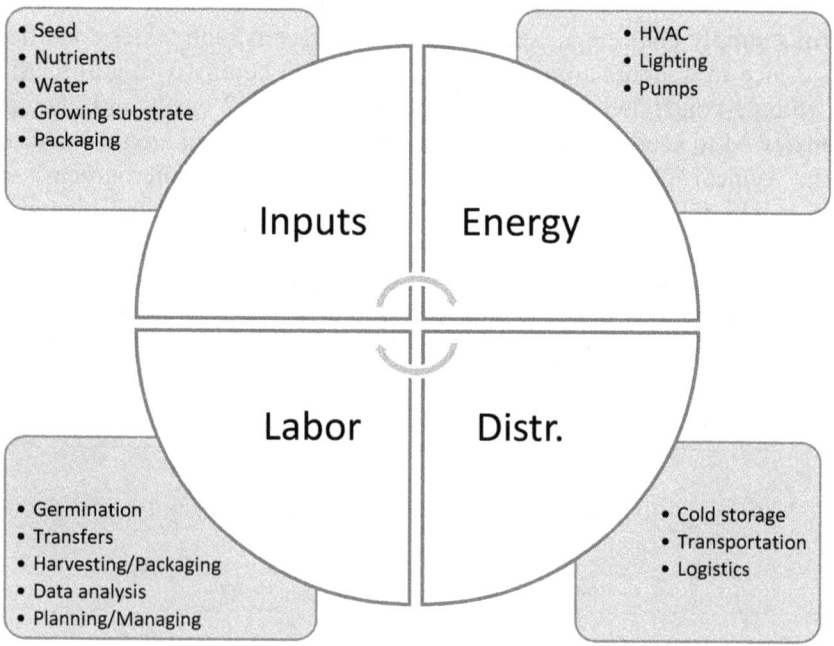

Figure 6.   Direct production costs for indoor farms.

input costs include seed, grow media, water, nutrients, water conditioners, and packaging. It should be noted that trucking is an increasing component of cost for farmers and has emerged as one financial justification for indoor vertical farms. For instance, prices to transport produce from California to the East Coast of the US in a 48-foot, 40,000-pound refrigerated truck range from $6,600 to 9,000 per load.[4] On the other hand, prices for the same from Florida to the Northeast (e.g., New York, Boston, and Philadelphia) are about a third as much.[5] Locating production facilities closer to large population centers thus reduces transportation miles and is one of the cost justifications for building indoor vertical farms adjacent to large urban areas.

3.3. *Indoor Farm Management and Control Systems*

Four primary inter-related systems need to be managed in an indoor farm's production environment to minimize costs and to optimize crop value (e.g., yields and quality) and hence revenues: (1) the infrastructure climate system, (2) the grow system, (3) the plant system, and (4) the operations system (see Figure 7). These systems are necessarily socio-technical and include labor, infrastructure, equipment, and digital technologies. In addition to labor with specialized horticultural knowledge, one or more managers will oversee the functioning of the indoor farm production systems.

The infrastructure *Climate System* (CS) is an integrated building control system that manages all aspects of heating, ventilation, and cooling (HVAC) to maintain optimal levels of temperature, humidity, and airflow for the plants. The CS also is responsible for monitoring and controlling the use of energy for the farm. Energy use is attributed to pumps, fans, heating, cooling, and lighting. The high use of energy for lighting is particularly significant in indoor vertical farms or "plant factories". Renewable energy (e.g., solar and geothermal) may be incorporated into the infrastructure design to offset lighting, heating, and cooling costs.[6]

---

[4] USDA Agricultural Marketing Service. Data retrieved on 11/25/2023.
[5] *Ibid.*
[6] For example, Ceres Greenhouses incorporates geothermal energy systems into their greenhouse designs.

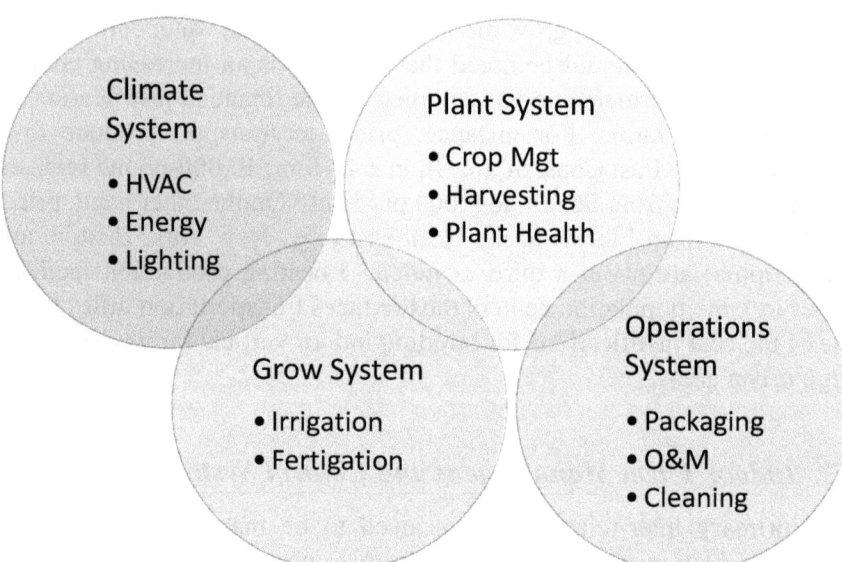

Figure 7. The interconnected systems of an indoor farm production system.

The *Grow System* (GS) includes the racking system where the plants are grown, the PVC pipes and valves (e.g., the plumbing) that transport nutrient-rich water, the nutrient reservoir tanks, and the fertigation system that controls nutrient levels and PH. The key control parameters of the GS include fluid flow rates, water temperature, dissolved oxygen, nutrient levels (e.g., EC), and PH.

The *Plant System* (PS) is the most labor-intensive component of the farm, which is typically performed by plant technicians and horticultural specialists. Plant technicians are responsible for all aspects of crop management, e.g., seeding, transplanting, pruning, culling, harvesting, and packaging. Horticultural specialists are responsible for the health of the plants and use their knowledge to detect disease, nutrient deficiencies, and the presence of pests, such as aphids.

The *Operations System* (OS) is also labor intensive and includes all activities related to facility and production management. Facility personnel are responsible for all operations including but not limited to cleaning, maintenance, and waste disposal. Operations also include packaging operations and logistics in preparation for distribution.

4. Opportunities for Digital Technologies in Indoor Farming

4.1. *Digitizing the Indoor Farm Work Environment*

One of the primary challenges for any indoor farm facility trying to implement Industry 4.0 capabilities is to fully digitize the production work environment. This is especially true for legacy farms that may have implemented older electro-mechanical devices for monitoring and control. The challenge is to send the signals from various sensors and controllers to a data analytic engine for automated control or to a dashboard that can accurately convert the raw inputs (e.g., voltage) to parameters needed for human decision-making, such as temperature, humidity, and PH. Complicating this goal is building a system that allows for the interoperability of devices coming from different manufacturers, each of which may have its own protocols and standards. Other requirements for IIoT facilities like indoor farms include being scalable, adaptive, reliable, and secure (Amjad *et al.*, 2021; Mirani *et al.*, 2022).

One of the solutions to these challenges is to create digital twins of the sub-systems that make up the farm production environment. For a comprehensive review of the literature on digital twins, please see Verdouw *et al.* (2021), Pylianidis *et al.* (2021), and Slob and Hurst (2022). A digital twin is a real-time, data-driven, digital replica of a real-world object or environment, which may be used for decision-making, systems analysis, and automated control. More precisely, digital twins may function in six different ways as noted in Table 1: (i) imaginary, (ii) monitoring, (iii) predictive, (iv) prescriptive, (v) autonomous, and (vi) recollective (Verdouw *et al.*, 2021).

The general structure of the transformation of the attributes of the physical object to the digital twin is illustrated in Figure 8. The digital twin can represent the past (p), current (c), or future (f) states of the attributes of the physical object.

Let's examine an example of the digitization requirements of an indoor farm growing lettuce (see Figure 9).

The physical objects would include components of each of the four systems outlined in Figure 7: *Plant System* (e.g., lettuce plants and crop management activities), *Climate System* (e.g., air, HVAC, energy, and lighting), *Grow System* (e.g., nutrient water in tanks, pipes, and channels), and the *Operations System* (e.g., cleaning, packaging, and logistics).

Table 1.   Six types of digital twins according to function.

Type	Description
Imaginary	Conceptual entities that depict and simulate reference objects that are not yet connected to objects that physically exist in the real world.
Monitoring	Digital representations of the real-time state and behavior of physical objects.
Predictive	Digital projections of the future state and behavior of physical objects using predictive analytics and based on real-time data of the physical objects.
Prescriptive	Smart digital objects that add intelligence for recommending corrective and preventive actions on real-life objects.
Autonomous	Operate autonomously and fully control the behavior of real-life objects without on-site or remote intervention by humans.
Recollection	Maintain the history of physical objects.

Source: Adapted from Verdouw *et al.* (2021).

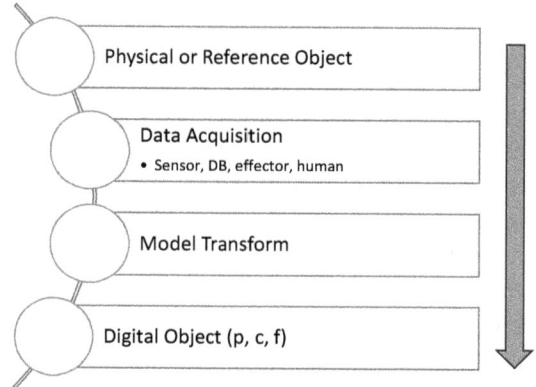

Figure 8.   General structure of a digital twin.

Source: Inspired by Verdouw *et al.* (2021).

The twin would be fed data from sensors on air temperature and humidity, water temperature, oxygen and EC, light levels, energy use in kWh, plant images, and so on. The digital twin would then represent that data in its current state, a past state, or a future state according to one of the six functions noted in Table 1. An example of an indoor farm digital twin dashboard built by software company Microclimates, Inc. is illustrated in Figure 10.

Figure 9. Illustration of modern indoor farm system.

Each of the parameters displayed has a physical equivalent data acquisition device. Sensors may be wired directly or connected to the central edge computing hub via a LoRaWAN network. The raw data are processed into user-meaningful measures and represented by the digital twin cards, thus serving as decision support for human farm operators. A farm managed by digital twins may also operate autonomously without AI and without human intervention as well. The feedback loop between the physical environment, data collected by sensors, and the digital twins allows for optimal management of the work environment. Additionally, the rich dataset generated by the digital twins may be used to train machine learning models, which may be deployed for predictive analysis, anomaly detection, and optimization of environmental processes. Digital twins thus act as a bridge between the physical and virtual realms, which can empower humans or AI to make informed decisions and contribute to more sustainable and resource-efficient production management. In a

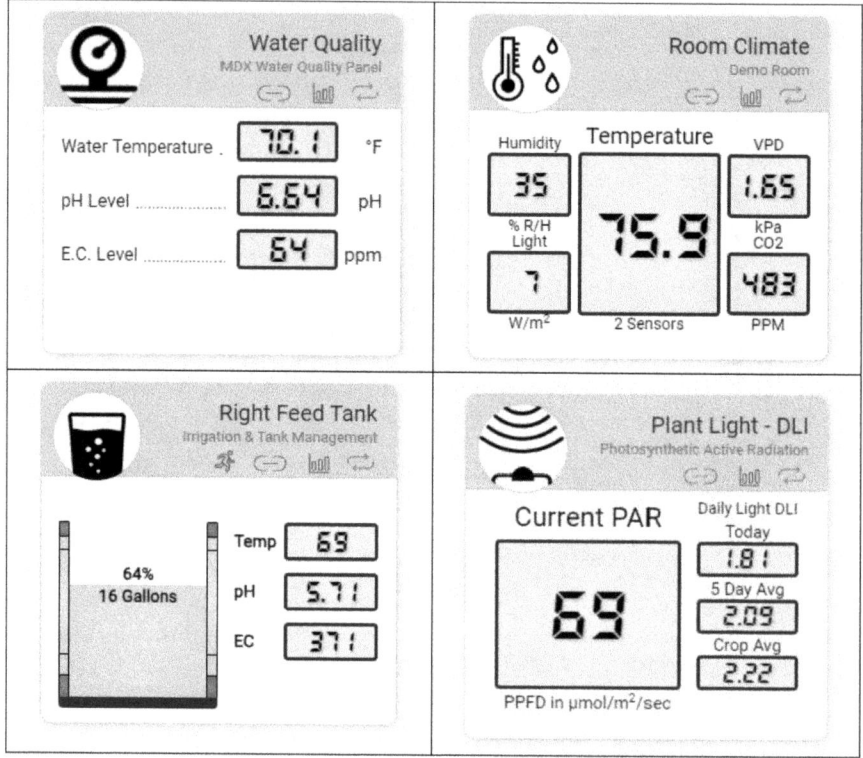

Figure 10. Example of an indoor farm digital twin dashboard for decision support.
Source: Images courtesy of Microclimates, Inc., https://www.microclimates.com/.

fully automated farm, data would be fed directly to an AI model that would autonomously issue commands without human intervention. We explore how one company is working to achieve this goal in the case study section of this chapter.

4.2. Strategic Applications of Digital Technologies That Impact the Business Model

Fundamentally, all business strategy is derived from the business model, i.e., how the firm makes money in the long run. The strategic application of digital technologies for the digital transformation of agriculture (or any industry) is a function of the likely impact on the business model throughout the value chain. Digital transformation thus emerges from the relationships between the value chain, the business model, and the enabling digital technologies. We designate this as the *Digital Transformation Nexus*.

These relationships are also reflected in the equation

$$\textbf{Profits = Revenues – Costs,}$$

which can also be written as

Revs – (Variable Costs + Fixed Costs)

=> $(p*q) - (c*q)$ – Fixed Costs

=> **Profits = $q\,(p - c)$ – Fixed Costs,**

where p stands for price, q is quantity, and c is the unit cost of the product. We can use this iteration to analyze the likely impact of various digital transformations. For instance, some IT applications may lower unit costs (e.g., labor) while other applications may increase the value of the crop (e.g., quality), resulting in the ability of the firm to raise prices to reflect the superior value proposition. These relationships are illustrated in the context of an indoor farm in Table 2.

For example, we can see that the [IoT-AI/ML-Robotics-BD] cluster can play a key role in reducing the amount of labor required for crop management (e.g., pruning and harvesting) and managing plant health (e.g., detecting diseases, pests, and nutrient deficiencies). The [IoT-AI/ML] cluster can have an impact on both reducing energy costs and increasing yields and quality. Blockchain can be used to effectively manage incoming supplies thus reducing material costs as well as helping to track the distribution of products to retailers and derive metrics on shrinkage. Quality is also directly impacted by the quality of the raw materials in supply chains (Bettin-Dıaz, 2018). Blockchain can also impact quality during the distribution phase by ensuring that the product has been maintained at USDA-recommended temperatures. Another interesting application of advanced digital technologies is in lighting and energy management. For example, some LED lights accept variable voltage input so that light recipes can be customized according to wavelength, photoperiod, intensity, and other variables that greatly impact energy costs as well as plant quality and yield. These dynamic lighting solutions include network architectures, software, and hardware that can be dash-boarded from the cloud. Another exciting development is the addition of Class 4 fault-managed power and cabling systems to NEC code (e.g., Article 726). The primary feature is that circuits are current-limited for faults between a Class 4 transmitter and receiver and will shut off within milliseconds (Ode, 2023). Furthermore, the technology allows for the simultaneous transmission of rich data (e.g., images, video, and text) and power (up to

Table 2. Main applications of Industry 4.0 technologies to indoor farm sub-systems.

Value Chain Systems >>	Supply Chain	Plant System	Plant System	Climate System	Climate System	Grow System	Ops System	Ops System	Distr. Chain
Functions	Raw Inputs	Crop Mgt	Plant Health	HVAC	Energy & Light	Fertigation Irrigation	O&M Clean	Packing Logistics	Transport
IoT		√	√	√	√	√	√	√	
AI/ML		√	√	√	√	√	√	√	
Robotics		√	√				√	√	
Big Data		√	√						
Blockchain	√								√
Business Variables	C/R	C	C/R	C/R	C	C/R	C	C	C
Business Impact	Input/ Quality	Labor/ Quality	Labor/ Quality	Energy Yield Quality	Energy Yield Quality	Inputs Yield Quality	Labor	Labor	Output/ Quality

Notes: (√) indicates an Industry 4.0 technology application area. *C*=cost. *R*=revenue. *C/R*=both. We have also included both inbound logistics (i.e., supply chain) and outbound logistics (distribution chain).

450V peak AC or DC) via IoT, smart building systems, and ethernet over longer distances (Ode, 2023). These capabilities dovetail nicely with indoor farms, which need to distribute power to lights and other devices as well as transmit data from sensors over the grow area.

5. Case Study

5.1. *Growing Strawberries in Greenhouses Using Robots*

Growing strawberries indoors under controlled conditions in indoor farms and greenhouses (Kubota, 2021) has been the focus of increasing research and industry interest in the past few years. A recent search using Proquest of peer-reviewed journals using the keywords "strawberry" and "greenhouse" in the article title produced over 215 results. USDA data and recent studies have shown that strawberry demand is on the rise (Samtani *et al.*, 2019). From an economic perspective, strawberries are an attractive crop because they command relatively high prices at the wholesale and retail levels. For example, a standard one-pound package of organic strawberries can sell retail for upwards of $6.49/lb[7] while vertically farmed berries in upscale retail markets such as NYC and LA can cost $20 or more for less than a pound (Hines, 2022). Unlike the production of leafy greens such as lettuce and microgreens, strawberries must be pollinated mechanically or using beneficial insects (e.g., bees) at the right time to produce flowers and fruits. Strawberries also require 2–3 times as much light as leafy greens, which contributes to the energy cost, especially in indoor vertical farms where energy requirements for lighting are much more significant. Another challenge to growing strawberries is that they are relatively fragile plants prone to disease, which require considerable care in handling, managing, cleaning, and packaging, thus adding to labor costs.

To address the challenge of lowering labor costs while maintaining quality, one indoor farm start-up, Zordi, is leveraging advanced digital technologies including robots and AI analytics to grow strawberries in relatively low-cost greenhouses (see Figure 11). The company was founded by Dr. Gilwoo Lee, a graduate of MIT, Carnegie Mellon, and the University of Washington in computer science, robotics, and AI. According to Lee, Zordi's mission is to "feed the world with high-quality, sustainable food".[8]

---

[7]USDA Agricultural Marketing Service data dated 9/1/2023.
[8]Personal communication. 12/31/2023.

Figure 11.   Scouting robot collecting visual data on strawberries in greenhouse.
Source: Image courtesy of Zordi, Inc., https://www.microclimates.com/.

The company has received $20M in venture funding (Hortidaily, 2023). At the time of writing, the price of a ½ lb package of Zordi strawberries was $18 at a retail partner in New York City.[9] Although the company is still in start-up mode and doing R&D, according to the company's estimates, each farm high tunnel is expected to yield gross profits of 50–60% with a projected capital payback of approximately three years.[10] According

---

[9]Price on 12/29/23 of an 8 oz package of strawberries at Butterfield Market, a retail partner in New York, NY listed on Zordi's website.
[10]Personal communication. 12/3/2023.

to Lee, these projections are based on selling strawberries directly to retail grocery stores in major metro areas at competitive prices at scale.[11]

Zordi's R&D farm is located in Oakfield, NY, near Buffalo and features several inter-connected gabled medium technology greenhouses designed to test sensors, robots, and its analytic models. Its second farm, which is designed for commercial production using high tunnel greenhouses, is located in Vineland, NJ, on the site of a former farm. High tunnels (or hoop houses) are relatively inexpensive structures that are built using galvanized metal piping bent in a semi-circle. Transparent plastic poly film is used to clad the structure, which protects the plants from cold, wind, rain, and snow while still admitting sufficient light for the plants. Greenhouses typically require lower energy costs than indoor vertical farms, although heating with natural gas or propane may be required in northern latitudes and cooling may be necessary in warmer climates. Zordi has chosen to invest in robotics and AI (as opposed to the building structure itself) to reduce labor costs associated with the plant and operations systems while enabling high yield and quality at scale (see Table 3). At the time of this writing, energy, lighting, and other components of cost are not linked to the AI analytic model but could be at a future date.[12] The long-term goal is presumably to lower the total cost of goods sold (COGS) sufficiently to enable the firm to increase gross margins and/or to expand market share by lowering prices.

The company's approach to digital transformation is grounded in the idea of a central "AI farm manager" making decisions based on data it receives from stationary IoT sensors and roving robots (see Figure 12).

In this architecture, three types of robots perform functions that closely resemble line production workers, whereas the AI farm manager serves to augment or replace skilled labor and horticultural specialists at the production facility. The harvesting robots do plant maintenance activities such as pruning, cutting, harvesting, as well as sorting and packing of fresh produce based on the maturity of the plants (see Figure 13). The scouting robots traverse the aisles between plants and collect data on the visual appearance of the plants, the presence of insects, and other parameters related to plant health and the environment (See Figure 11). These data are relayed to the central AI farm manager, which houses the processing, BD database, and models. The AI farm manager parses the data and

---

[11] Personal communication. 12/31/2023.

[12] *Ibid.*

Table 3.   Current applications of Industry 4.0 technologies at Zordi.

Value Chain Systems >>	Supply Chain	Plant System	Plant System	Climate System	Climate System	Grow System	Ops System	Ops System	Distr. Chain
Functions	Raw Inputs	Crop Mgt	Plant Health	HVAC*	Energy/ Light*	Fertigation/ Irrigation*	O&M Clean	Packing Logistics	Transport
IoT		√	√						
AI/ML		√	√					√	
Robotics		√	√					√	
Big Data		√	√						
Blockchain									
Business Variables	C/R	C	C/R	C/R	C	C/R	C	C	C
Business Impact	Input/ Quality	Labor/ Quality	Labor/ Quality	Energy Yield Quality	Energy Yield Quality	Inputs Yield Quality	Labor	Labor	Output/ Quality

Notes: Primary digital technology applications currently deployed at Zordi are highlighted with checkmarks. Future applications of Industry 4.0 tech are indicated with an asterisk (*). Standard automation for HVAC, energy, and fertigation is currently implemented but not indicated in the table.

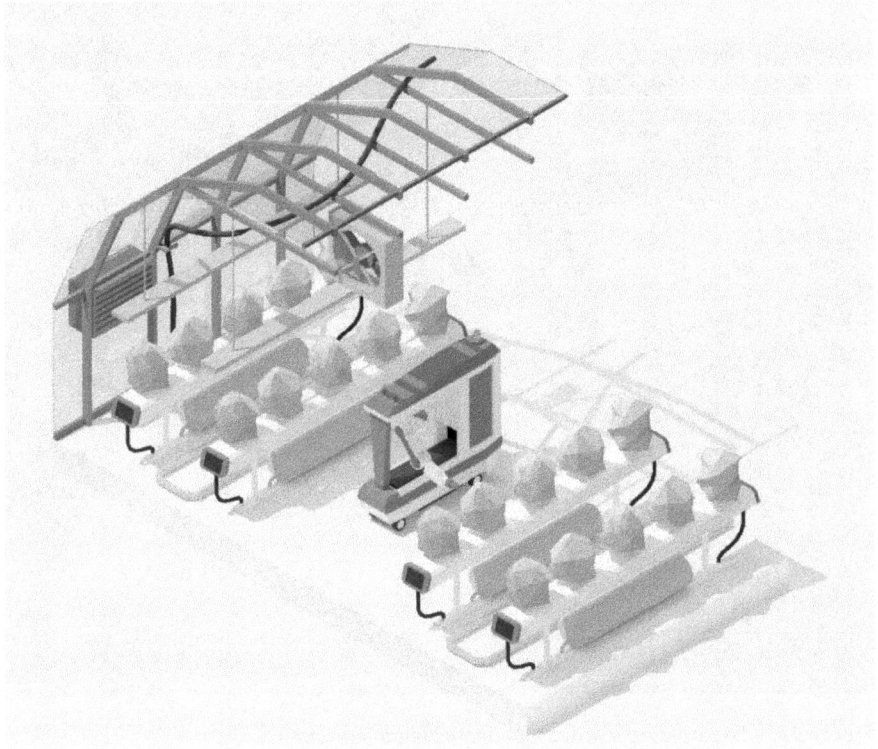

Figure 12.   Illustration of smart greenhouse.

uses analytical models to process the information into tasks. For example, it might use pattern matching, machine learning, and other AI techniques to detect disease, nutrient deficiencies, and other plant anomalies, leading to specific actions that need to be taken. For example, an outbreak of predatory insects might trigger the need for a foliar spray at specific locations. A 3rd-party robot customized to Zordi's specifications will then administer foliar sprays when needed. In summary, the AI farm manager monitors the farm over time and generates work orders to optimize production to meet the farm's objectives, such as yield and quality. In this sense, it is a good example of a socio-technical system. The AI farm manager and human analysts may also use operations data to improve the functioning of the farm over time.

Figure 13.   Examples of Zordi robot harvesting mature fruit.
Source: Image courtesy of Zordi, Inc.

6. Challenges and Risks

While there are many opportunities for the application of Industry 4.0 technologies to indoor farming, there are several challenges and risks:

- Financial Requirements
- Human and Machine Training
- Business and Management
- Social and Environmental Impacts.

One of the biggest challenges is financial. Modern indoor farms require significant capital for land, planning, design, construction, R&D, and operations. Capital expenditures for land and buildings can be mitigated by locating in rural areas but production equipment (e.g., lighting, grow systems, and HVAC) can range from \$150 to 400/ft^2 or more (Stein, 2021), resulting in facilities costing tens and even hundreds of millions of dollars. For example, AppHarvest needed a \$91 million construction loan to build a 60-acre greenhouse in Richmond, KY (AppHarvest, 2021), which was on top of other funding it received in the hundreds of millions. Planning and design may take several months or years to prepare architectural plans, secure permits for water and electricity, construction, and install racking, fertigation systems, lighting, and other equipment to facilitate operations. Capital costs for lights alone can be in the hundreds of thousands or millions of dollars. Operating costs can also be expensive, especially for indoor vertical farms that require artificial lighting running 365 days a year for 18 hours or more per day at intensities of 5–10 times the amounts required for standard building interiors. For example, growing cultivars at illumination rates of 10–15 watts per ft^2 using high efficacy LEDs (DOE, 2020) can result in operating costs for lighting alone that run 2–3 million dollars per year for a 100,000 ft^2 farm. This fact runs counter to the narrative that vertical farms are fully sustainable. While from a land and water use perspective, they can be, from an energy perspective, they are not (Stein, 2021).

Adding to these infrastructure costs are R&D costs for robots for crop management and training AI/MI to recognize plant pathologies and nutrient deficiencies. Training an AI model can be extremely expensive including costs for software, hardware, processing, and personnel and run into the millions (Vanian & Leswing, 2023). Another risk for indoor farms is managerial: Is the farm being run as a business and is the business model sound? There are numerous examples of failure in the industry. AppHarvest, which at one point had a market value of 3.68 billion in 2021 (ACG Kentucky, 2021), went out of business after declaring Chapter 11 in late 2023. Their failure was a function of poor management, human training deficiencies, and below-average yields in terms of quality and quantity rather than a lack of automation. In short, IT alone cannot solve all problems. Fifth Season, a high-tech indoor vertical farm located outside Pittsburgh, went out of business in 2022 after having received over \$80 million in venture capital spent mostly on automation, robotics, and AI. Founded by three Carnegie Mellon graduates in 2015, the farm is a textbook example of investing too much in technology and not enough in people and the business model. A former VP of the company, Chris Cerveny remarked, "Startups should be mindful of what automation they're putting in and whether there is a return on investment. Don't auto-mate for the sake of automation; carefully decide where you will automate and have a progression.... Also, the burn [in vertical farming] is very high — not just in the utilities and the growing but in the cost of customer acquisition and all the things that you have to do to try to build a national brand" (Marston, 2023). In summary, at the end of the day, a farm is a business, and we have to ask ourselves the following: Is it cost effective to spend tens or hundreds of millions of dollars on facilities that produce low-margin commodities such as lettuce and tomatoes? A profitable indoor farm will not produce 5× or 10× ROI but can expect modest returns of 15–20% (Pollard, 2023). With that kind of return, it will take several years to write off capital depreciation alone.

7. Conclusion

These caveats aside, we see opportunities for greenhouses and vertical farms to continue to transform into autonomous or semi-autonomous pro-duction systems as the price of Industry 4.0 digital technologies falls. Future farms will benefit from well-trained AI/MI algorithms available "off the shelf". The price of farm robots will continue to go down. IoT platforms will better support big data applications in indoor farm settings. We also see a continued de-coupling of hardware and software for indoor farm environments. For example, many of the solutions for energy management, fertigation, and lighting began with equipment developed by hardware manufacturers. Although the latter offer proprietary software interfaces for their equipment, the market is moving to hardware-independent digital twin software solutions offered on a subscription basis,[13] thus promoting flexibility, interoperability, and affordability. Finally, we see successful indoor farm enterprises placing a premium on their people as well as production. Integrating human beings into complex socio-technical farm enterprises run by robots and AI can be disorienting and may result in low morale and high turnover rates. Future farm organizational designs must take into account the needs of employees and their training in tandem with the design of the farm automation and decision-support systems.

---

[13] For example, Microclimates, Inc.

Acknowledgments

The author wishes to thank the following people and organizations for their support and contributions to this work: Dr. Gilwoo Lee, CEO of Zordi, Inc.; Neda Vaseghi (CEO) and Loren West (CTO) of Microclimates, Inc.; Sepehr Archard, CEO of iGrow News and Suzanne Pruit, Events Director at Indoor Ag-Con.

References

Aceto, G., Persico, V., & Pescapé, A. (2019). A survey on information and communication technologies for Industry 4.0: State-of-the-art, taxonomies, perspectives, and challenges. In *IEEE Communications Surveys & Tutorials*, *21*(4), 3467–3501 (Fourthquarter). DOI: 10.1109/COMST.2019.2938259.

ACG Kentucky. (2021). AppHarvest — A SPAC IPO, merger & acquisition and $3.68B success story. March 18, 2021. Retrieved from https://www.acg.org/kentucky/events/appharvest-spac-ipo-merger-acquisition-and-368b-success-story#:~:text=Since%20listing%20on%20the%20NASDAQ,Special%2DPurpose%20Acquisition%20Company.

Agarwal, R., Guodong, G., DesRoches, C., & Jha, A. K. (2010). The digital transformation of healthcare: Current status and the road ahead. *Information Systems Research, 21*(4), 796–809.

Al-Kodmany, K. (2018). The vertical farm: A review of developments and implications for the vertical city. *Buildings, 8*, 24. DOI: 10.3390/buildings8020024.

Amjad, A., Azam, F., Anwar, M. W., & Butt, W. H. (2021). A systematic review on the data interoperability of application layer protocols in industrial IoT. *IEEE Access, 9*, 96528–96545. DOI: 10.1109/ACCESS.2021.3094763.

AppHarvest.com (2021). AppHarvest secures $91 million financing arrangement with equilibrium capital for construction of rapidly growing network of high-tech controlled environment agriculture facilities. Retrieved from https://investors.appharvest.com/node/7471/pdf.

Benke, K. & Tomkins, B. (2017). Future food-production systems: Vertical farming and controlled-environment agriculture. *Sustainability: Science, Practice and Policy, 13*, 13–26. DOI: 10.1080/15487733.2017.1394054.

Bettin-Díaz, R., Rojas, A. E., & Mejía-Moncayo, C. (2018). Methodological approach to the definition of a blockchain system for the food industry supply chain traceability. In Gervasi, O., *et al. Computational Science and Its Applications — ICCSA 2018*. ICCSA 2018. Lecture Notes in Computer Science (Vol. 10961). Cham: Springer. https://doi-org.ezaccess.libraries.psu.edu/10.1007/978-3-319-95165-2_2.

Bharadwaj, A., El Sawy, O., Pavlou, P., & Venkatraman, N. (2013). Digital business strategy: Toward a next generation of insights. *MIS Quarterly*, *37*(2), 471–482.

Botta, A., Cavallone, P., Baglieri, L., Colucci, G., Tagliavini, L., & Quaglia, G. (2022). A review of robots, perception, and tasks in precision agriculture. *Applied Mechanics*, *3*(3), 830–854. https://doi.org/10.3390/applmech3030049.

Chance, E., Ashton, W., Pereira, J., *et al.* (2018). The plant — An experiment in urban food sustainability. *Environmental Progress & Sustainable Energy*, *37*, 82–90.

Department of Energy (DOE), Office of Energy Efficiency and Renewable Energy (2020). Energy savings potential of SSL in agricultural applications. June 2020. Retrieved from https://www.energy.gov/sites/prod/files/2020/07/f76/ssl-agriculture-jun2020.pdf on 12/15/2023.

Despommier, D. (2010). The vertical farm: controlled environment agriculture carried out in tall buildings would create greater food safety and security for large urban populations. *Journal für Verbraucherschutz und Lebensmittelsicherheit*, *6*, 233–236.

Di Pierro, M. (2017). What is the blockchain? *Computing in Science & Engineering*, *19*(5), 92–95. DOI: 10.1109/MCSE.2017.3421554.

Eigenbrod, C. & Gruda, N. (2014). Urban vegetable for food security in cities. A review. *Agronomy for Sustainable Development*, *35*, 483–498.

Favaretto, M., De Clercq, E., Schneble, C. O., & Elger, B. S. (2020). What is your definition of big data? Researchers' understanding of the phenomenon of the decade. *PLoS One*, *15*(2), e0228987. February 25, 2020. DOI: 10.1371/journal.pone.0228987. PMID: 32097430; PMCID: PMC7041862.

Fitzgerald, M., Kruschwitz, N., Bonnet, D., & Welch, M. (2014). Embracing digital technology — A new strategic imperative. *MIT Sloan Management Review*, *55*(2), 1–12.

Gabriel, A. & Gandorfer, M. (2023). Adoption of digital technologies in agriculture — An inventory in a European small-scale farming region. *Precision Agriculture*, *24*, 68–91. https://doi.org/10.1007/s11119-022-09931-1.

Gnauer, C., Pichler, H., Tauber, M., *et al.* (2019). Towards a secure and self-adapting smart indoor farming framework. *E & i Elektrotech Informationstechnik*, *136*, 341–344.

Gong, C. & Ribiere, V. (2021). Developing a unified definition of digital transformation. *Technovation*, *102*, 102217. https://doi.org/10.1016/j.technovation.2020.102217.

Hines, M. (2022). *USA Today*. July 26, 2022. Retrieved from https://www.usatoday.com/story/life/food-dining/2022/07/26/omakase-berry-price-taste-about/10101658002/.

Hortidaily (2023). $20M in funding and second AI-powered robotic greenhouse for Zordi. 10/23/2023. Retrieved from https://www.hortidaily.com/article/9568807/us-nj-20m-in-funding-and-second-ai-powered-robotic-greenhouse-for-zordi/.

Hossain, M. M., Rahman, M., Chaki, S., Ahmed, H., Haque, A., Tamanna, I., Lima, S., Ferdous, M., & Rahman, M. (2023). Smart-Agri: A smart agricultural management with IoT-ML-blockchain integrated framework. *International Journal of Advanced Computer Science and Applications*, *14*, 985–996. DOI: 10.14569/IJACSA.2023.01407107.

Janiesch, C., Zschech, P., & Heinrich, K. (2021). Machine learning and deep learning. *Electron Markets*, *31*, 685–695. https://doi.org/10.1007/s12525-021-00475-2.

Khan, M. A. & Salah, K. (2018). IoT security: Review, blockchain solutions, and open challenges. *Future Generation Computer Systems*, *82*, 395–411. https://doi.org/10.1016/j.future.2017.11.022.

Khin, S. & Ho, T. C. (2019). Digital technology, digital capability and organizational performance: A mediating role of digital innovation. *International Journal of Innovation Science*, *11*(2), 177–195. https://doi.org/10.1108/IJIS-08-2018-0083.

Kozai, T., Niu, G., & Takasaki, M. (eds.) (2016). *Plant Factory*. Amsterdam, The Netherlands: Academic Press.

Kubota, C. (2021). Get the inside scoop on why greenhouse strawberries are trending. Greenhouse Grower. April 14, 2021. Retrieved from https://www.greenhousegrower.com/crops/get-the-inside-scoop-on-why-greenhouse-strawberries-are-trending/.

Liu, L. & Liu, K. (2023) Can digital technology promote sustainable agriculture? Empirical evidence from urban China. *Cogent Food & Agriculture*, *9*(2), 2282234. DOI: 10.1080/23311932.2023.2282234.

Liu, Y., Ma, X., Shu, L., Hancke, G. P., & Abu-Mahfouz, A. M. (2021). From Industry 4.0 to Agriculture 4.0: Current status, enabling technologies, and research challenges. *IEEE Transactions on Industrial Informatics*, *17*(6), 4322–4334. June 2021. DOI: 10.1109/TII.2020.3003910.

Marston, J. (2023). Q&A: Fifth Season's former VP on why it failed and how vertical farming must change. *Agfunder News*. April 23, 2023. Retrieved from https://agfundernews.com/fifth-seasons-former-vp-on-why-it-failed-and-how-vertical-farming-must-change.

Mirani, A. A., Velasco-Hernandez, G., Awasthi, A., & Walsh, J. (2022). Key challenges and emerging technologies in industrial IoT architectures: A review. *Sensors* (Basel), *22*(15), 5836. August 4, 2022. DOI: 10.3390/s22155836. PMID: 35957403; PMCID: PMC9371229.

Mushi, G. E., Di Marzo Serugendo, G., & Burgi, P.-Y. (2022). Digital technology and services for sustainable agriculture in Tanzania: A literature review. *Sustainability*, *14*(4), 2415. https://doi.org/10.3390/su14042415.

Ode, M. (2023). Class 4 fault-managed power systems: An overview of this new classification in the 2023 NEC. ECmag.com. April 14, 2023. Retrieved from https://www.ecmag.com/magazine/articles/article-detail/class-4-fault-managed-power-systems-an-overview-of-this-new-classification-in-the-2023-nec.

OECD (2014). Recommendation on digital government strategies — OECD. Retrieved from http://www.oecd.org/gov/digital-government/recommendation-on-digital-government-strategies.htm.

Ossewaarde, M. (2019). Digital transformation and the renewal of social theory: Unpacking the new fraudulent myths and misplaced metaphors. *Technological Forecasting and Social Change, 146,* 24–30. DOI: 10.1016/j.techfore.2019.05.007.

Owoseni, A. (2023). What is digital transformation? Investigating the metaphorical meaning of digital transformation and why it matters. *Digital Transformation and Society, 2*(1), 78–96. https://doi.org/10.1108/DTS-10-2022-0049.

Pennisi, G., Pistillo, A., Orsini, F., Cellini, A., Spinelli, F., Nicola, S., Fernandez, J., Crepaldi, A., Gianquinto, G., & Marcelis, L. F. M. (2020). Optimal light intensity for sustainable water and energy use in indoor cultivation of lettuce and basil under red and blue LEDs. *Scientia Horticulturae, 272,* 109508. DOI: 10.1016/j.scienta.2020.109508.

Piccinini, E., Gregory, R. W., & Kolbe, L. M. (2015a). Changes in the producer consumer relationship-towards digital transformation. In *Wirtschaftsinformatik Conference,* Osnabrück (pp. 1634–1648). Germany: AIS Electronic Library.

Piccinini, E., Hanelt, A., Gregory, R., & Kolbe, L. (2015b). Transforming industrial business: The impact of digital transformation on automotive organizations. *International Conference of Information Systems,* Forth Worth, TX.

Pollard, A. (2023). Venture capital's AI-run lettuce farms start to go bust. Bloomberg.com. June 16, 2023. Retrieved from Venture Capital's AI-Run Lettuce Farms Start to Go Bust — Bloomberg.

Porter, M. E. (1985). *Competitive Advantage: Creating and Sustaining Superior Performance.* New York: Simon and Schuster.

Protopop, I. & Shanoyan, A. (2016). Big data and smallholder farmers: Big data applications in the agri-food supply chain in developing countries. *The International Food and Agribusiness Management Review, 19*(A), 173–190. https://doi.org/10.22004/ag.econ.240705.

Pylianidis, C., Osinga, S., & Athanasiadis, I. N. (2021). Introducing digital twins to agriculture. *Computers and Electronics in Agriculture, 184,* 105942. https://doi.org/10.1016/j.compag.2020.105942.

Samtani, J. B., Rom, C. R., Friedrich, H., Fennimore, S. A., Finn, C. E., Petran, A., Wallace, R. W., Pritts, M. P., Fernandez, G., Chase, C. A., Kubota, C., & Bergefurd, B. (2019). The status and future of the strawberry industry in the United States. *HortTechnology Hortte, 29*(1), 11–24. https://doi.org/10.21273/HORTTECH04135-18.

SharathKumar, M., Heuvelink, E., & Marcelis, L. F. M. (2020). Vertical farming: Moving from genetic to environmental modification. *Trends in Plant Science, 25.* DOI: 10.1016/j.tplants.2020.05.012.

Slob, N. & Hurst, W. (2022). Digital twins and industry 4.0 technologies for agricultural greenhouses. *Smart Cities*, *5*(3), 1179. https://doi.org/10.3390/smartcities5030059.

Sorri, K., Mustafee, N., & Seppänen, M. (2022). Revisiting IoT definitions: A framework towards comprehensive use. *Technological Forecasting and Social Change*, *179*, 121623. https://doi.org/10.1016/j.techfore.2022.121623.

Stein, E. W. (2020). What is indoor farming? Center of Excellence for Indoor Agriculture. July 9, 2020. Retrieved from https://indooragcenter.org/what-is-indoorfarming/.

Stein, E. W. (2021). The transformative environmental effects large-scale indoor farming may have on air, water, and soil. *Air, Soil and Water Research, 14*. DOI: 10.1177/1178622121995819.

Tey, Y. S. & Brindal, M. (2021). A meta-analysis of factors driving the adoption of precision agriculture. *Precision Agriculture*, 1–20. https://doi.org/10.1007/s11119-021-09840-9.

Thomaier, S., Specht, K., Henckel, D., Dierich, A., Siebert, R., Freisinger, U., & Sawicka, M. (2014). Farming in and on urban buildings: Present practice and specific novelties of Zero-Acreage Farming (ZFarming). *Renewable Agriculture and Food Systems*, *30*, 1–12. DOI: 10.1017/S1742170514000143.

Trevino, L. K., Webster, J., & Stein, E. W. (2000). Making connections: Complementary influences on communication media choices, attitudes, and use. *Organization Science*, *11*(2), 163–182. https://doi.org/10.1287/orsc.11.2.163.1251054.

Turing, A. (1950). Computing machinery and intelligence. *Mind*, *LIX*(236), 433–460. DOI: 10.1093/mind/LIX.236.433.

Urbinati, A., Chiaroni, D., Chiesa, V., & Frattini, F. (2018). The role of digital technologies in open innovation processes: an exploratory multiple case study analysis. *R&D Management*, *50*, 136–160. 10.1111/radm.12313.

Vanian, J. & Leswing, K. (2023). ChatGPT and generative AI are booming, but the costs can be extraordinary. CNBC.com. March 13. Retrieved from https://www.cnbc.com/2023/03/13/chatgpt-and-generative-ai-are-booming-but-at-a-very-expensive-price.html.

Verdouw, C., Tekinerdogan, B., Beulens, A., & Wolfert, S. (2021). Digital twins in smart farming. *Agricultural Systems*, *189*, 103046. https://doi.org/10.1016/j.agsy.2020.103046.

Vial, G. (2019). Understanding digital transformation: A review and a research agenda. *Journal of Strategic Information Systems*, *28*(2), 118–144. DOI: 10.1016/j.jsis.2019.01.003.

Vijay, S. & Ponnusamy, V. (2023). A review on application of robots in agriculture using deep learning. *AIP Conference Proceedings*, *2946*(1), 050005.

Westerman, G., Calméjane, C., Bonnet, D., Ferraris, P., & McAfee, A. (2011). *Digital Transformation: A Roadmap for Billion-Dollar Organizations* (pp. 1–68). MIT Center for Digital Business and Capgemini Consulting.

Xu, M., Chen, X., & Kou, G. (2019). A systematic review of blockchain. *Financial Innovation, 5*(1), 1–14. https://doi.org/10.1186/s40854-019-0147-z.

Yaseen, H. & Obaid, A. (2020). Big data: Definition, architecture & applications. *JOIV: International Journal on Informatics Visualization, 4*. DOI: 10.30630/joiv.4.1.292.

Chapter 5

Digital Transformation in Universities as a Double-Sided Challenge

Roberto C. S. Pacheco[*,†], **Adriana Veríssimo Karam Koleski**[‡], **and Larissa Mariany Freiberger Pereira**[§]

Programa de Pós-Graduação em Engenharia, Gestão e Mídia do Conhecimento (EGC) — Universidade Federal de Santa Catarina (UFSC), Florianópolis, Brazil

[†]*roberto.pacheco@ufsc.br*

[‡]*adriana@opet.com.br*

[§]*freiberger.lm@gmail.com*

1. Introduction

The prevailing university model that shaped the landscape from the 20th century to the present day was formulated by Wilhelm von Humboldt. As a diplomat, philosopher, and co-founder of the University of Berlin in 1810, Humboldt believed that fostering students' creativity goes beyond traditional teaching methods and involves an active exchange between students and professors. According to Humboldt, a university could only truly cultivate critical thinking and creativity by integrating teaching with research and the generation of novel knowledge (Östling, 2018). The Humboldtian university, as it came to be known, emphasizes academic

---

[*]Corresponding author.

freedom in teaching and practical education, where faculty engage in ongoing research to stay abreast of the latest developments in their fields. The core principles also include the practical application of research findings, extending knowledge to society through outreach, partnerships, and collaborative agreements in the technical-scientific realm.

Over the course of the 20th century, Humboldt's model significantly influenced the structure of higher education and global academic research, contributing to notable advancements in education, research methodologies, and their interactions with broader societal contexts.

Another influential university model in the 20th century was brought by Vannevar Bush (1945). Worried about the impact of technological advancements on American competitiveness aftermath of World War II, Bush successfully persuaded President Roosevelt to create the National Science Foundation. This initiative was grounded in the notion that investments in basic science would eventually lead to applied research outcomes. Following experimental development phases, such as prototyping, these outcomes would evolve into tangible technologies and, ultimately, foster innovation. According to this perspective, the measurable academic merit primarily, if not exclusively, hinges on the production of high quality.

Both Humboldt's and Bush's visions exhibit a linear interconnection among teaching, research, outreach, and technological development. This linearity is apparent in departmentalized structures, lengthy content-based courses, regulatory models, bureaucratic processes, and notably, the ingrained practices within academic culture and tradition.

Nevertheless, in the last fifty years, linear perspectives have become inadequate to fulfill complex phenomena. Linearity falls short in elucidating the impacts of digital connectivity on society, as illustrated by Henry Jenkins' concept of the "digital renaissance" (2001), and on global socioeconomic relations, as evidenced in Thomas Friedman's idea of the "flat world" (2005). Furthermore, it struggles to account for intricate innovation systems, as seen in various proposals emerging from the "Sabato triangle" (Sábato & Botana, 1968) to the OECD's systemic model (OECD, 1999). It also grapples with understanding contemporary society's interactions with science, including Allan Irwin's perspectives on "citizen science" (1995) and Robert Frodeman's concept of "co-production transdisciplinarity" (2013).

On a broader perspective, linear and disciplinary views have been overpassed by Digital Transformation (DT) phenomena — a culture, social, economic, and organizational change demanded by digital society

(Stolterman & Fors, 2004). In all economic sectors, organizations have been facing DT in different dimensions: from internal and external processes and from individual and institutional stakeholders.

In educational sector, we refer to DT as Digital Education (DE), a phenomenon in which the challenge is to develop personal and professional skills to meet the demands of the digital society, with social, economic, and environmental responsibility. DE has challenged universities, research institutions, and academia, in general, to change structures, practices, and especially their training and knowledge production offerings to society. These challenges have revealed a demand for shorter cycles of organizational innovation and, especially, for the university's participation and co-production with other socio-economic actors.

In this chapter, we present two instruments recently developed to help academic managers to face digital transformation challenges: (i) *DTU Metamodel* — an interdisciplinary framework developed to help universities to create and implement an organizational DT model and (ii) *IAA/DS Method* — a research mission-oriented method to help research leaders to implement digital science as a set of practices in Transdisciplinarity, openness, and technology. Initially, we explore Digital Education (DE) as a dual-faceted phenomenon for the university: a transformation in its mission-oriented processes and a shift in organizational management and governance structures.

2. Digital Education as a Double-Sided Phenomena

In all sectors, DT challenges organizational leaders to assess their vision, positioning, operations, and relationships with all stakeholders enrolled or affected by the organization value generation chains (Henriette *et al.*, 2015). As represented in Figure 1, DT aims to align organizational effectiveness to digital society demands, by changing its operational and managerial efficiencies.

In the educational sector specifically, the dimensions illustrated in Figure 1 refer to how universities and schools deliver their educational, research, and outreach services to students and society (DT effectiveness) and how they organize their personnel, processes, and technology to ensure the efficiency of operations and management in delivering these services.

It is a dual challenge because, from one side, it requires that students (and other social stakeholders) receive services that meet contemporary digital society demands and, to do so, universities have to evolve their

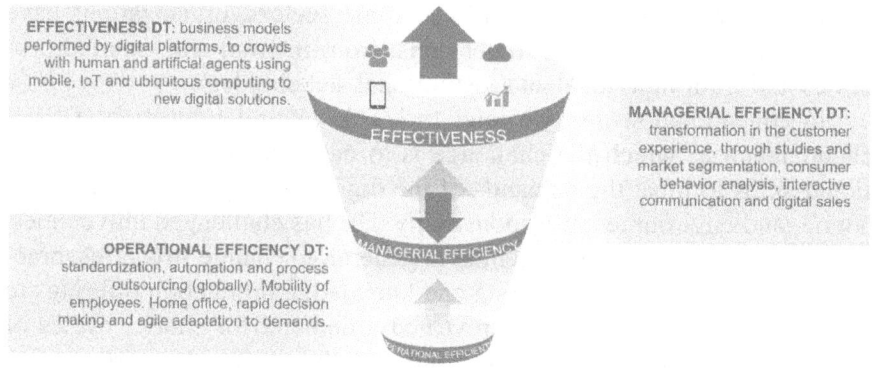

Figure 1.   Organizational dimensions of digital transformation.
Source: Pacheco *et al.* (2020).

traditional Humboldtian structures and culture. The first challenge is a mission-oriented DT, and the second is an organizational-oriented DT. In the following sections, we discuss further these two dimensions and two approaches that illustrate how universities can develop organizational projects to implement each kind of DT.

3. An Organizational-Oriented DTU Metamodel

While extensive literature has discussed the challenges posed by digital society for universities (Alenezi, 2021; Barber *et al.*, 2013; Goldin, 2016; Luna, 2020; Pacheco *et al.*, 2020; Pucciarelli & Kaplan, 2016; Rof *et al.*, 2020; Sandkuhl & Lehmann, 2017), there remains a gap in systemic approaches for implementing DT in these organizations (Benavides *et al.*, 2020; Bernhard-Skala, 2019; Hess *et al.*, 2016; Marks *et al.*, 2020; Matt *et al.*, 2015; Menendez *et al.*, 2016; Pacheco *et al.*, 2020; Rof *et al.*, 2020).

We recently encountered this challenge by developing a model founded on Organizational Change Theory, acknowledging that organizational change and digital transformation are unique for each higher education institution (Jacobs *et al.*, 2013; Ostrom, 2007). The DTU Metamodel (Karam-Koleski, 2023) was designed to assist university leaders in understanding and addressing DT by establishing an organizational culture and structure to design their own digital transformation model. DTU is a metamodel because, when applied, it creates a specific organizational model (Mendling, 2008).

The DTU Metamodel comprises four concurrent elements, distributed in layers: (1) journey for digital transformation in universities, (2) lenses and factors to be considered during DTU implementation, (3) stakeholders to be included in the process of DTU, and (4) digital transformation spiral (Karam-Koleski, 2023).

The DTU Metamodel consists of four concurrent elements distributed across layers: (i) *the DTU Journey (DTJ)*: the pathway for digital transformation; (ii) *the DTU Criteria (DTC)*: lenses and factors to be considered during DTU implementation; (iii) *the DTU stakeholders (DTS)*: players to be involved in the DTU process; and (iv) *the DTU spiral*: the digital transformation cycle (Karam-Koleski, 2023).

3.1. *Digital Transformation Journey (DTJ)*

The digital transformation journey (DTJ) represents the path the university should follow from planning to implementing DT. In the DTU Metamodel, we propose an organizational journey by combining the perspectives of Kotter's model for organizational change management (2014) with Wade *et al.*'s model for orchestrating digital transformation (2019).

In the DTU Metamodel, the DTJ comprises nine stages: (1) *digital strategy*: planning the university's strategic movement and digital strategy; (2) *digital urgency*: creating a sense of urgency for DTU; (3) *guiding team*: establishing leadership for DTU and creating a dual operating system; (4) *project*: formulating a strategic vision and initiatives to implement DTU; (5) *engage*: communicating the strategic vision, engaging, and recruiting volunteers; (6) *cocreate in networks*: making execution of DT initiatives possible with intra and interorganizational networks; (7) *celebrate*: celebrating short term, visible, and meaningful results; (8) *reinforce*: staying vigilant, reinforcing, learning from results, and accelerating DT initiatives; (9) *root*: institutionalizing DTU changes (Karam-Koleski, 2023). These nine interactive stages are illustrated in Figure 2.

Even though Figure 2 presents the DTJ stages in a sequential order, it is crucial to underscore that the implementation of digital transformation is not a linear progression. To account for this, they are depicted in a circular arrangement, emphasizing their nonlinearity. This is evident in the central gradient, indicating the potential for connections in various orders and directions once DTU is initiated.

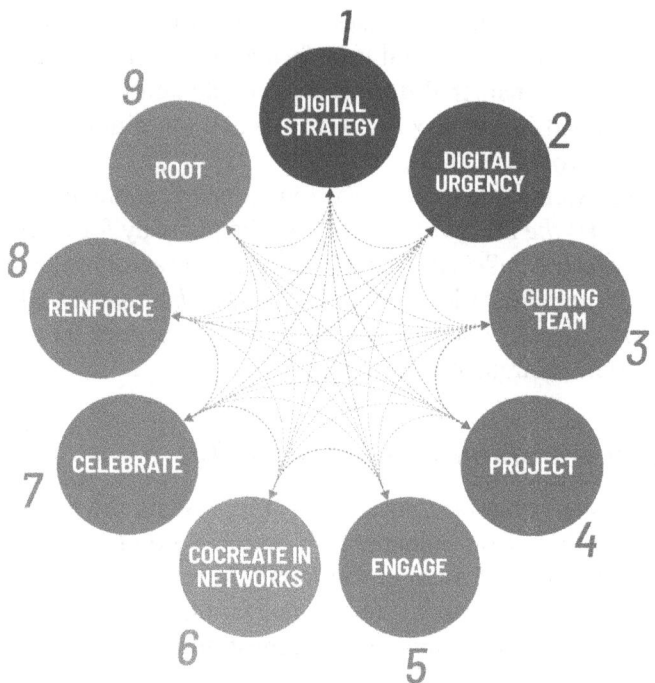

Figure 2.   Digital transformation journey (DTJ) in universities.
Source: Karam-Koleski (2023, p. 195).

3.2. *Digital Transformation Criteria (DTC)*

Organizational change models usually assume that change is a result of strategic leadership decision and can be implemented in a linear and rational way (Carnall, 1995; Carr, 1996; Peterson, 1995, 1997). However, digital transformation is a multifaceted and complex endeavor (Benavides *et al.*, 2020; Bernhard-Skala, 2019; Marks *et al.*, 2020; Menendez *et al.*, 2016).

To deal with DTU complexity in universities, Kezar (2014) considers the following organizational change (OC) theories: *scientific administration* (Peterson, 1995, 1997; Carnall, 1995; Carr, 1996; Kotter, 1996), *cultural* (Schein, 2004; Simsek & Louis, 1994; Smircich, 1983; Cameron, 1991; Collins, 1998; Neumann, 1993), *sociocognitive* (Morgan, 1986; Weick, 1995; Argyris, 1999; Schon, 1992), *political* (Bolman & Deal, 1991; Gumport, 1993; Balridge, 1971; Bergquist, 1992; Lindquist, 1978), *evolutionary* (Sporn, 1999; El-Kawas, 2000), and *institutional* (Hannan &

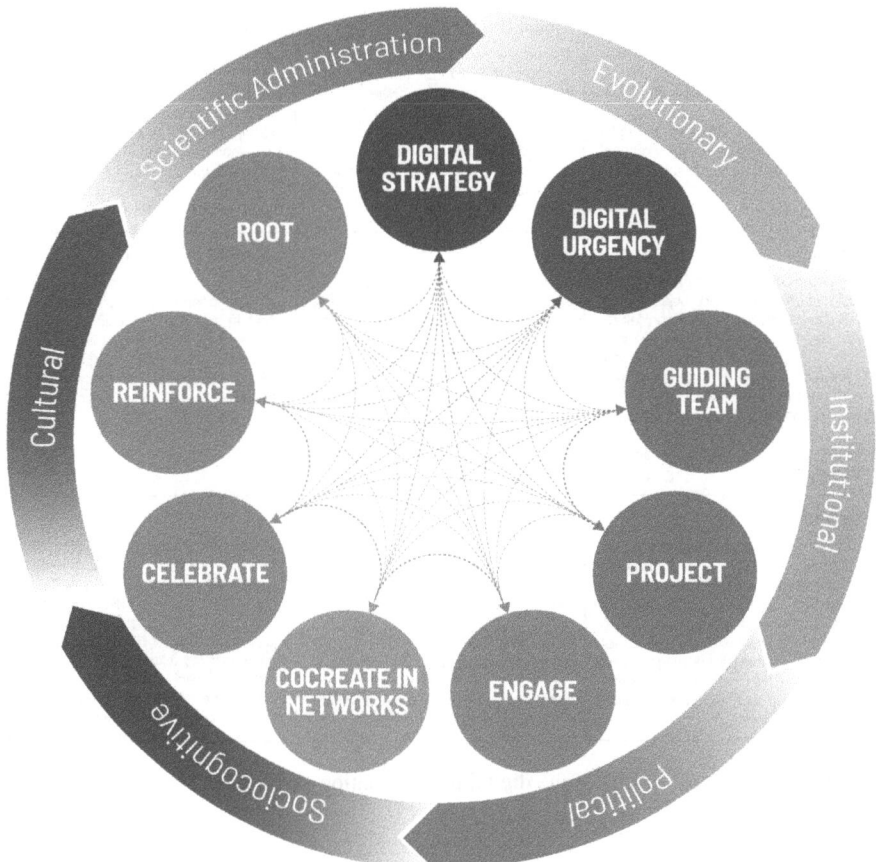

Figure 3. Change theories applied to DTJ for HEI.

Source: Karam-Koleski (2023, p. 196).

Freeman, 1984; Leitch & Fennel, 2008; Hanson, 2001; Di Maggio & Powel, 1983). In DTU Metamodel, we have combined these OC paradigms that set a background for the second layer of the metamodel. As illustrated in Figure 3, each OC theory offered criteria and factors to enrich leadership´s analysis and assessment and to support the implementation of DTU.

By combining different OC theories, DTU Metamodel has 112 factors to be elucidated during DTJ stage. These factors are related to the courses of action which allows the university to design its own digital transformation model. Their objective is to make the contribution of DT factors in a tangible and synthetic manner.

Digital strategy	Digital Urgency	Guiding team
Create a digital/organizational strategy and network business model shaped by leadership empowered with knowledge about TD, taking into account the university's culture and values, digital maturity,intra and interorganizational aspects, as well as its institutional field and external context.	Establish a clear and compelling articulation of the opportunities and vision that DT offers to the university, considering the imperative for embracing change, adherence to institutional field rules, overcoming resistance, and, notably, fostering the essential internal and external connections required to instill digital urgency	Define a DT coordinator and a guiding team comprising diverse stakeholders with a shared vision of DT. This team has to be legitimized and empowered to act in an agile manner within a structure separate from the hierarchical framework but closely aligned with it.
Project	**Engage**	**Cocreate in networks**
Develop a collaborative university's strategic vision and primary objectives for DT implementation; strategic initiatives and monitoring mechanisms aligned with the institution's strategic planning, considering its identity, potential cultural and political resistances, collaboration with the ecosystem, internal and external contexts, and the essential competencies for the realization of the next two stages.	Establish a volunteer team consisting of university members and individuals from its ecosystem to collaboratively create transformative initiatives. This involves sharing and legitimizing a DT vision that incorporates the appreciation of rituals, cultural nuances, and existing knowledge	Create strategic initiatives prioritized and developed by transformation networks in an agile and flexible manner, aligning with the desired culture, and monitoring and addressing cultural, political, structural, and knowledge barriers.
Celebrate	**Reinforce**	**Root**
Sustain and grow internal team and engagement within the ecosystem by showcasing and celebrating immediate results. This is done with the backing of opinion leaders, taking into account the interests and needs of various stakeholders, existing cultural practices, as well as the introduction of new practices and language that align with the TD mindset.	Expediting DTU initiatives and adapting the strategy based on lessons learned and key performance indicators (KPIs), with particular emphasis on resisting reverting to previous states. This involves continuous digital learning and the upkeep of communication and co-creation channels with internal structures and the ecosystem.	Integrate initiatives created by transformation networks into the university's hierarchical structure, reviewing governance documents, managing practices, and promoting organizational learning. This also includes introducing new narratives aligned with DTU and solidifying mechanisms that institutionalize the relationship between the university and its ecosystem.

Figure 4.   Expected results of the digital transformation journey.

Source: Karam-Koleski (2023, p. 198).

Given the concise focus of this chapter on presenting the metamodel, the detailed DT factors are not provided here but are available in the original research thesis (Karam-Koleski, 2023). The integration of these factors is articulated through the anticipated outcomes of each stage, as illustrated in Figure 4.

3.3. *Digital Transformation Stakeholders (DTS)*

The third layer of the DTU Metamodel identifies key stakeholders for each stage of the journey: top leadership, management, staff, faculty, students, ecosystem partners, and tactical and operations personnel. Engaging both internal and external stakeholders enriches the DT process by incorporating diverse perspectives and needs. Throughout the DTJ, various stakeholders contribute to the digital transformation,

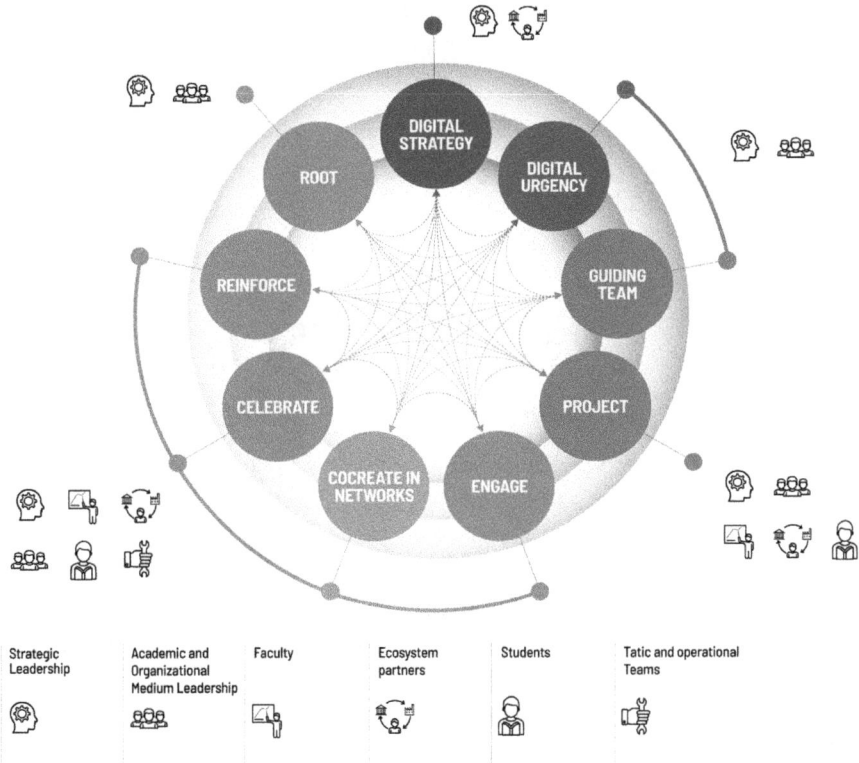

Figure 5. Stakeholders to be involved in DTU.

Source: Karam-Koleski (2023, p. 199).

except for strategic leadership, which consistently guides planning, lead-ership, and sustainability efforts. This process is illustrated in Figure 5, where we relate each DT stage with the correspondent university stakeholders.

3.4. *Digital Transformation Spiral*

The fourth component of the DTU Metamodel is the Digital Transformation Spiral (Karam-Koleski, 2023), highlighting DTU as an ongoing journey rather than a one-time effort (Grajek, 2022; Kotter, 2014). As illustrated in Figure 6, this involves continuously adapting organizational structures (Hanelt *et al*., 2020). Starting with low-complexity transformation activi-ties that produce tangible results, the DTU establishes a foundation for

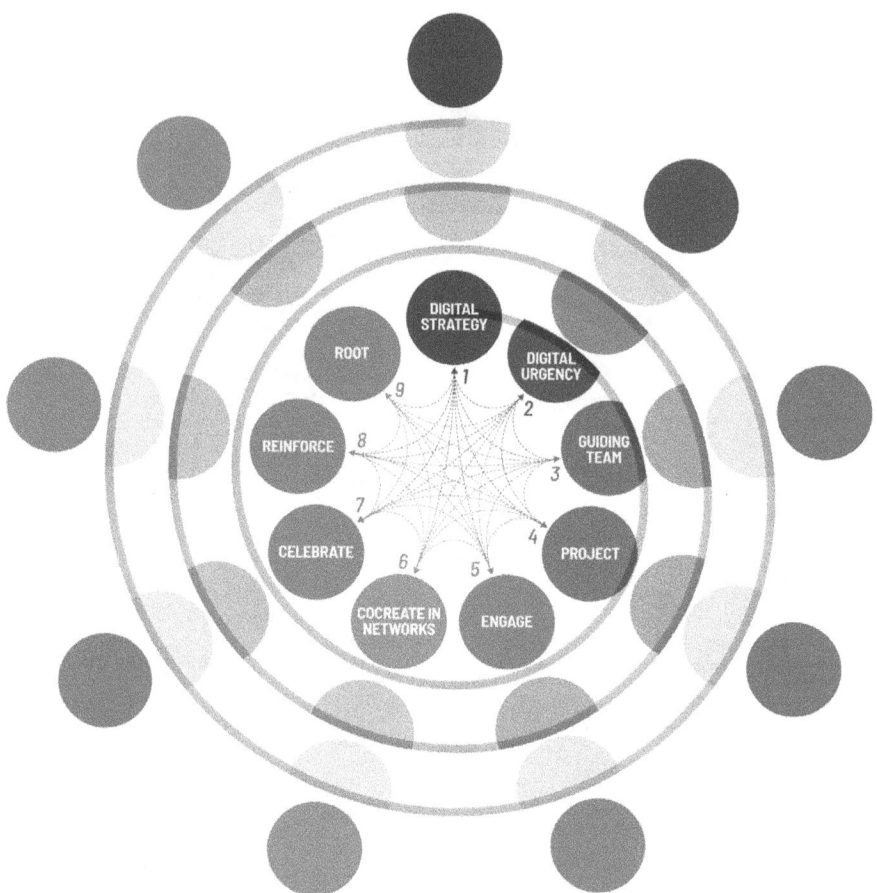

Figure 6.   Spiral cycle of DTU.

Source: Karam-Koleski (2023, p. 200).

developing a digital culture and the necessary competencies for digital transformation. Essentially, this journey cultivates organizational competencies and culture for DTU.

As mentioned, the four layers of the metamodel were conceived to work concurrently: the DTJ stages should be executed while considering various OC theoretical perspectives, incorporating contributions from multiple stakeholders in a nonlinear and iterative approach. The Metamodel for Digital Transformation in University provides strategic leadership in universities with a framework to address DT and make choices tailored to the unique context of each institution. Organizational and academic dimensions should be approached in an integrated manner when implementing transformation initiatives.

4. IAA/DS: A Mission-Oriented DTU Method

The DTU Metamodel is an example and recent development to approach DT as an organizational change process. As we mentioned earlier, DT can also be reached as a mission-oriented task. At universities, this can be done from educational, research, or outreach perspectives.

In this section, we present IAA/DS — the Digital Science Adherence Assessment Instrument — also a recent development to help universities in DT projects, specifically in their research mission. IAA/DS project was inspired by the study of the impact of DT on scientific knowledge production. In Science, DT has been effective in incorporating digital tools into processes, such as data collection and research evaluation (Aalbersberg *et al.*, 2014), as well as by changing the way people collaborate (Dougherty & Dune, 2012), making science more open, collaborative, global, and creative, thereby bringing it closer to society (EC, 2013).

This disruptive change in the nature of science is referred to as *Digital Science,* defined as "a system shared by scientific and social communities engaged in solving complex problems based on common good and sharing a set of methods, data, information, technological and methodological infrastructure" (Pacheco *et al.*, 2018, p. 382).

The landscape of Digital Science has evolved beyond academic actors to encompass citizens and individuals affiliated with government, industry, and society at large. Digital Science provides tools and methods for multisector co-production, serving as a conduit for collaborative endeavors (EC, 2013; Pacheco *et al.*, 2018).

By enhancing research processes with new collaboration and co-production tools, Digital Science not only promotes transparency, efficiency, and effectiveness but also fosters the emergence of novel research practices, scientific paradigms, and research fields that were previously non-existent. In this context, Transdisciplinarity plays a central role in Digital Science (EC, 2013; Pacheco *et al.*, 2018).

4.1. *Research Lifecycle Models*

In order to meet contemporary demands and expectations from all stakeholders, universities have to align their research and digital policies (Rodrigues, 2017; Benavides *et al.*, 2020). The ongoing digital transformation of universities, shaped by their distinctive missions, is observable across several institutions globally. This phenomenon is manifest in the development of individualized research life cycles by many universities, notably emphasizing the digitization of the research process.

The digital transformation of universities based on their specific mission is already taking place in many institutions worldwide. This reality is evident when we encounter numerous IES developing their own research life cycles, with a particular emphasis on digitizing the research process.

One of the first steps in a DT project is to comprehend the current organizational process to be changed. In Figure 7, we list a set of universities that have established an organizational lifecycle for research.

Although the research lifecycles differ in terms of number of stages and organizational stakeholders considered, they share a set of phasis

UNIVERSITY	RESEARCH LIFECYCLE PHASIS						
Monash	Concept & Planning (P) (F)	Exploring & Organizing (R)	Collection & Analysis (R)	Output & Publications (PB)	Impact & Engagement (A)		
Bournemouth	Research Strategy (P)	Proposal (F)	Research Process (R)	Publication (PB)			
Sheffield	Awareness of Scheme (P)	Idea Generation (P)	Bid Writing (P)	Funding Granted (F)	Project (R)	Impact (PB) (A)	
Nottingham	Planning (P) (F)	Implementation (R)	Publishing (PB)	Discovery & Impact (A)	Preservation (PV)	Reuse (PV)	
Queen's	Plan (P)	Create (R)	Process (R)	Analyze (A)	Disseminate (PB)	Preserve (PV)	Reuse (PV)
Ohio	Planning (P) (F)	Conducting (R)	Publishing (PB)	Increasing Impact (A+PV+PB)			
RMTI	Research Design (P)	Planning (P) (F)	Primary Research (R)	Analyzing, writing and Creating (R)	Publishing and Communicating (PB)	Impact & Getting Noticed (A) (PB)	
Washington Univ.	Plan/Propose (P) (F)	Setup (R)	Manage (R)	Closeout (A) (PB)			
Western Sidney	Research Idea (P)	Formulate Research Question (P)	Secure Funding (F)	Conduct Research (R)	Disseminate Research Findings (PB)	Identify Related/ Further Research Questions (A) (PV)	
	1 - Planning (P)	2 - Funding (F)	3 - Researching (R)	4 - Assessing (A)	5 - Preserving (PV)	6 - Publicizing (PB)	

Figure 7.   Research lifecycles from several universities.

from planning to closing a research project, with tasks such as the following:

1. *Planning*: idea generation, benchmarking research questions, writing a research proposal, defining staff, infrastructure, and budget, data management policies, research committee and policies, ethics committee, and intellectual property rights and policies.
2. *Funding*: grant and funds procurement, contracts, contacting investors, and sponsors.
3. *Researching*: literature review, supervising research, information and data literacy, collaboratories, citizen science (data collection), and writing.
4. *Assessing*: altmetrics, impact analysis, and defining/using metrics.
5. *Preserving*: data standards, data lakes, store, and reusing.
6. *Publicizing*: writing about research results, licensing products, publicizing in social media, and open access.

Once the institutional research lifecycle has been established, a digital transformation project consists of deciding which and how factors of knowledge production can be fostered/modified by digital society demands. In the following section, we present a recent method to approach these research stages based on digital science.

4.2. *Instrument for Analyzing the Adherence of University to Digital Science (IAA/DS)*

Digital transformation in university's research dimension can be associated with a project that aims to bring digital science to academics. In the IAA/DS project, this goal was achieved by developing guidelines in three digital science dimensions: Technology, Transdisciplinarity, and Openness Culture (Pereira, 2023).

The Technology dimension encompasses the use of computer systems, data, information resources, digital sensory networks, and others integrated from end to end, enabling collaboration in conducting research (NSF, 2007; Pacheco *et al.*, 2018). Therefore, it is not merely the insertion of technologies into the scientific process (Ribes & Lee, 2010) but also the strategic incorporation of different digital technologies into this process to achieve knowledge co-production.

Table 1.   Dimensions, factors, and analysis criteria of IAA/DS.

Dimension	Factor	Criteria
Transdisciplinarity	Common Good	Research Motivation
		Nature of the Problem
	Complex Problems	Training Profile and Research Intentionality
		Setting up Research Project Teams
	Coproduction	Prediction of Team Actors according to University's Research Policy
Technology	Interoperability	Purpose of Web Technologies
	Technological Infrastructure	IT Infrastructure Support for Services
	Data Culture and Literacy	Data-driven Performance of Research Project Team
		Data-driven Professional Support for Research
	Human Capital in Technology	Performance of IT Professionals
Openness Culture	Knowledge Sharing	Research Results Publishing Profile
		Research Data Storage Profile
	Knowledge Dissemination	Research Portfolio Dissemination
		Research Results Dissemination Policy
	Cooperative Work	Co-authorship Profile
	Systemic Change	Evolution of Institutional Policy
		Adherence to Open Science

Source: Pereira (2023).

The Transdisciplinarity dimension involves transforming scientific processes to enable the resolution of complex problems for the common good (Schuttenberg & Guth, 2015).

Finally, if Digital Transformation is a phenomenon that influences all aspects of human life, Openness Culture dimension solidifies the practice of openness in the scientific community (Kunkel & Matthess, 2020; Santarius *et al.*, 2020; Truong, 2022). This ensures that the knowledge produced generates relevant impacts on society in general.

After literature review and domain expert validation, the IAA/DS instrument was designed with 11 factors and 17 criteria (Table 1) to assess the adherence of a University research to each of those three Digital Science dimensions.

The IAA/DS has objective, single-choice questions with a five-point Likert psychometric response scale. Respondents can indicate their perception of University's level concerning each criterion, by answering an online questionnaire, organized into sections, with each section addressing one dimension. IAA/DS questionnaire has a brief explanatory text about the dimension and the factor under consideration, followed by the corresponding questions.

The Transdisciplinarity dimension is assessed through five single-choice objective questions, taking into account three factors (Common Good, Complex Problems, and Coproduction) and their respective analytical criteria. The Technology dimension is also evaluated using five single-choice objective questions, considering four factors (Interoperability, Technological Infrastructure, Data Culture and Literacy, and Human Capital in Technology), along with their analysis criteria. Finally, the Openness Culture dimension is appraised through seven single-choice objective questions, considering four factors (Knowledge Sharing, Knowledge Dissemination, Cooperative Work, and Systemic Change), and their respective analytical criteria.

The goal of IAA/DS is not to assess each criterion through objective indicators that can be quantified or instrumentally measured. Instead, this tool aims to build an analysis of a university's adherence to Digital Science based on the respondents' perceptions of the university's performance concerning each analysis criterion. Consequently, each respondent individually analyzes these criteria, considering their distinct worldview, which may vary from that of other respondents.

Prior to the formal administration of the questionnaire, a preliminary phase is essential, during which the IAA/DS is introduced to the respondents. The objective is to ensure a shared understanding of the dimensions, factors, and analysis criteria among the participants. It is also crucial to emphasize to the respondents that the IAA/DS should be completed with consideration for the entire university rather than specific or individual circumstances.

The IAA/DS needs to be implemented across all levels of the university: strategic, tactical, and operational. To achieve this, the instrument should assess the same dimensions, factors, and criteria. However, the formulation of questions must be adapted to the perspective held by individuals at each organizational level. For instance, in examining the

Technology dimension, the strategic level should be evaluated based on how this dimension is considered in strategic actions and institutional policies. The tactical level should be assessed in terms of aspects like technological infrastructure and the training of IT professionals. Lastly, the operational level should be appraised concerning the ability to utilize the technologies provided by the university.

After the questionnaire has been distributed, it is essential to conduct a follow-up phase, such as a workshop, where respondents can discuss their responses and collectively answer a common questionnaire. This approach facilitates not only the exploration of individual perceptions but also the development of a shared and aligned understanding among the participants.

With these findings, the University gains insights for decision-making to refine its strategy and policies, aiming for higher levels of adherence to Digital Science. Utilizing a radar chart to visualize the responses allows for the identification of well-evaluated criteria and pinpointing weaknesses in the institution's adherence to Digital Science.

5. Final Remarks

The journey of Digital Transformation in universities presents a double-sided challenge, encompassing both a transformation in mission-oriented processes and a shift in organizational management and governance structures. The traditional paradigms such as Humboldtian and Bushian models became inadequate to face the complexities introduced by digital connectivity, societal shifts, and global interactions.

In this chapter, we introduced two models — the DTU Metamodel and IAA/DS Method: the first to illustrate how DT can be conducted as an organizational change process and the latter as an example that, in universities, DT can also be a mission-oriented project. Both models acknowledge the uniqueness and complexity of Digital Transformation in universities, emphasizing the need for individualized strategies and approaches. They underscore the importance of engaging stakeholders, fostering a culture of openness, and continuously adapting to the evolving digital landscape.

In essence, universities must embark on a strategic journey, reaffirming their mission and identity within their organizational ecosystem. The interplay of digital technology, transdisciplinarity, and openness culture requires a holistic and adaptive approach. The models presented are examples of tools for academic managers and research leaders to navigate this transformative journey, aligning their institutions with the demands of digital society. As universities grapple with the ongoing challenges posed by Digital Transformation, these models serve as guideposts, facilitating informed decision-making and charting a course toward a more digitally resilient and mission-aligned future.

References

Aalbersberg, I. J., Atzeni, S., Koers, H., Specker, B., & Zudilova-Seinstra, E. (2014). Bringing digital science deep inside the scientific article: The Elsevier article of the future project. *Liber Quarterly*, *23*(4), 274–299.

Alenezi, M. (2021). Deep dive into digital transformation in higher education institutions. *Education Sciences*, *11*(770), 1–13. https://doi.org/10.3390/educsci11120770.

Argyris, C. (1999). *On Organizational Learning*, 2nd edn. Oxford, UK: Wiley-Blackwell.

Balridge, J. V. (1971). *Power and Conflict in the University: Research in the Sociology of Complex Organizations*. New York, NY: Wiley.

Barber, M., Donelly, K., & Rizvi, S. (2013). *An Avalanche Is Coming: Higher Education and the Revolution Ahead*. London: Institute for Public Policy Research — IPPR.

Bazanini, R., *et al.* (2020). A teoria dos stakeholders nas diferentes perspectivas: controvérsias, conveniências e críticas. *Revista Pensamento e Realidade*, *35*(2), 43–58.

Benavides, L. M. C., *et al.* (2020). Digital transformation in higher education institutions: A systematic literature review. *Sensors*, *20*, 3291. DOI: 10.3390/s20113291. Disponível em: https://www.mdpi.com/1424-8220/20/11/3291.

Bergquist, W. H. (1992). *The Four Cultures of the Academy: Insights and Strategies for Improving Leadership in Collegiate Organizations*. San Francisco: Jossey-Bass.

Bernhard-Skala, C. (2019). Organisational perspectives on the digital transformation of adult and continuing education: A literature review from a German-speaking perspective. *Journal of Adult and Continuing Education*, *25*(2), 178–197. DOI: 10.1177/1477971419850840.

Bolman, L. & Deal, T. (1991). *Reframing Organizations: Artistry, Choice, and Leadership*. San Francisco: Jossey-Bass.

Bush, V. (1945). *The Endless Frontier, Report to the President on a Program for Postwar Scientific Research*. Washington: Office of Scientific Research and Development.

Cameron, K. S. (1991). Organizational adaptation and higher education. In Peterson, M. W., Chaffee, E. E., & White, T. H. (eds.), *Organization and Governance in Higher Education*. Needham Heights, MA: Ginn Press.

Carnall, C. (1995). *Managing Change in Organizations*. London: Prentice-Hall.

Carr, C. (1996). *Choice Change and Organizational Change: Practical Insights from Evolution for Business Leaders and Thinker*. New York: AMACON.

Collins, D. (1998). *Organizational Change: Sociological Perspectives*. London, UK: Routledge.

Di Maggio, P. J. & Powell, W. W. (1983). The iron cage revisited: Institutional isomorphism and collective rationality in organizational fields. *American Sociological Review, 48*(2), 147–160.

Dougherty, D. & Dunne, D. D. (2012). Digital science and knowledge boundaries in complex innovation. *Organization Science, 23*(5), 1467–1484.

European Commission (EC) (2013). Digital science in horizon 2020.

Freeman, R. E., Phillips, R., & Sisodia, R. (2020). Tensions in stakeholder theory. *Business and Society, 59*(2), 213–231. DOI: 10.1177/0007650318773750.

Friedman, T. (2005). It's a flat world, after all. *The New York Times*. 3 April.

Frodeman, R. (2013). *Sustainable Knowledge: A Theory of Interdisciplinarity*. Boston: Springer.

Goldin, C. (2016). Human capital. In Diebold, C., Haupert, M. (eds.), *Handbook of Cliometrics* (pp. 55–86). Heidelberg, Germany: Springer-Verlag. https://dash.harvard.edu/handle/1/34309590.

Grajek, S. (2022). Dx, um caminho para a jornada de transformação digital. In Fábio, R. (org.). Educação Superior além da crise (p. 192). São Paulo: Instituto SEMESP.

Gumport, P. J. (1993). The contested terrain of academic program reduction. *The Journal of Higher Education, 64*(3), 283–311. DOI: 10.1080/00221546.1993.11778433.

Hanelt, A., *et al.* (2020). A systematic review of the literature on digital transformation: Insights and implications for strategy and organizational change. *Journal of Management Studies*, (1), 1–39. DOI: 10.1111/joms.12639.

Hannan, M. T. & Freeman, J. (1984). Structural inertia and organizational change. *American Sociological Review, 49*(2), 149–164. DOI: doi.org/10.2307/2095567.

Hanson, M. (2001). Institutional theory and educational change. *Education Administration Quarterly, 37*(5), 637–661. DOI: 10.1177/2F001316101219 69451.

Henriette, E., Feki, M., & Boughzala, I. (2015). The shape of digital transformation: A systematic literature review. In *Mediterranean Conference on Information Systems. MCIS 2015 Proceedings* (pp. 1–19).

Hess, T. *et al.* (2016). Options for formulating a digital transformation strategy. *MIS Quarterly Executive, 15*(2), 123–139.

Irwin, A. (1995). *Citizen Science: A Study of People, Expertise and Sustainable Development*. Londres: Routledge.

Jacobs, G., Van Witteloostuijn, A., & Christe-Zeyse, J. (2013). A theoretical framework of organizational change. *Journal of Organizational Change Management*, *26*(5), 772–792. DOI: 10.1108/JOCM-09-2012-0137.

Jenkins, H. (2001). Convergence? I diverge. *Technology Review*, *104*(5), 93–93. June 2001.

Kezar, A. (2014). *How Colleges Change: Understanding, Leading and Enacting Change*. New York, London: Routledge.

Karam-Koleski, A. V. K. (2023). Metamodelo para implementação de transformação digital em instituições de educação superior: jornada de transformação por meio de abordagem multiteórica de mudança organizacional. Tese de Doutorado em Engenharia e Gestão do Conhecimento — Universidade Federal de Santa Catarina. Orientador: Roberto Carlos dos Santos Pacheco.

Kotter, J. (1996). *Leading Change*. Boston, MA: Harvard Business School Press.

Kotter, J. P. (2014). *XL8: Accelerate*. Boston, MA: Harvard Business Review Press.

Kunkel, S. & Matthess, M. (2020). Digital transformation and environmental sustainability in industry: Putting expectations in Asian and African policies into perspective. *Environmental Science & Policy*, *112*, 318–329.

Leitch, K. & Fennel, M. (2008). Who staffs the US leaning tower? Organizational change and diversity. *Equal Opportunities International*, 1.

Lindquist, J. (1978). *Strategies of Change*. Washington, D.C.: Council of Independent Colleges.

Luna, F. D. S. (2020). Instituições de ensino superior brasileiras e sua jornada para a transformação digital. *Universidade de São Paulo*.

Marks, A. *et al.* (2020). Digital transformation in higher education: A framework for maturity assessment. *International Journal of Advanced Computer Science and Applications*, *11*(12), 504–513. DOI: 10.14569/IJACSA.2020.0111261.

Matt, C., Hess, T., & Benlian, A. (2015). Digital transformation strategies. *Business & Information Systems Engineering*, *57*(5), 339–343. DOI: 10.1007/s12599-015-0401-5.

Mendling, J. (2008). Metrics for Process Models: Empirical Foundations of Verification, Error Prediction and Guidelines for Correctedness, 1st edn. Heidelberg, Germany: Springer, Berlin: Heidelberg. http://www.springer link.com/content/vj505800l4376717.

Menendez, F. A., Machado, A. M., & Esteban, C. (2016). Analysis of the digital transformation of higher education institutions: A theoretical framework. *Edmetic*, *6*(1), 180–202.

Morgan, G. (1986). *Images of Organization*. Newburry Park, CA: SAGE Publications.

National Science Foundation (NSF) (2007). *Cyberinfrastructure Vision for 21st Century Discovery*. National Science Foundation, Cyberinfrastructure Council.

Neumann, A. (1993). College planning: A cultural perspective. *Journal of Higher Education Management, 8*(2), 31–41.

Östling, J. (2018). *Humboldt and the Modern German University: An Intellectual History.* Lund: Lund University Press.

Ostrom, E. (2007). Institutional rational choice: An assessment of the institutional analysis and development framework. In Sabatier, P. A. (ed.), *Theories of the Policy Process* (pp. 21–64). Boulder, Colorado: Westview. DOI: 10.4324/9780367274689.

Pacheco, R. C. S., Nascimento, E. R., & Weber, R. O. (2018). Digital science: Cyberinfrastructure, e-science and citizen science. In *Knowledge Management in Digital Change* (pp. 377–388). Cham: Springer.

Pacheco, R., Santos, N., & Wahrhaftig, R. (2020). Transformação digital na educação superior: modos e impactos na universidade. *Revista Nupem, 12*(27), 94–128. DOI: 10.33871/nupem.2020.12.27.94-128.

Parmar, B. L., *et al.* (2010). Stakeholder theory: The state of the art. *The Academy of Management Annals, 4*(1), 403–445. http://annals.aom.org/lookup/doi/10.1080/19416520.2010.495581.

Pereira, L. M. F. (2023). IAA/ICD: Instrumento de Análise da Ciência Digital para Instituições de Ensino Superior Brasileiras. 2023. Tese de Doutorado em Engenharia e Gestão do Conhecimento) — Universidade Federal de Santa Catarina. Orientador: Roberto Carlos dos Santos Pacheco. https://repositorio.ufsc.br/bitstream/handle/123456789/251901/PEGC0795-T.pdf?sequence=1&isAllowed=y. Acesso em: 14 December, 2023.

Peterson, M. W. (1995). Images of university structure, governance, and leadership: adaptive strategies for the new environment. In Dill, D. & Sporn, B. (eds.), *Emerging Patterns of Social Demand and University Reform: Through a Glass Darkly.* Oxford: Pergamon.

Peterson, M. W. (1997). Using contextual planning to transform institutions. In Peterson, M., Dill, D., & Mets, L. (eds.), *Planning and Management for a Changing Environment.* San Francisco: Jossey-Bass.

Pucciarelli, F. & Kaplan, A. (2016). Competition and strategy in higher education: Managing complexity and uncertainty. *Business Horizons, 59*(3), 311–320. http://dx.doi.org/10.1016/j.bushor.2016.01.003.

Ribes, D. & Lee, C. P. (2010). Sociotechnical studies of cyberinfrastructure and e-research: Current themes and future trajectories. *Computer Supported Cooperative Work (CSCW), 19*, 231–244.

Rodrigues, L. S. (2017). Challenges of digital transformation in higher education institutions: A brief discussion. In *Proceedings of 30th IBIMA Conference.*

Rof, A., Bikfalvi, A., & Marquès, P. (2020). Digital transformation for business model innovation in higher education: Overcoming the tensions. *Sustainability* (Switzerland), (12), 1–15. DOI: 10.3390/su12124980.

Sábato, J., Botana, N. (1968). La ciencia y la tecnología en el desarrollo futuro de América Latina. *Revista de la Integración, 1*(3), 15–36.

Sandkuhl, K. & Lehmann, H. (2017). Digital transformation in higher education: The role of enterprise architectures and portals. In Rossman, A. & Zimmermann, A. (eds.), *Digital Enterprise Computing 2017*, Bonn. Anais [...] (p. 12). Bonn: Gesellschaft fur Informatik.

Santarius, T., Pohl, J., & Lange, S. (2020). Digitalization and the decoupling debate: Can ICT help to reduce environmental impacts while the economy keeps growing? *Sustainability, 12*(18), 7496.

Schein, E. H. (2004). *Organizational Culture and Leadership: A Dynamic View*, 4th edn. San Francisco: Jossey-Bass.

Schön, D. (1992). Formar professores como profissionais reflexivos. In Novoa, A. (ed.), *Os professores e sua formação*. Lisboa: Dom Quixote.

Schuttenberg, H. Z. & Guth, H. K. (2015). Seeking our shared wisdom: A framework for understanding knowledge coproduction and coproductive capacities. *Ecology and Society, 20*(1).

Simsek, H. & Louis, K. S. (1994). Organizational change as a paradigm shift: Analysis of the process of a large, public university. *Journal of Higher Education, 65*(6), 670–695.

Smircich, L. (1983). Organizations as shared meanings. In Pondy, L. R., Frost, P. J., Morgan, G., & Dandridge, T. C. (eds.), *Organizational Symbolism*. Greenwich, CT: JAI Press.

Sporn, B. (1999). Towards more adaptive universities: Trends of institutional reform in Europe. *Higher Education in Europe, 24*(1). DOI: 10.1080/037977 2990240103.

Stolterman, E. & Fors, A. C. (2004). Information technology and the good life. In Kaplan, B., *et al.* (eds.), *Information Systems Research: Relevant Theory and Informed Practice*. Boston: Springer.

Truong, T. C. (2022). The impact of digital transformation on environmental sustainability. *Advances in Multimedia, 2022*, 1–12.

Wade, M., *et al.* (2019). *Orchestrating Transformation: How to Deliver Winning Performance with a Connected Approach to Change*. Lausanne: IMD.

Chapter 6

The Journey of Societies from the Real World to the Metaverse World with the Support of Digital Transformation and Artificial Intelligence

Kemal Gökhan Nalbant

Department of Software Engineering, Faculty of Engineering and Architecture, Istanbul Beykent University, Istanbul, Türkiye

kemalnalbant@beykent.edu.tr

1. Introduction

The term "metaverse" refers to a speculative world that surpasses the boundaries of tangible existence and is characterized by its perpetual and permanent qualities. The multiuser environment effectively integrates aspects of physical reality and digital virtuality in a seamless manner. This phenomenon is based on the integration of many technologies that enable the engagement of people with virtual environments, digital entities, and other individuals through various modes, such as virtual reality (VR) and augmented reality (AR). Hence, the metaverse might be characterized as an intricate system of interconnected immersive encounters inside enduring multiuser platforms, enabling social interactions and networking (Mystakidis, 2022).

A metaverse refers to a composite entity including interconnected, permanent, three-dimensional virtual environments that are shared among several users and integrated with the physical world, resulting in a unified and enduring VR. The metaverse is undergoing a notable shift from being a concept in science fiction to being an impending actuality, mostly due to recent advancements in several emerging technologies, such as blockchain, VR, digital twins, extended reality (XR), and AR. Individuals get access to the metaverse by means of avatars, which serve as their virtual representations and enable them to engage in interactions with other users as well as with the many entities comprising the metaverse, including items, programs, services, and organizations (Soliman *et al.*, 2023).

With the advent of Industry 4.0, corporations began to adopt the Fifth Industrial Revolution, sometimes referred to as Industry 5.0. Industry 5.0 is widely recognized as an approach that recognizes the potential of the industrial sector to contribute to societal objectives beyond employment and economic growth. It aims to transform production practices to align with the limitations of our planet and prioritize the welfare of industry workers as a central aspect of the production process (Xu *et al.*, 2021).

Evidence of the escalating rate of technological advancement is pervasive, as indicated by the notable indications of significant societal and economic shifts emerging from concepts, such as the "metaverse" and "Web3". Although the precise definition of these notions remains somewhat elusive, the process of digital transformation persists and is, in fact, progressing rapidly because of the economic pressures brought about by the COVID-19 epidemic (Ciuriak, 2021).

The field of science and engineering is currently experiencing a significant shift known as transformational development. This shift involves the fast integration of machine intelligence and human intelligence, resulting in the emergence of cyber-physical-social intelligence (CPSI). CPSI serves as the foundation for the increasing interconnections between cyberspace, physical space, and social space. The interactions occurring within our current landscape are giving rise to a multidimensional reality that is both developing and transforming. This phenomenon has led to the emergence of several novel notions and frameworks, including parallel intelligence, digital twins, and the metaverse (Wang *et al.*, 2023).

2. Metaverse Platforms

The transition from Industry 4.0 to Industry 5.0 entails a shift from a technology-centric industrial framework to a value-centric one that prioritizes human needs. This transformation also involves a departure from tangible physical environments toward immersive virtual realms, facilitated by the integration of various developing technologies. The utilization of artificial intelligence (AI) technologies has significantly transformed the way individuals engage in interpersonal communication. The implementation of the recent domestic epidemic quarantine policy has resulted in a significant surge in online activity throughout society. As a result, with the development of AI, a novel type of "home economy" has emerged. This development has created fresh opportunities for production and daily life, public health, education and employment, economy and finance, national security, and various other domains. People are discovering that the physical world does not fully meet their demands as online platforms become more and more integrated into daily life. Consequently, a digital realm known as the metaverse is emerging, serving as a parallel dimension that bridges the gap between the online and offline spheres (Li *et al.*, 2023).

A metaverse platform has the potential to incorporate several levels (Radoff, 2021; Huynh-The *et al.*, 2023):

- The infrastructure encompasses several technological components, such as 5G and 6G networks, WiFi connectivity, cloud computing, data centers, central processing units (CPUs), and graphics processing units (GPUs).
- The human interface encompasses a range of technological devices, such as mobile phones, smartwatches, smartglasses, wearable gadgets, and head-mounted displays, as well as interaction methods, such as gestures, voice commands, and electrode bundles.
- Decentralization encompasses several technological components, such as edge computing, AI agents, blockchain, and microservices.
- Spatial computing encompasses several technologies and methodologies, such as 3D engines, Virtual Reality (VR), Augmented Reality (AR), Extended Reality (XR), geographic mapping, and multitasking.
- The creator economy encompasses several components, such as design tools, asset markets, e-commerce, and workflow.
- The discovery of several technological advancements has significantly impacted the digital landscape. These include advertising networks, virtual storefronts, social curation, rating systems, avatars, and chatbots.
- Areas of experience are gaming, social media, e-sports, e-commerce, festivals, events, education, and employment.

3. Artificial Intelligence in Metaverse

The progress achieved in the field of AI has led to significant technical improvements across several domains. AI is currently being incorporated into several industries, such as healthcare, education, and smart-city services. The conceptualization of these technological advancements would have been implausible without the utilization of efficient, reliable, and fault-tolerant communication mediums. Immersive service environments provide challenges for traditional processing, communication, and storage technologies as they struggle to uphold optimal user experience and scalability. Individuals can engage in the metaverse, a virtual environment that exists in three-dimensions (3D), by utilizing advanced technologies, such as VR and AR. The synthesis of imagination and reality is employed in this universe to construct an artificial environment. The development of a setting of this nature is now underway and will require much study to achieve the utmost level of perfection (Murala & Panda, 2023).

In a similar vein, the utilization of AI-based technology inside the metaverse holds significant potential for providing valuable assistance to those afflicted with diverse psychological disorders. For instance, individuals diagnosed with borderline personality disorder (BPD) exhibit a significantly heightened propensity for engaging in suicidal behaviors. Individuals who engage in suicidal behavior often do so due to a sense of hopelessness, heightened anxiety, and impulsive tendencies. An AI-powered conversational agent that functions as a virtual assistant or virtual companion has the potential to offer a reliable presence to individuals, thereby assisting in mitigating occasionally overwhelming emotions. Virtual assistants have the capability to be designed in such a way that they may provide replies based on the principles and techniques of dialectical behavioral therapy (DBT). Indeed, individuals diagnosed with BPD who had made prior suicide attempts have reported that they had distressing cognitive patterns that served as triggers. However, due to feelings of shame and embarrassment, they refrained from seeking assistance and therefore engaged in self-destructive behaviors with the intention of ending their lives. According to several accounts, individuals expressed a growing sense of emotional void and a lack of available confidants. A virtual assistant has the potential to offer patients a readily available platform for sharing their concerns and seeking support, regardless of the time of day. Nevertheless, patients frequently experience a sense of alleviation when they perceive empathy from another individual, as demonstrated by non-verbal signs, such as body language. This form of non-verbal communication is a challenge for artificial intelligence systems to imitate. Theoretically, the constraints mentioned might be solved by relocating these programs to the metaverse, where virtual characters and avatars are present (Ahuja *et al.*, 2023).

AI and the metaverse have been suggested as potential solutions for fashion firms to automate several aspects of their operations, including product suggestion, customer segmentation, and inventory management. AI and the metaverse have the potential to enhance client interaction methods and enable more effective, tailored advertising campaigns. AI and the metaverse have the potential to enhance the implementation of digital marketing strategies for organizations. By leveraging data-driven insights and analysis, these technologies can provide a deeper understanding of client demands and preferences, enabling firms to optimize their marketing efforts more efficiently. The utilization of AI and Metaverse predictive marketing analytics enables firms to strategically develop and enhance their marketing efforts, as well as discern the consumer categories that provide the most profitability. Furthermore, the utilization of AI-driven consumer segmentation and targeting algorithms may assist organizations in optimizing the allocation of budget and resources, resulting in enhanced efficiency. In conclusion, the integration of AI with Metaverse automation offers organizations the opportunity to streamline marketing operations, such as customization, customer segmentation, incentives, and promotions, thus enhancing the overall customer experience (Rathore, 2023).

4. Industry 5.0 and Metaverse

The advent of the metaverse and Industry 5.0 has significantly altered the way we engage with technology and one another, presenting new prospects for both enterprises and individuals. The components of Industry 5.0 that are crucial to the development of the metaverse encompass the following (Agarwal & Alathur, 2023):

- The integration of human and machine intelligence to enhance outcomes is a core element of Industry 5.0. The metaverse presents a prospective resolution through the establishment of immersive virtual environments that enable synchronous cooperation between people and technology.
- The implementation of personalized virtual worlds that dynamically adjust to individual user preferences has the potential to achieve this within the metaverse.

- The use of smart automation in the metaverse has the potential to streamline repetitive tasks and enhance virtual interactions through the utilization of intelligent virtual assistants.

Decentralization: Within the Metaverse, the implementation of decentralized virtual marketplaces has the potential to optimize operational efficiency and provide cost savings by facilitating the exchange of virtual products and services among users.

The utilization of data analytics in the metaverse has the potential to enhance the user experience and optimize virtual operations by means of virtual environments that collect and analyze user data.

Numerous adverse outcomes and ancillary ramifications arise when one fails to adequately assess the potential influence of adopting digital technology and neglects to undertake a conscientious digital transformation. Blockchain technology enables the identification and subsequent mitigation of counterfeit goods, exemplifying its potential in this regard. Nevertheless, the utilization of blockchain technology necessitates a substantial quantity of energy, hence rendering it ecologically unsustainable. The implementation of AI technology has various impacts on the decision-making process, enhancing it in a proactive manner. However, enterprises are required to gather information from ecosystem seeds to utilize AI effectively. This leads to additional expenses arising from information dispersion and the necessity for validation. In a similar vein, the implementation of robots, 3D printing, and digital twins enables companies to digitize their manufacturing facilities, resulting in enhanced operational efficiency. Regrettably, these advancements can also lead to unemployment and the need for individuals to acquire new skills. The Internet of Things (IoT) has the capability to provide ongoing and transparent insights into the ecosystem. Nevertheless, the social sustainability of this approach may be compromised because of concerns around data security and the safeguarding of privacy (De Giovanni, 2023).

5. Artificial Intelligence Technologies for Metaverse

The presence of vast quantities of data within the metaverse necessitates the utilization of highly rapid and efficient computational processes to facilitate its operation. To tackle the computational challenge at hand, it is imperative to explore various computation strategies for both central platforms, such as cloud computing, and distributed devices, such as edge computing. Additionally, it is crucial to consider emerging computation architectures, such as in-memory computing, and novel computation paradigms, such as optoelectronic computing. Over the past several years, there has been a significant transformation in people's everyday lives because of the advancements in AI. Nevertheless, the substantial volume of data and the extensive number of terminal devices impose a significant strain on both the cloud computing system and the data transportation network. Consequently, there has been a growing interest in a distributed edge computing framework among both business and academics. This is mostly due to its capacity to extend computational capabilities to a vast number of edge devices, thereby alleviating the strain on cloud computing resources. The proliferation of edge devices has facilitated the advancement of AI approaches in several practical domains, including industrial manufacturing, healthcare, and urban security. However, the utilization of sophisticated AI approaches in practical applications is hindered by several challenges, such as inadequate data quality and restricted computational resources. These limitations result in the models' limited capability to effectively handle different practical situations. The utilization of contemporary deep-learning methodologies in AI necessitates substantial computing and storage resources due to the extensive number of neurons employed and the inherent computational intricacy involved. Nevertheless, meeting such demand on the periphery of the IoT device is impractical and challenging. In many instances, it is necessary to simplify huge and intricate AI models to get a dual benefit in terms of accuracy and efficiency prior to their deployment on edge AI hardware (Guo *et al.*, 2022).

The recent renaming of Facebook to Meta and the substantial investments made by firms such as Microsoft in the metaverse have garnered significant attention, positioning the metaverse as a prominent forthcoming technical innovation. Numerous significant domains of technology, such as natural language processing (NLP), machine vision, blockchain, networks, deep learning, and neural interface, have been subject to extensive investigation. Additionally, a diverse array of application fields, encompassing healthcare, manufacturing, smart cities, gaming, and decentralized finance (DeFi), have been explored. The examination of AI-based solutions has demonstrated the significant potential of AI in enhancing system design, enhancing built-in services inside virtual environments, and improving the immersive experience in three-dimensional settings (Soto & Leon, 2022).

AI has lately exhibited its capacity to enhance the allocation of networking resources and enhance overall system performance. The anticipated 6G network is projected to effectively manage a wide range of diverse devices for metaverse applications, all while ensuring optimal communication efficiency by leveraging AI. Nevertheless, the proliferation of extensive data and the increasing number of devices pose a significant obstacle in the realm of network management, leading to network congestion and a decline in quality of service (QoS). Digital twins refer to the virtual representation of real-world entities within the metaverse, necessitating the replication of their physical attributes and sensory capabilities. The utilization of a generative adversarial network (GAN) has considerable potential in the realm of producing digital replicas that possess the capability to produce diverse ensembles, hairstyles, and facial expressions within the context of three-dimensional (3D) imagery. AR and VR applications integrate the virtual and real worlds by utilizing computer vision (CV)-based analysis and computation. The advancement of AI and communication technologies has led to notable enhancements in the visual capabilities of AR/VR systems. Consequently, these upgraded AR/VR systems have found widespread use across several sectors, such as industrial settings and medical treatments. The utilization of AI to govern non-player characters (NPCs) holds significant significance in many metaverse applications. NPCs are obligated to engage with players in a manner that resembles human behavior. Various advanced learning-based approaches, including reinforcement learning (RL), support vector machines, and decision trees, are commonly utilized in the development of decision-making systems for NPCs (Peng *et al.*, 2022).

All entities inside the metaverse, including digital replicas, virtual representations of individuals, and intricate spatial representations, are comprised only of numerical data. However, the storage capacity of servers is always required due to the vast amount of data. In contrast, the conventional centralized design has constraints on uploading data to cloud servers because of restricted network resources. Conversely, the implementation of a metaverse system that relies on a centralized design may give rise to potential hazards, including the establishment of monopolies and the exertion of unlawful control. Within the metaverse, the immersive encounters, virtual office environments, and perceptual communication of users are contingent upon the utilization of network communication technologies that possess characteristics, such as high bandwidth, low latency, and high dependability. In the metaverse, the storage of all users' data on a single server is prohibited owing to concerns around security and privacy. The server's collapse can lead to a significant disruption in the Metaverse system, resulting in the potential compromise of users' private data. On the contrary, under the decentralized storage system, any participating organization has the potential to function as a storage node. Computer vision is a technological field that facilitates the interaction between the digital realm and the physical world, serving as a fundamental component for image processing in the context of XR implementation. Computer vision is primarily utilized in several applications inside the metaverse, including visual localization and mapping, human position and eye tracking, general scene identification and understanding, as well as picture recovery and augmentation. The execution of virtual 3D scenes necessitates a significant amount of computational and storage resources. The increasing prominence of the metaverse is expected to drive a heightened need for cloud computing services, owing to its robust computational capabilities and dependable network infrastructure. The ongoing advancement and maturation of virtual applications need an escalation in the capacity and real-time processing demands of the metaverse. Edge computing, as an extension of cloud computing, is widely recognized as a pivotal catalyst in the ongoing technological revolution and is anticipated to play a crucial role in the development of the metaverse (Chang *et al.*, 2022).

6. Artificial Intelligence and Metaverse for Digital Transformation

Constructing a metaverse with a solitary human holds no inherent significance. The metaverse may be seen as a virtual environment with a potentially vast user base ranging from millions to billions. Within this context, the facilitation of distant collaboration among users emerges as a significant and integral aspect of the metaverse's functionality. The central inquiry revolves around the means of establishing connectivity and facilitating the exchange of information between individuals, regardless of their geographical separation. This question serves as the primary focal point for the exploration and development of cooperation and communication methodologies. The collaboration inside the metaverse encompasses several elements, such as communication strategies facilitating information sharing among users, blockchain techniques enabling decentralized data storage, and cybersecurity techniques ensuring the security of collaborative activities in the metaverse. The significance and use of a virtual environment are rendered null and void in the absence of user interaction and the ability to effectively utilize it in the pursuit of certain objectives. Hence, interaction serves as a fundamental aspect of the metaverse, facilitating the connection between individuals in the physical world and the virtual realm. Human–computer interaction has been a prominent subject of research in this domain for an extended period. It encompasses essential functionalities that facilitate contact between humans and computers. Moreover, the field of brain–computer interaction has garnered significant attention in recent years. AI plays a significant role in both research subjects, serving to enhance and advance these methodologies. The optimization of human–computer interaction (HCI) is a fundamental concern in the metaverse. The levels of HCI encompass perception, presentation, and comprehension, all of which need enhancement to provide a real-time, natural, and immersive user experience. In a similar vein, the fundamental technological concerns encompass multimodal active perception technology, holographic display technology, and the approach to comprehending interactive goals that incorporate context and psychology. AI plays a significant and influential role in the cutting-edge study of HCI (Guo *et al.*, 2022).

The concept of the metaverse has the capacity to significantly impact business digital transformation and the advent of Industry 5.0. The promotion of user-friendly digital environments fosters a transition toward dematerialization when the act of purchasing items online supplants the acquisition of physical products (Dwivedi *et al.*, 2022; Agarwal & Alathur, 2023). Furthermore, the integration of manufacturing, information, and communication technologies (ICTs), and social technologies leads to the execution of tasks within the framework of the social-cyber-physical system (SCPS) that surpass the cognitive abilities of workers who have been educated in conventional manufacturing practices characterized by the division of labor. To facilitate collaboration across cyber, physical, and social domains, it is imperative for workers to possess a comprehensive understanding of the environment within which their interactions take place. The process of training and retraining staff is an unavoidable aspect of organizational operations. Industrial revolutions tend to induce alterations within human civilization, serving as catalysts for societal progress and expediting societal transformations. The concepts of Industry 4.0 and 5.0 aim to facilitate the progression of civilization into an advanced stage known as civilization 5.0, characterized by its high level of intelligence and wisdom. Industry 5.0, also known as Society 5.0, is distinguished by its emphasis on human-centric customization and personalization, which is facilitated by the utilization of SCPS (Yao *et al.*, 2022).

The digitization of the fashion industry has two primary goals: (1) to improve the effectiveness of designing, producing, and managing tangible products in the real world and (2) to work toward the goal of achieving sustainability via the use of a variety of digital technologies. The arrival of the metaverse, which is a VR parallel universe, has, despite this, ushered in a fresh era of digital fashion. The developments in digital fashion can be categorized into four distinct categories, which are as follows: (1) digital design and electronic prototype, (2) digital business and promotional strategies, (3) digital representation of humans and virtual environments, and (4) digital garments and intelligent electronic technology (Sayem, 2022).

The progression from a disparate assemblage of discrete virtual realms to a cohesive network of interconnected three-dimensional virtual domains, commonly referred to as the metaverse, is reliant on advancements in four key domains: immersive realism, widespread accessibility and identification, interoperability, and scalability. The metaverse refers to a network including interconnected three-dimensional virtual worlds (Dionisio *et al.*, 2013).

7. Conclusion

In the envisioned metaverse, individuals demonstrate a predilection for utilizing their virtual wardrobe to select digital attire, while corporations embark on the promotion of virtual skins, virtual garments, and virtual properties at exorbitant costs, thereby hindering a substantial portion of gamers from engaging in the metaverse. Hence, it is crucial to establish precise governance frameworks within the realm of global business cooperation. Furthermore, the unsolved issue pertains to the construction of a digital currency system that effectively allows the transfer of monetary value between the metaverse and the actual world. Moreover, it is expected that the volume and frequency of transactions within the metaverse will exceed those witnessed in the physical domain to a considerable degree. Hence, the matter of efficiently enabling transactions with large volumes and frequencies is a substantial difficulty in the potential metaverse. A further possible issue that might arise in relation to the forthcoming metaverse pertains to the inflationary consequences stemming from the extensive utilization of cryptocurrencies inside a decentralized economic structure founded on blockchain and AI (Yang *et al.*, 2022).

The emergence of the metaverse is expected to bring significant changes to many industries, creating new job prospects and enabling substantial improvements in remote collaboration capabilities. Teams of specialized experts who are geographically separated can come together in a metaverse environment, enabling collaborative innovation. This facilitates the collective creation of prototypes for emerging products before they enter the production phase. The metaverse, as a conceptual framework, holds promise for the emergence of innovative virtual economies. Users within these economies can accumulate and employ virtual currencies while also participating in the generation and exchange of virtual goods. The metaverse, as a conceptual framework, has promise for generating innovative opportunities for economic engagement and facilitating the virtual trade of goods and services among people. The incorporation of machine learning methodologies for harnessing data created within the metaverse is crucial for the integration of AI functionalities within the metaverse ecosystem. AI possesses the capacity to examine data with the objective of identifying patterns and then leveraging these patterns to improve its own performance. Individuals and organizations are currently employing metaverse technology to create new opportunities that offer social benefits. There is great enthusiasm for the beneficial results that the metaverse is producing, including immersive educational and training experiences as well as unique opportunities in healthcare and the workplace. A multitude of technological enterprises and developers are now involved in the advancement of their respective versions of the metaverse, mostly aimed at enhancing internet accessibility. The potential replacement of specific elements of the tangible realm with the metaverse is a forthcoming notion that might potentially manifest in the next few years or possibly decades. Significant advancements in technology amplify the potential for the metaverse to surpass the physical world. Experts anticipate that the metaverse could potentially replace certain elements of the physical world in the foreseeable future, although this transition may take several years to even many decades. The subject of interest is the possibility of the metaverse replacing conventional physical office spaces. To a certain extent, the metaverse possesses the capacity to replace in-person human interaction. In prospective times, it is conceivable that its importance might perhaps approach that of social media in our contemporary lives. The plausibility of the metaverse replacing jobs is a probable possibility. The metaverse economy's potential significance parallels that of the real-world economy.

References

Agarwal, A. & Alathur, S. (2023). Metaverse revolution and the digital transformation: Intersectional analysis of Industry 5.0. *Transforming Government: People, Process and Policy, 17*(4), 688–707.

Ahuja, A. S., Polascik, B. W., Doddapaneni, D., Byrnes, E. S., & Sridhar, J. (2023). The digital metaverse: Applications in artificial intelligence, medical education, and integrative health. *Integrative Medicine Research, 12*(1), 100917.

Chang, L., Zhang, Z., Li, P., Xi, S., Guo, W., Shen, Y., Xiong, Z., Kang, J., Niyato, D., Qiao, X., & Wu, Y. (2022). 6G-enabled edge AI for Metaverse: Challenges, methods, and future research directions. *Journal of Communications and Information Networks, 7*(2), 107–121.

Ciuriak, D. (2021). On the Metaverse, Web3 and prospering in the digital transformation. *Published under the Title, 'Dan Ciuriak: Intangible Intellectual Property and Data-The Most Important Assets of the New Economy,' Commentary, in Chinese Views of Non-traditional Security, 13*(1).

De Giovanni, P. (2023). Sustainability of the Metaverse: A transition to Industry 5.0. *Sustainability, 15*(7), 6079.

Dionisio, J. D. N., Iii, W. G. B., & Gilbert, R. (2013). 3D virtual worlds and the metaverse: Current status and future possibilities. *ACM Computing Surveys (CSUR), 45*(3), 1–38.

Dwivedi, Y. K., Hughes, L., Baabdullah, A. M., Ribeiro-Navarrete, S., Giannakis, M., Al-Debei, M. M., Dennehy, D., Metri, B., Buhalis, D., Cheung, C. M. K., Conboy, K., Doyle, R., Dubey, R., Dutot, V., Felix, R., Goyal, D. P., Gustafsson, A., Hinsch, C., Jebabli, I., Janssen, M., Kim, Y.-G., Kim, J., Koos, S., Kreps, D., Kshetri, N., Kumar, V., Ooi, K.-B., Papagiannidis, S., Pappas, I. O., Polyviou, A., Park, S.-M., Pandey, N., Queiroz, M. M., Raman, R., Rauschnabel, P. A., Shirish, A., Sigala, M., Spanaki, K., Tan, G. W.-H., Tiwari, M. K., Viglia, G., & Wamba, S. F. (2022). Metaverse beyond the hype: Multidisciplinary perspectives on emerging challenges, opportunities, and agenda for research, practice and policy. *International Journal of Information Management, 66.* DOI: 10.1016/j.ijinfomgt.2022.102542.

Guo, Y., Yu, T., Wu, J., Wang, Y., Wan, S., Zheng, J., Fang, L., & Dai, Q. (2022). Artificial intelligence for metaverse: A framework. *CAAI Artificial Intelligence Research, 1*(1), 54–67.

Huynh-The, T., Pham, Q. V., Pham, X. Q., Nguyen, T. T., Han, Z., & Kim, D. S. (2023). Artificial intelligence for the metaverse: A survey. *Engineering Applications of Artificial Intelligence, 117,* 105581.

Li, Y., Ma, Z., & Zhang, L. (2023). Research on interaction design based on artificial intelligence technology in a metaverse environment. In *International Conference on Human-Computer Interaction* (pp. 193–209). Cham: Springer Nature Switzerland.

Murala, D. K. & Panda, S. K. (2023). Artificial intelligence in the development of metaverse. *Metaverse and Immersive Technologies: An Introduction to Industrial, Business and Social Applications* (pp. 407–436).

Mystakidis, S. (2022). Metaverse. *Encyclopedia, 2*(1), 486–497.

Peng, H., Chen, P. C., Chen, P. H., Yang, Y. S., Hsia, C. C., & Wang, L. C. (2022). 6G toward metaverse: Technologies, applications, and challenges. In *2022 IEEE VTS Asia Pacific Wireless Communications Symposium (APWCS),* August 2022 (pp. 6–10). IEEE.

Radoff, J. (2021). The metaverse value-chain. https://medium.com/building-themetaverse/the-metaverse-value-chain-afcf9e09e3a7.

Rathore, B. (2023). Digital transformation 4.0: Integration of Artificial intelligence & metaverse in marketing. *Eduzone: International Peer Reviewed/ Refereed Multidisciplinary Journal, 12*(1), 42–48.

Sayem, A. S. M. (2022). Digital fashion innovations for the real world and metaverse. *International Journal of Fashion Design, Technology and Education, 15*(2), 139–141.

Soliman, M. M., Darwish, A., & Hassanien, A. E. (2023). The threat of the digital human in the metaverse: Security and privacy. In *The Future of Metaverse in the Virtual Era and Physical World* (pp. 247–265). Cham: Springer International Publishing.

Soto, I. B. R. & Leon, N. S. S. (2022). How artificial intelligence will shape the future of metaverse. A qualitative perspective. *Metaverse Basic and Applied Research, 1,* 12.

Wang, F. Y., Tang, Y., & Werbos, P. J. (2023). Guest editorial: Cyber–physical–social intelligence: Toward metaverse-based smart societies of 6I and 6S. *IEEE Transactions on Systems, Man, and Cybernetics: Systems, 53*(4), 2018–2024.

Xu, X., Lu, Y., Vogel-Heuser, B., & Wang, L. (2021). Industry 4.0 and Industry 5.0 — Inception, conception and perception. *Journal of Manufacturing Systems, 61,* 530–535.

Yang, Q., Zhao, Y., Huang, H., Xiong, Z., Kang, J., & Zheng, Z. (2022). Fusing blockchain and AI with metaverse: A survey. *IEEE Open Journal of the Computer Society*, 3, 122–136.

Yao, X., Ma, N., Zhang, J., Wang, K., Yang, E., & Faccio, M. (2022). Enhancing wisdom manufacturing as industrial metaverse for industry and society 5.0. *Journal of Intelligent Manufacturing*, *35*(1), 235–255.

Chapter 7

Digital Transformation (DX), Platform Strategy, and Knowledge Leadership

Yayoi Hirose

Information Networking for Innovation and Design,
Toyo University, Japan

yayoi.hirose@iniad.org

1. Introduction

This chapter claims that (1) Digital Transformation (DX)-related business knowledge has become more complex due to DX platform strategy and that (2) a DX leader needs to adopt "knowledge leadership" to create new knowledge to effectively conduct a DX strategy. While many global enterprises actively conduct DX, they need to execute more complex strategies. They build their industry-specific digital cloud platform, which is an open ecosystem for developers and users to generate various kinds of DX applications. On a DX platform, both DX application users and developers learn from each other and create new DX knowledge. The organizations that use the new DX applications need to transform their conventional operations for utilizing these applications and enhance customer engagement. The developer organizations can co-create DX systems and applications with their platform company, users, and other developers on the platforms. They need to create new knowledge by transforming their engineering knowledge for platform principles and user organizations that aim to effectively utilize the DX applications.

Thus, every DX stakeholder needs to transform their conventional mindset, openly exchange their knowledge, and create new DX knowledge with participating organizations on their industrial DX platform. The platform leaders need to encourage every stakeholder to participate in this knowledge journey. It is difficult and exhausting work for the leader because while many global enterprises actively conduct DX strategy, more than 70% of DX projects fail (Bonnet, 2022). This chapter emphasizes the importance of knowledge for transformation and aims to present how DX platform leaders should address various kinds of participating individuals and organizations in their DX industrial platforms.

2. Digital Competitive Situation

2.1. *DX and Digital Platform Strategy*

For a decade, many global enterprises have conducted DX strategy and developed DX application software to enhance customer engagement and create new DX operations. DX is defined as a business transformation strategy by enhancing and engaging relationships with customers and other stakeholders using advanced digital technologies, including AI, VR/AR, and robotics. To present a picture of the recent competitive environment related to DX strategy, it is necessary to mention the relationship with digital platform strategy. To effectively promote a DX business strategy, DX leaders have built digital cloud platforms for organizations that use the DX software and developers who use the APIs to create new DX applications. Figure 1 shows a visualization of the recent situation. While the main players are IT vendors in infrastructure as a service (IaaS) and platform as a service (PaaS) layers, several global companies that used to implement IT solutions have developed their industrial cloud platforms for around a decade. The digital platform has been developed in both intra-organizational and inter-organizational modes. In the case of a platform for the automobile industry, the users would be drivers, and in the case of the pharmaceutical industry, the users would be doctors, patients, etc. After spreading word of their useful DX applications within their organizations, the enterprises aimed to increase their DX application users; they expanded the industry-specific DX software to other companies in the same industries. They also invited other companies to participate in their cloud platform and utilize their DX software.

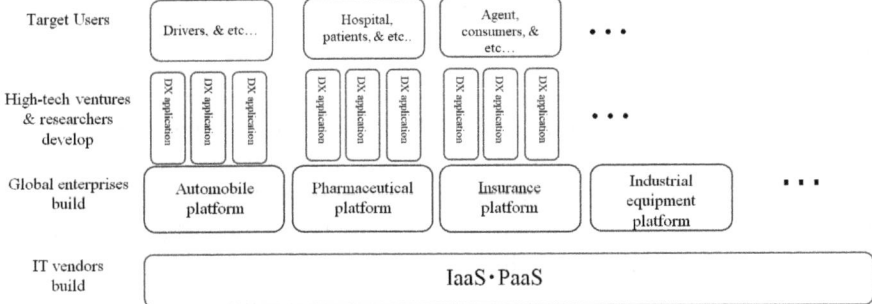

Figure 1. DX and industrial cloud DX platform.

One can see that they adopt a *de facto* standard strategy by expanding users and developers for their platform to be a global standard of their industry. They aim to create new DX applications based on their new value chain. They also aim to standardize their value chain in their industry and let other companies use their DX applications. Once user companies adopt and use the DX application, they are locked in and tend to continue using them. Furthermore, increasing participating organizations suggests that their platform will be able to obtain competitive advantage by analyzing accumulated digital data and developing new DX applications using AI technology. To increase the number of users, the platform companies have also financially supported developers and high-tech ventures to develop killer DX applications that many user organizations want to utilize to promote DX strategies. To maintain the superiority of the company's platform, it is necessary for them to popularize killer applications that are useful to many users. They believe that by having their platform used more than that of anyone else in their industry, they can dominate in terms of digital strategy in their industry. By providing the platform it has built as a solution specific to that industry, the company aims to develop its business in a different way from that of giant platform vendors, such as Google, Apple, Facebook, and Amazon (GAFA), which target consumers in general. In other words, global enterprises build digital platforms that enable numerous companies and innovators to generate new DX solutions. This means that to create new DX solutions, organizations need to share their knowledge with other fields, other organizations, and nations to generate new business knowledge.

2.2. *DX Platform Integrated SDGs*

Recently, to differentiate their platform from others, enterprises have adopted solutions for Sustainable Development Goals (SDGs) as well as digital business. To generate killer DX applications, global DX platform companies have started promoting the development of DX applications considering SDGs for differentiation. This chapter discusses two types of SDGs integrated into DX platforms: production value chain and after-production service. Figure 2 shows the following value chain type: a DX platform strategy for EV battery production. A platform leader company built a new DX value chain for EV battery production and aimed to globally standardize their value chain process. They can also accumulate and analyze the manufacturing data collected from the stakeholders and utilize Circular Economy (CE)-related digital passport data for their platform to be more competitive.

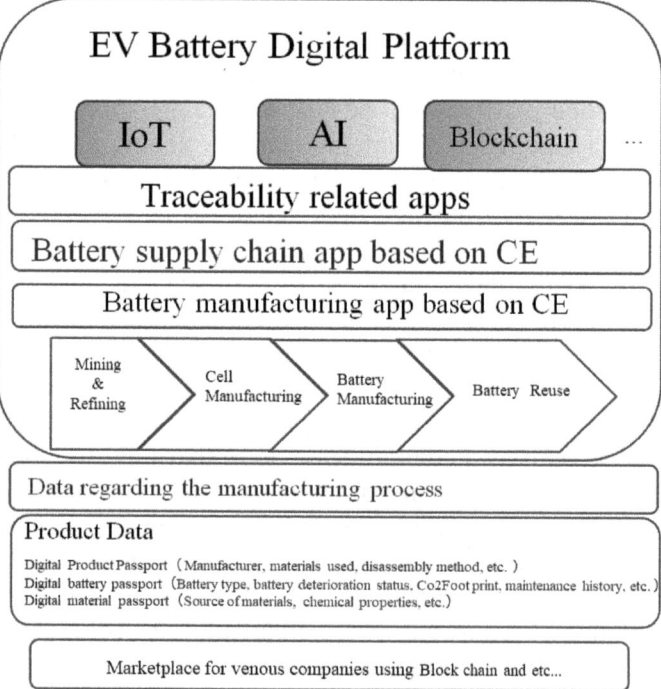

Figure 2.   EV battery digital platform.

To differentiate their value chain from others, this EV battery company integrated SDG discipline into their DX application. For example, the company has envisioned transforming the entire EV battery value chain into one based on CE and will invite material manufacturers and other suppliers to participate, making the entire manufacturing value chain more efficient. They create a reusable and long-life product specification based on a circular economy discipline and encourage the alliance partner companies to follow this specification. The platform company also develops DX software using blockchain technology. The blockchain-based traceability system built by the group is currently limited to tracking down to the parts level, but the company suggests that in the future, it can build a system that traces all the way up to mines and smelters. Many metals are used in lithium-ion batteries, and if more and more of these products are manufactured sustainably, the value chain process of a wide range of industries — from mining to metal manufacturing processes, as well as EVs in general — will be affected. The application also requires mining companies that participate in the EV battery platform to input data that certifies zero child labor to the blockchain software.

Figure 3 shows the following after-service type: a DX platform after the production service of industrial equipment. While in the past, equipment was discarded when it expired, circular economy discipline requires longer product life. In the DX industrial equipment platform, the life of the product can be prolonged by an IoT monitoring system. CE requires both production companies and users to extend the lifespans of machines. When a platform company focuses on a market wherein CE requirements are stringent and competitors fail to popularize the Internet of Things (IoT) monitoring service, that company expects to standardize its application and dominate the global market.

This suggests that DX platform enterprises need to adopt more leadership so as to apply a wider range of new business knowledge for their ecosystem DX platform to be competitive. Figure 4 exemplifies the variation of business knowledge regarding industrial equipment between company DX and industrial platform DX. In company DX, the equipment company needs to create new knowledge by integrating digital technology with their machine-production know-how and customer needs. A DX leader needs to announce the DX vision to shareholders and suppliers by telling them how the company will transform and create DX knowledge, which can be competitive. It is important to adjust the discussion between digital producers, such as developers and engineers, and digital users,

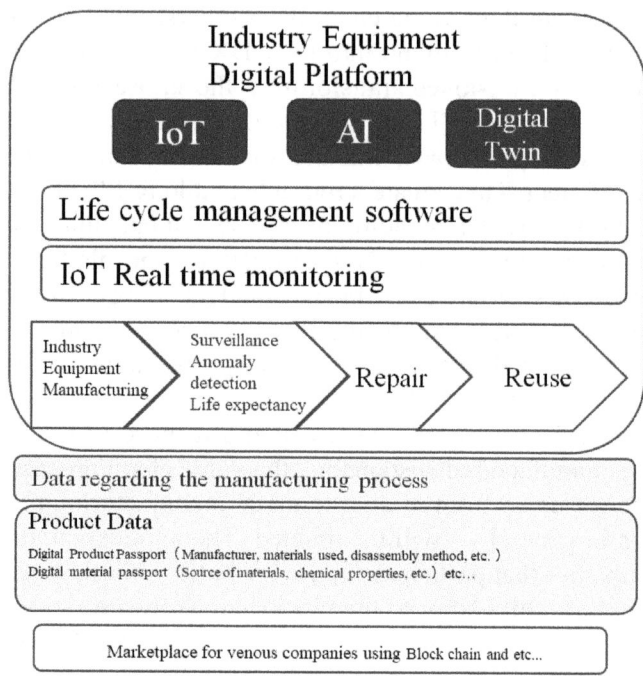

Figure 3.   DX platform after the production service of industrial equipment.

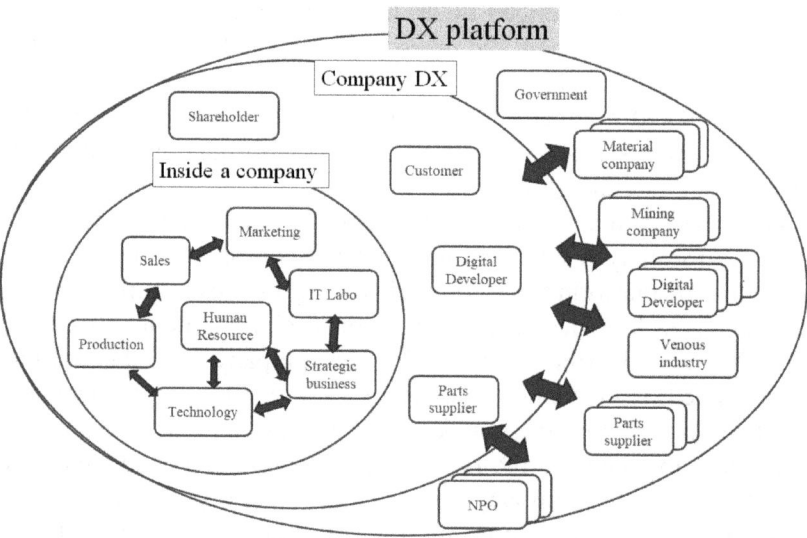

Figure 4.   Variation of stakeholders' business knowledge: Industrial Equipment Company.

such as business and marketing departments. On the other hand, in industrial platform DX, knowledge increases and widens as the number of participants and DX applications increases.

The knowledge would then become more complicated because it needs to integrate SDG principles into DX business. Thus, DX platform leaders need to organize the value chain, convince a wider range of participating organizations to understand SDGs' value, disrupt their conventional mindset, integrate it with their DX strategy, and create new business knowledge to be competitive and standardized.

3. The Role of DX Platform Leadership

For their platform to be competitive, every DX participant needs to transform their conventional mindset, deepen their relationships with other stakeholders and customers, openly exchange knowledge, and create new DX knowledge with participating organizations on their industrial DX platform. Then, how should DX platform leaders act for various kinds of participants to create new business knowledge in their DX industrial platforms?

3.1. *Past Discussions on DX Leadership within a Company*

Past literature on DX leadership discusses how a leader should behave within a company. They claim that in order to promote DX inside a company, the CEO should take the leadership role in implementing a transformational system. The CEO announces a clear strategic DX vision, which includes the message of why DX is necessary, organizes the DX department, and assigns the Chief Digital Officer (CDO). The DX literature claims the importance of clarifying a strategic vision and organizing a new division for transformation (Rogers, 2016; Wade, 2019). The DX department is required to frequently communicate with business departments under the CDO's initiative to implement the DX system to transform their conventional operations and practices and launch a new business (Rogers, 2016; Wade *et al.*, 2019).

Business leadership literature claims that a business leader who aims to transform a conventional organization should enable his/her staff and middle managers to understand the necessity of disrupting the conventional approach and present them with a new business direction (Heifetz *et al.*, 2009; Rogers, 2016). Heifetz *et al.* (2009) emphasize that an executive leader should present the threat by continuing conventional business and evaluating challenges for adapting to a new environment. Kotter (1996) identifies the importance of promoting staff's crisis awareness, organizing collaborative teams for transformation, presenting a strategic vision, and encouraging staff initiative.

3.2. *Difficulty in Understanding Transformative Business Knowledge*

However, companies that implemented transformative business knowledge — including how to conduct a new strategic vision and incur profit through new projects — have not successfully transformed their action. A business survey reveals that organizational leaders believe that while it is relatively easy to implement a new technology, it is extremely difficult to change the employees' business mindsets and how the employees work together (Kane, 2019). The survey also shows that around 80% of companies that effectively use digital technologies recognize the necessity of new business leadership. In order to transform a company, organizational people need to disrupt their conventional ways of thinking and implement a new approach. However, as large-sized firms struggle with bureaucratic structures that sap initiative, they tend to maintain a conventional way of thinking; it is hard for them to understand new transformative business knowledge (Hamel & Zanini, 2018).

Carlile (2004) highlights the different requirements for managing the transfer of different types of knowledge between individuals and groups from different contexts (Figure 5). In essence, what this tells us is the greater the distance between the giver and the receiver's context, the more one has to do to enable the knowledge to get from Actor A to Actor B whether they are individuals, groups, or organizations. The base of the triangle includes common knowledge, including technical knowledge, maybe using the common language of mathematics, which can be transferred via information processing, because the giver and receiver share a basic common understanding of the technicalities involved. As there are a lot of shared understandings of vocabulary and definitions between organizations, the knowledge can easily be transferred. The middle part includes tacit knowledge, which requires translation in order to create shared meaning between actors. To fill the role of a translator, organizations often create cross-functional teams or use various software methodologies.

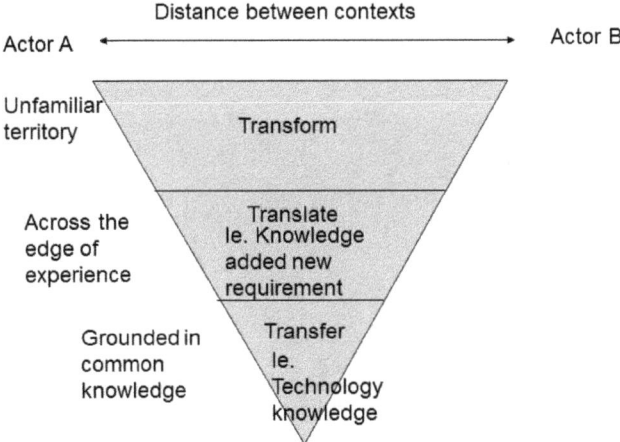

Figure 5. Carlile (2004) framework for managing knowledge.

The upper part of Figure 5 includes knowledge created in a very different context. Carlile (2004) claims that in the case of managing knowledge that was generated in a fundamentally different context, simply transferring knowledge is not possible partly because shared vocabulary and definitions between knowledge providers and receivers are no longer useful for understanding new knowledge. But more particularly, the knowledge needs to be adapted to suit the different conditions in the new context in order for it to be seen as relevant and useful. Thus, in the case of implementing knowledge that has been generated in a DX context, which is different from conventional business, the knowledge receiver needs to transform his or her path dependency based on his or her conventional values. To activate a DX industry-specific platform, individual stakeholders need to understand DX knowledge and generate new DX knowledge by interacting with others. In other words, it is difficult for many participants in DX platform to understand DX and SDG business knowledge because the new knowledge has been generated in different contexts from conventional businesses.

3.3. *Complexities in Transformative Business Knowledge in DX Platforms*

Figure 6 shows the complexity of DX platform knowledge. The knowledge required on the DX platform is a complex mixture of various

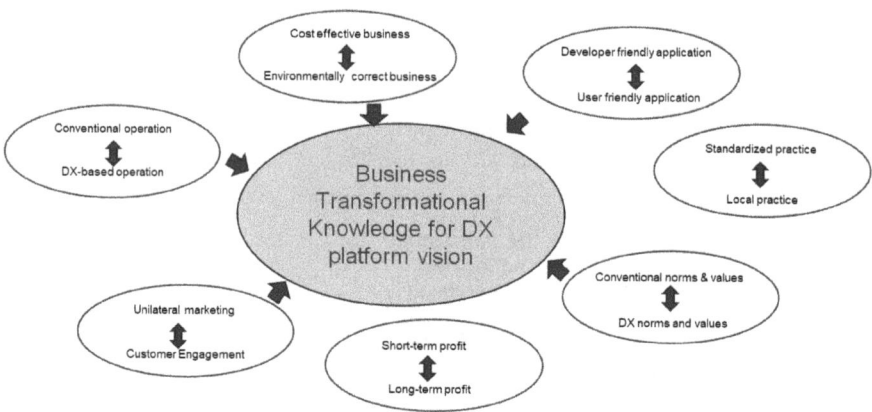

Figure 6.   Complexity of DX platform knowledge.

viewpoints and values, so rather than simply changing one viewpoint, for example, changing the conventional mindset for creating high-quality products and integrating customer experience is preferred. It takes even more time to understand this knowledge as it is necessary to think from multiple perspectives. For example, a business division that has focused on producing high-quality products may have to consider whether it is environmentally correct, whether it is possible to standardize the manufacturing process as application software, or whether it is possible to make full use of AI. They also need to consider other factors, such as what should be done to quickly reflect the user needs that marketing staff who emphasize customer engagement regularly purchase and hold discussions with each person in charge to create knowledge. Business managers who have previously focused on profits on a yearly basis now need to understand the business based on the medium-term success vision that DX aims for. To do so, they must disrupt traditional practices and norms, and it is necessary to discuss this with various stakeholders and create practices that are also understood by alliance partners outside the company.

This suggests that past discussions lack insight into how to handle participants' difficulty in understanding new business knowledge at the individual level. Although the literature on leadership for transformation focuses on how a business leader ought to be and what a business leader should do (Heifetz, 2009; Hughes, 2016; Kotter, 1996; McKnight, 2013; Mitzberg, 2004; Rogers, 2016; Wade, 2019), it does not discuss how employees can transform their way of thinking or how they understand transformative business knowledge to the degree of actualizing the knowledge from an employee perspective. When a global enterprise aims to generate a new DX platform, the enterprise needs stronger leadership than a company-level transformation as more various fields of stakeholders participate in the platform so that various kinds of "conventional business methods" may exist in the platform.

4. Knowledge Leadership in DX Ecosystem Industrial Platform

4.1. *Leadership Encourages Understanding the Threshold Concept*

When implementing DX, leaders indicate the vision they want to achieve through DX. Employees are expected to understand why DX is necessary and then proceed with it. On the other hand, the DX platform vision needs to consider various perspectives, such as stopping conventional practices and norms, changing the relationship with customers, considering constraints due to environmental issues, and incorporating the knowledge of DX developers, managers, and staff, who may be confused about which customs, norms, and knowledge they need to adopt and which ones to stop adopting.

Thus, creating the complex knowledge discussed in Figure 6 cannot be achieved simply by listening to the DX vision that the platform company announces to all the stakeholders and being organized as members to take charge of it. Even if the business leaders understand that transformation is necessary, they will not be able to take effective actions because they subconsciously imagine their business in a way that adheres to traditional values or they come up with business plans that are focused on short-term profits. It is not easy for people who have focused on manufacturing high-quality products to create a method to manufacture environmentally sensitive products in a way that software engineers can understand while also considering the use of artificial intelligence (AI). The more successes such business leaders have had, the less likely it is that they would understand why they should invalidate their past successes in order to pursue new endeavors that they do not know will be profitable. This path dependency can be referred to as *knowledge inertia*.

A DX leader should consider that participants do not have deep enough understanding to take transformative action, so he or she needs to disrupt the participants' knowledge inertia. From a knowledge perspective, a platform leader first needs to disrupt each participant's knowledge inertia — which includes judgment based on conventional practices, rules, and norms — and encourage him or her to understand new, transformative knowledge. For example, a leader can encourage participants who have been focusing on cost-efficient production to integrate new values, such as SDGs.

Before focusing on creating knowledge that incorporates various multidisciplinary viewpoints into the DX platform, a leader needs to confirm that all participants sufficiently understand the DX platform vision to take transformative actions because they might suffer from knowledge inertia. To do so, the leader can use the threshold concept approach. The threshold concept for business transformation is the ability to imagine successful business at the individual level through transformation (Hirose, 2023). The most important point is that every participant should have a successful vision at the individual level because this vision differs depending on the participants. By receiving a leader's encouragement to understand the threshold concept, the participants will be able to imagine the goal from their own perspectives rather than from the perspectives of the DX platform or their companies. For example, the production staff of an EV battery company needs to imagine collaborating with the department staff in a circular economy, the DX staff, and the supplier company staff to generate DX business knowledge. This view will enable the production staff to disrupt simple cost-efficient production and to understand how to integrate CE principles, DX knowledge, and suppliers' know-how with their product. On the other hand, DX application developers of the EV battery need to learn battery-value-chain know-how and adopt a CE mindset and customer needs.

The threshold concept has been developed more fully in the field of education rather than business solutions (Barradell, 2013; Meyer & Land, 2003, 2005, 2006). Past discussion on threshold concepts has focused on how learners understand more complex knowledge that is not accessible to novices, such as how to use a statistical lens to understand statistics (Beitelmal *et al.*, 2022; Luoma, 2006; Meyer & Land, 2005). DX platform leaders can utilize the threshold concept by encouraging employees to understand DX platform knowledge because the threshold concept serves as a gateway function that may prove troublesome for the learners to integrate with what they already know but that, once learned, is both transformative and irreversible. "Transformative" refers to a complete and radical change in a learner's understanding, interpretation, and view of a phenomenon, topic, and/or practice (Meyer & Land, 2003, 2005). It can be a portal or a step progression that enables a person to understand more complex knowledge that is inaccessible to a novice (Luoma, 2006; Meyer & Land, 2005). When a DX platform leader aims to promote a transformational project, he or she needs to consider the gateway function because participants may be novices in the field of transformation. For example, when the participants do not have experience in collaborating with SDG experts, a platform leader should support the participants to understand the expert's knowledge and value. Since DX platform knowledge is a mixture of various perspectives and knowledge, stakeholders need to define what knowledge they should discard and what they should absorb. To do so, each person needs to imagine what kind of success he or she will have.

Threshold concepts completely alter the learner's view of the world and his or her way of thinking and behaving (Meyer & Land, 2005; Trafford, 2008). They change learners' internal mental structures with respect to the way they perceive and interact with external reality (Yip & Raelin, 2012). The concept is also irreversible. Once a learner has deeply embedded knowledge into his or her mindset, it is hard to unlearn because the conceptual framework used to interpret experiences has been reconfigured as a result of a novel integration of new thinking that applies to many phenomena (Davies & Mangan, 2007; Meyer & Land, 2005). When stakeholders participate in the DX platform, they need to completely disrupt their conventional ways of thinking, and this disruption can be irreversible. For example, it is difficult for industrial equipment sales representatives who used to periodically sell expensive machines to transform their mindsets to seek a contract for an IoT monitoring system. They are not always proactive about changing their sales method from hardware to services, making it difficult for services centered on this application to become widespread. Moreover, such representatives had been assessed based on their sales figures for these expensive machines, so they may be resistant to increasing the number of contracts with IoT monitoring systems instead of periodic replacement because the monitoring contracts are less expensive. Many customers also may not necessarily prefer this IoT service because they are accustomed to the traditional method of replacing old devices after a certain period rather than maintaining and using them for a longer time. In other words, both users and internal staff may be reluctant to abandon traditional operations and adopt new methods to utilize DX applications. A DX platform leader thus needs to make the sales representatives and customers recognize a new world where customers continue using their industrial equipment for a longer period instead of periodically purchasing new equipment. This leadership action is expected to encourage them both to take the next step of contributing to creating a useful IoT monitoring system by collaborating with each other.

A threshold concept is also integrative in that it makes sense of and combines past knowledge through a different logic so that a learner can relate factors that have been previously hidden or separated (Meyer & Land, 2005). Davies and Mangan (2007) argued that a threshold concept integrates past dimensions in complex ways by transforming conventional perception. For instance, a platform leader can support participants to understand how to integrate new DX and SDG transformative knowledge into their business knowledge by encouraging them to understand the threshold concepts. Figure 7 shows the role of leadership in the process of participants' multidisciplinary knowledge creation in the DX platform.

Participants who have belonged to traditional organizations may have difficulty understanding transformative business knowledge because they are used to focusing on conventional markets. In other words, it may be difficult for them to disrupt their knowledge inertia and to understand and integrate new DX and SDG values into their business. The threshold concept can be useful for them to disrupt their conventional ways of thinking and learn new business knowledge.

To promote this transformation, a business leader needs to consider the individual levels of participants in overcoming the impediments to understanding transformative business knowledge. When promoting corporate DX, a C-level executive needs to clearly articulate the DX vision, announce it to various departments, and take the lead. However, at the individual level, knowledge inertia is at work, making it difficult to take action. Thus, the DX platform leaders should encourage individuals to understand the threshold concept for DX platform knowledge.

Each participant needs to imagine in detail the individual goal of implementing a business by incorporating various types of knowledge as a gateway for understanding complex and new knowledge. It is important to imagine themselves working energetically by determining who their stakeholders are, with whom they constantly communicate and have discussions, to whom they report, and what to do. By having their own DX platform visions, they will understand what knowledge to adopt or discard and better understand DX platform knowledge.

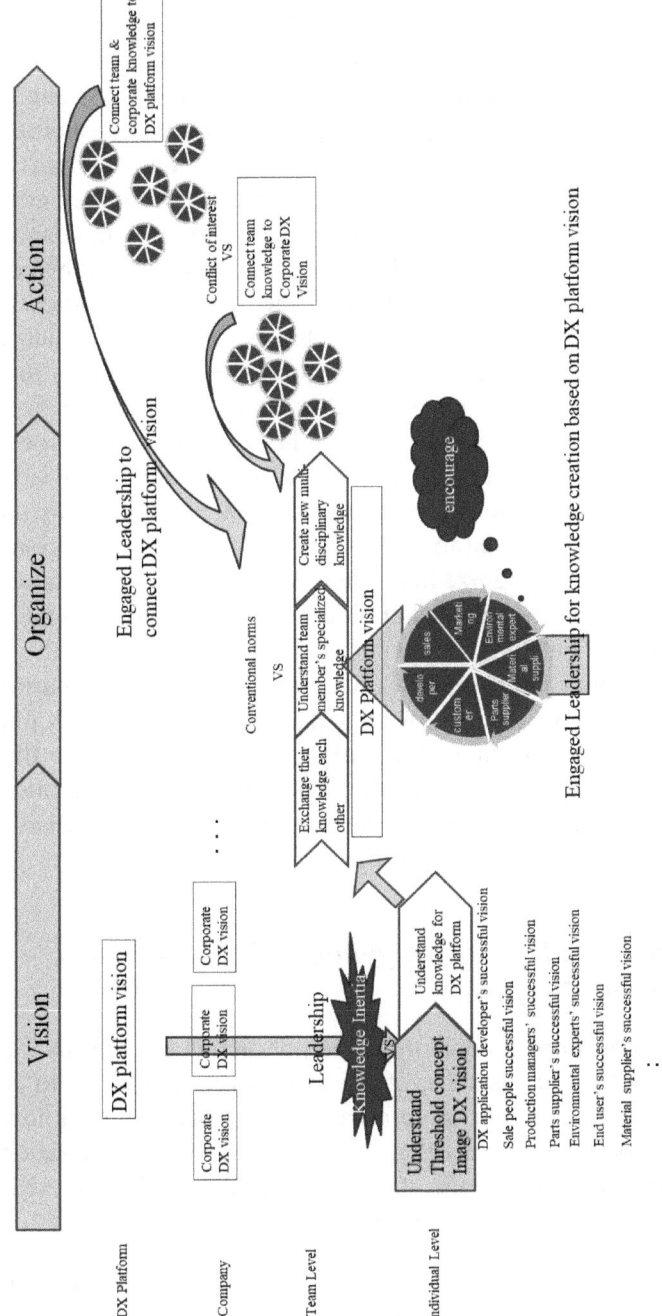

Figure 7. Leadership in DX platform knowledge creation process.

Figure 7 also shows the participants' subsequent process of knowledge creation: After understanding new DX platform knowledge, participants exchange their knowledge with others and create multidisciplinary new knowledge with team members. The team's new knowledge necessarily follows the corporate DX and DX platform visions. In this stage, the platform leader should visualize the team's goal. Since the participants understand the threshold concept, they can imagine how they contribute to their team; they become more able to collaborate with colleagues who similarly overcame the same challenge and thus generate knowledge that supports their business transformation. In the DX platform, knowledge is more complex, and the number of stakeholders increases, which further impedes understanding and action. Therefore, it is important for leaders to foster understanding on a personal level and then create a system to encourage knowledge exchange. By understanding others' specialized knowledge, team members will be able to create new knowledge that relates to the vision of the company and the DX platform. This makes it possible for each participant to understand his or her own position on the DX platform and to recognize his or her own role after understanding the intentions of the surrounding stakeholders. By comprehending the threshold concepts, participants can deepen their understanding of the knowledge of other teams and companies with which they want to partner, and they can expect to create the knowledge necessary for a new DX platform. In subsequent stages, because the participants understand the threshold concept at their individual levels, they can be expected to connect their successful images to corporate DX and DX platform visions, disrupt conventional norms, and contribute to their DX platforms.

4.2. *Engaged Leadership Struggling with Conventional Norms and Conflict*

However, several impediments may keep participants from taking transformative actions. For instance, at the team level, adherence to conventional practice may hinder generating new transformative knowledge, and, at the corporate level, conflict of interest between organizations may suppress movement and make it difficult to take action. To overcome these impediments, a DX platform leader should practice engaged leadership.

A DX platform leader needs to avoid top-down leadership in which he or she simply announces the DX strategic vision, creates a new DX department, allocates financial and human resources, and requires stakeholders to follow the DX vision. Instead, the leader needs to be more engaged with each participant by communicating with the participants and supporting them as they solve problems that impede their understanding of DX platform knowledge. According to several studies (Mintzberg, 2004; Marquardt, 2007), a business leader should first reflect on him or herself and frequently communicate with his or her frontline staff to take effective action for transformation. A key question for the leader is how to create effective dialog with staff members in a conventional mindset (Szulanski, 1996). This goal can only be accomplished through a complex process of dialog, practice, experimentation, and adaptation or transformation, as knowledge needs to be transformed so as to create common interest among actors, which requires a big practical effort (Carlile, 2004). Thus, DX platform leaders also need to create opportunities for participants to solve problems and to learn from others' perspectives, successes, and mistakes.

5. Summary: The Role of the Leader in the DX Platform

In this chapter, the DX platform strategy is reviewed and discusses how knowledge in a DX platform is a complex mixture of various perspectives. As mentioned, many global enterprises have developed DX applications on their industry cloud platforms. For their DX platforms to obtain competitive advantages, the platform leader needs to organize a wider range of value chains that are globally standardized and understand that the knowledge becomes more complex and multidisciplinary as various kinds of stakeholders participate in the DX platform.

Moreover, two types of knowledge leadership are emphasized: (1) the leadership that overcomes knowledge inertia and enables participants to understand DX platform knowledge and the threshold concept, which is the individual's view of business success, and (2) engaged leadership, which overcomes conventional norms and organizational conflict of interest and enables participants to understand and exchange knowledge with other participants and generate new DX knowledge on DX platforms. The platform leaders should think about creating a system that carries out these two types of knowledge leadership.

A DX platform strategy that unilaterally announces and tries to convince stakeholders of the importance of transformation is ineffective. Although past research on DX leadership has described the DX leader as having a transformative vision, being forward-looking, and being change-oriented, the DX platform leader should have a multidisciplinary, transformative vision and lead the wider value chain by involving all the stakeholders. Such a leader needs to encourage stakeholders to understand the threshold concept so that it aligns with the DX platform vision. The DX platform leader also needs to encourage stakeholders' knowledge exchange and creation so that they create new knowledge by collaborating with one another. Thus, engaged leaders enable stakeholders to broaden their perspectives and understand others' ways of thinking.

References

Barradell, S. (2013). The identification of threshold concepts: A review of theoretical complexities and methodological challenges. *Higher Education, 65,* 265–276.

Beitelmal, W. H., Littlejohn, R., Okonkwo, P. C., Hassan, I. U., Barhoumi, E. M., Khozaei, F., & Bonnet, D. (2022) 3 Stages of a Successful Digital Transformation, *Harvard Business Review.* https://store.hbr.org/product/3-stages-of-a-successful-digital-transformation/H077PJ.

Carlile, P. R. (2004). Transferring, translating, and transforming: An integrative framework for managing knowledge across boundaries. *Organization Science, 15*(5), 555–568.

Davies, P. & Mangan, J. (2007). Threshold concepts and the integration of understanding in economics. *Studies in Higher Education, 3*(6), 711–726.

Hamel, G. & Zanini, M. (2018) The end of bureaucracy: How a Chinese appliance maker is reinventing management for the digital age. *Harvard Business Review*, (November–December). 51–59.

Hassan, A. M. & Alkaaf, K. A. (2022). Threshold concepts theory in higher education — Introductory statistics courses as an example. *Education Sciences, 12*(11), 748.

Heifetz, R. A., Linsky, M., & Grashow, A. (2009). *The Practice of Adaptive Leadership: Tools and Tactics for Changing Your Organization and the World.* Harvard Business Review Press, Brighton, Massachusetts.

Hirose, Y. (2023). Threshold concept for promoting business transformation. In *Proceedings of the 24th European Conference on Knowledge Management, ECKM 2023,* Vol. 1, pp. 550–556.

Hughes, M. (2016). Leading changes: Why transformation explanations fail. *Leadership, 12*(4), 449–469.

Kane, G. (2019). The technology fallacy- people are the real key to digital transformation. *Research-Technology Management, 62*(6), 44–49.

Kotter, J. (1996). *Leading Change*. Harvard Business School Press, Brighton, Massachusetts.

Liao, S., Fei, W., & Liu, C. (2008). Relationships between knowledge inertia, organizational learning and organization innovation. *Technovation, 28*(4), 183–195.

Luoma, M. (2006). A play of four arenas. *Management Learning, 37*(1), 101–123.

McCarthy, P., Sammon, D., & Alhassan, I. (2022) Digital transformation leadership characteristics: A literature analysis. *Journal of Decision Systems, 32*(1), 79–109.

McKnight, L. L. (2013). Transformational leadership in the context of punctuated change. *Journal of Leadership, Accountability and Ethics, 10*(2), 103–112.

Meyer, J. H. F. & Land, R. (2003). Threshold concepts and troublesome knowledge (1) — linkages to ways of thinking and practising. In Rust, C. (ed.), *Improving Student Learning — Ten Years On*. Oxford: OCSLD.

Meyer, J. H. F. & Land, R. (2005). Threshold concepts and troublesome knowledge (2): Epistemological considerations and a conceptual framework for teaching and learning. *Higher Education, 49*, 373–388.

Meyer J. H. F. & Land R. (2006). Threshold concepts and troublesome knowledge: Issues of liminality. In Meyer, J. H. F. & Land, R. (eds.), *Overcoming Barriers to Student Understanding: Threshold Concepts and Troublesome Knowledge* (pp. 19–32). London, England: Routledge.

Mintzberg, H. (2004). *Managers Not MBA: A Hard Look at the Soft Practice of Managing and Management Development*. San Francisco: Berett-Koehler Publishers Inc.

Rogers, D. L. (2016). *The Digital Transformation Playbook: Rethink Your Business for the Digital Age*. Columbia Business School Publishing.

Szulanski, G. (1996). Exploring internal stickiness: Impediments to the transfer of best practice within the firm. *Strategic Management Journal, 17*, 27–43.

Wade, R., Macauray, J., Noronha, A., & Barbier, J. (2019). *Orchestrating Transformation: How to Deliver Winning Performance with a Connected Approach to Change*. DBT Center Press, Lausanne, Switzerland.

Yip, J. & Raelin, J. (2012). Threshold concepts and modalities for teaching leadership practice. *Management Learning, 43*, 333–354.

https://doi.org/10.1142/9789811295140_0008

Chapter 8

Digital Transformation and Smart Home Appliances: An Examination through the Theory of Consumption Values

Joel Flink[†,§] and Soumitra Chowdhury[*,‡,¶]

†*Uppsala University, Uppsala, Sweden*

‡*Linnaeus University, Växjö, Sweden*

§*joelflink@gmail.com*

¶*soumitra.chowdhury@lnu.se*

1. Introduction

The Internet of Things (IoT) comprises objects interconnected to the internet through embedded sensors or computers. In the realm of IoT, communication involves the exchange of information between objects, networks, and humans, facilitated by conscious and/or unconscious actions initiated by an IoT agent or unit to another. This differentiates IoT from the regular internet, where human input is required for it to work (Radanlieva *et al.*, 2019). The global market for IoT has grown at a remarkable pace. As of late 2021, 12.3 billion devices were expected to be connected by the year end, with projections for over 27 billion devices by 2025 (IoT Analytics, 2021). By 2030, the IoT is estimated to enable $5.5 trillion to $12.6 trillion in value globally (Chui *et al.*, 2021).

---

*Corresponding author.

Smart homes are one of the most important IoT areas (Zhai *et al.*, 2014). According to a report from Zion Market Research (2018), the global market for smart homes will exceed $53 billion by 2022. A smart home consists of smart products and gadgets situated in the home. These homes vow to provide massive opportunities for our future lives through automation of the home, removing labor from housework and household activities (Zhai *et al.*, 2014). Modern homes utilizing smart products such as smart meters, appliances, and power outlets also make it possible to develop energy-aware smart homes (Stojkoska & Trivodaliev, 2017).

Smart home technologies (SHT) can be differentiated from other consumer technologies since they are ingrained into the personal routines of an individual more directly (Aldossari & Sidorova, 2020). SHTs' main features are the capabilities of acquiring information from the enclosing environment and responding in accord (Balta-Ozkan *et al.*, 2014). A form of SHT, smart home appliances (SHA), such as smart refrigerators, smart washer, and smart ovens (Kang *et al.*, 2017), offer value through energy management, information and content not otherwise available, as well as improvements upon the original functionality and general convenience (Kim & Baek, 2019).

Despite increased economic value projections, projections for the growth of IoT have been lowered in comparison to previous reports (Chui *et al.*, 2021). The slowed pace of consumer adoption is big disappointment for the industry, with companies risking consumer resistance to the products (Chouk & Mani, 2017).

Further deterrence comes from awkward input devices and proprietary systems. Smart gadgets and homes are some of the most convoluted both in terms of installing them and the actual usage of the devices since they still rely on a significant portion of do-it-yourself (DIY) skills. Learning to use all the devices and incorporating them into daily life can be so bothersome that the adoption of new solutions may grind to a halt (Bjelica, 2018).

Smart home appliances have shown a slow adoption rate compared to more entertainment-related smart devices. One of the factors for this is the price. There is, simply put, a large discrepancy in price between appliances that are connected and those that are not (Serrenho & Bertoldi, 2019). In 2020, the average extra cost for consumers was £855 for smart fridge-freezers, while dishwashers and tumble dryers set consumers back an additional £259 and £190, respectively, compared to their non-smart counterparts (Osborne, 2020).

Recent research shows that innovative technologies, such as SHA, suffer from a deficit in user acceptance testing, and especially there is a lack of research in the private setting (Balakrishnan *et al.*, 2018; Marikyan *et al.*, 2021). While SHT for health care has received ample attention from researchers, studies into acceptance and adoption of SHT from a private consumer perspective are sorely lacking (Nikou, 2019).

While the empirical studies into user acceptance of smart home technology are quite few, it is nonetheless an important area of research as it helps create an understanding of and explanation for users' acceptance of smart homes and the related technology, something that could help accelerate the rate of user adoption and general success for SHTs (Shuhaiber & Mashal, 2019).

While some studies have investigated the adoption and acceptance of smart products and the factors affecting adoption (Gao & Bai, 2014), earlier research has been mostly concerned with industry and the public sector, meaning there is a lack of research into the private setting of smart home technologies.

The purpose of this study is therefore to explore private consumers' views on the value of smart home appliances. We seek answers to the following question:

How do private consumers perceive the value of smart home appliances?

To seek answers to this question, in-depth interviews have been conducted with private consumers to investigate their views and perceptions of value within the research area. This study explores the value of smart home appliances from a consumer perspective, with the intention of creating a better understanding of the adoption and acceptance of smart home appliances in a private context. It does this by investigating what values private consumers see in smart home appliances. Since SHAs are the sole focus of this study, the results might not be applicable to other areas of smart products. Other limitations have occurred due to the time and resources available, such as the number of people interviewed. The study takes place in Sweden, which could pose limitations for the applicability of the findings to other countries.

2. Related Research

2.1. *Smart Home Technology*

Generally, the definition for "smart" whether it be smart homes, cities, or devices is that something is considered smart when it is either connected or has the ability to connect to other products or services through a network (Serrenho & Bertoldi, 2019). In regard to smart homes, there isn't one single definition that everyone uses, but most definitions generally fall into one of the two categories. Either they focus on the home aspect and what it can do for the inhabitants or they focus on the building itself and its connection with energy systems (Darby, 2017). One definition that focuses on the home aspect looks as follows:

"A smart home is a residence equipped with a communications network, linking sensors, domestic appliances, and devices, that can be remotely monitored, accessed or controlled and which provides services that respond to the needs of its inhabitants" (Balta-Ozkan *et al.*, 2014).

Some examples of smart home technologies include but are not limited to the following:

- smart TVs that can access online content through apps, such as streaming video and music;
- smart lighting that can be controlled and customized remotely as well as often being able to regulate themselves when sensing that residents are in the room, or in response to changing daylight;
- smart locks and door-openers giving users the possibility to grant access to visitors, as well as sensing when residents are near to automatically unlock doors;
- smart thermostats, using integrated Wi-Fi to enable users to remotely control temperature, as well as learning the residents' habits to automatically change settings in order to provide the highest level of comfort. Smart thermostats can also monitor energy consumption;
- smart appliances of all kinds are available, from coffee brewers to washing machines. See the following section for more information (Shea, 2020).

2.1.1. *Smart Home Appliances*

Smart appliances can be defined as appliances that are able to communicate, both with the user and other platforms and services. The ability to communicate can be used for several types of functionalities such as communication with a smart meter or to change its consumption pattern (Serrenho & Bertoldi, 2019). A smart appliance is connected to some form of central system and can be programmed or controlled remotely or even perform its functions autonomously, in response to input from sensors detecting light, activity, or temperature. Customarily, these appliances are designed to be able to work with other smart products as a part of a smart home (Ayla Networks, 2020).

There exist several definitions of Smart Home Appliances, where some include almost every smart home product from kitchen appliances to lighting, heating, security systems, and consumer electronics, while others only include kitchen and household appliances (Ayla Networks, 2020; PC Mag, n.d.). In this study, the latter definition is used, meaning Smart Home Appliances are household products such as ovens, washing machines, refrigerators, and coffee makers that are computerized and connected to the internet, through either the home Wi-Fi or Ethernet. Access to the internet allows the smart appliances to send alerts to users' computers or mobile devices, as well as allow remote control. These Smart Home Appliances often have the capability to automatically perform tasks at a programmed or learned time, such as a coffee maker brewing a fresh cup of coffee in the morning (PC Mag, n.d.; Shea, 2020).

The main benefits of smart appliances for customers lie in the convenience and usability. Utilizing the remote control and automation abilities of the products makes home life and everyday tasks easier (Ayla Networks, 2020). Other advantages come from accessibility, where people with disabilities might experience a more independent life, and from safety, where controlling remotely minimizes the risk of leaving hot appliances on (Dragani, 2020).

2.1.2. *Smart Refrigerators and Freezers*

Smart refrigerators and freezers are a type of smart home appliance. They do the same job as conventional refrigerators and freezers but are connected to the internet to offer some extra functionality. Depending on the model, the extra functionality can be to get notifications on your phone if the door is open and control the temperature remotely. More advanced models can let you see what is inside from your smartphone by utilizing cameras on the inside of the refrigerator/freezer. They also allow you to send and receive notes, messages, and calendar entries that appear on the screen on the door. On certain models, the built-in display can be used to order groceries online, play music, and access a smart personal assistant, such as Alexa or Google Assistant. Some models have a large, tinted glass panel on the door that becomes transparent when knocked on, letting the user see what's inside without opening the door. A door-in-door feature is also available on some models, allowing one to open the outer section of the door to access the items most often used, without having to fully open the refrigerator (Prospero, 2019).

In this chapter, we investigated smart refrigerators and freezers as the smart home appliances (SHA). Due to time and size limitations, investigating more products than this has been deemed unfeasible.

2.2. *Smart Technology Adoption and Acceptance*

According to Marikyan *et al.* (2021), only a few studies into technology acceptance in a private setting have been conducted. Among these are Brown and Venkatesh (2005), Venkatesh and Brown (2001), Balta-Ozkan, Davidson *et al.* (2013), and Balta-Ozkan *et al.* (2014). The latter two gave insights into the possible application of pervasive technology in houses but missed out on explanations for user perceptions of technology. Furthermore, the studies look at the implications in settings beyond the residential one, something that restricts the insights into technology usage in a private context.

Since there are very few studies into the private setting of technology acceptance and adoption, a significant portion of the related research had to be collected from outside this setting to identify themes in the research area.

2.2.1. *Monitoring and Control*

Studies have shown that intentions to adopt smart technology are positively affected by the usability of the product as well as the mobility. Yang *et al.* (2017) found that potential users saw particular value in remote capabilities such as being able to control, view, and manage their smart home appliances remotely from their mobile devices, without hindrance. Similar findings were reported by Yang *et al.* (2018a) who found that people did not want to relinquish control to automation but instead preferred to be able to control and monitor their smart home devices themselves.

Monitoring and control have been found to have a strong effect on other smart technologies as well. When ride-hailing services were investigated as a smart technology, these two attributes were found to be among the most important. Control was seen as a must-have function for drivers in the services (Kang *et al.*, 2020).

These sorts of functional values that monitoring and control represent have been proven to be so-called drivers of intentions to adopt smart technology. The advantages of smart home technologies have been proven to take this form by several researchers. Other studies have shown that it influences non-smart technology as well as mobile phones, green housing, and hyped technologies (Aldossari & Sidorova, 2020; Marikyan *et al.*, 2021; Sequeiros *et al.*, 2021; Papagiannidis & Davlembayeva, 2021; Bødker *et al.*, 2009; Petrovčiková & Sudzina 2018; Ali *et al.*, 2019; Hedman & Gimpel, 2010).

2.2.2. *Hedonic Dimension*

Hedonic values such as joy are an important factor in explaining the acceptance and adoption of smart home technologies. Together with the more utilitarian aspects, they are considered drivers to adopt smart technology. Studies show that the enjoyment of using a smart product correlates positively with consumers' choice to use a specific product. In fact, just the expectation that a product will provide hedonic values increases the intentions to adopt such a product (Aldossari & Sidorova, 2020; Marikyan *et al.*, 2021; Sequeiros *et al.*, 2021; Chang & Chen, 2021; Ahn *et al.*, 2016).

For smart home technologies, in particular, it has been shown that hedonic beliefs affect a consumer's use behavior. This extends to smart home healthcare systems as well, where it was shown that one of the facilitators of intentions to use a smart home healthcare system was emotional support (Marikyan *et al.*, 2019; Alaiad & Zhou, 2017).

Managing to trigger emotional values in consumers has been shown to act as a source of affiliation. The customer becomes more likely to continue using products from the company in question, creating a bond of loyalty (Poushneh & Vasquez-Parraga, 2019).

2.2.3. *Cost*

Researchers have shown that price is a deterrent that slows down technology adoption in general. This has been shown to hold true for smart technologies as well. Studies show that adoption of smart homes is affected by cost as a barrier hindering adoption. Individual smart home services are also affected by this, where the cost acts as a deterrent toward intentions to adopt. Furthermore, studies show that perceived cost also affects intentions to adopt smart technology negatively (Hsu & Lin, 2018; Balta-Ozkan *et al.*, 2013; Park *et al.*, 2018; Nikou, 2019).

While cost acts as a deterrent, it does not appear to be considered a risk by consumers. Hong *et al.* (2020) conducted a study into the barriers of adoption of smart home services. And they found that different kinds of risk, such as performance, privacy, and psychological risk, affected adoption of smart home services negatively. The only risk that did not have this effect in the study was financial risk.

2.2.4. *Users*

Students of higher education have been found to be more open-minded and flexible in regard to smart technologies when compared to working professionals. They are also more likely to accept trade-offs in some factors in order to get new features. Students have also been shown to be more positive to smart homes specifically, having exhibited a readiness to embrace the concept of smart homes, suggesting that smart homes should be developed specifically for this group. A possible explanation offered for the result was that this group is already using new technologies, reducing the barrier for adoption. Younger users in general have been shown to have more diverse reasons for choosing a smart technology. They are also more adept at interacting with smart technology, as well as at describing said technology in technical terms (Baudier *et al.*, 2020; Adapa *et al.*, 2018; Tsai, 2012).

In contrast, older adults show no natural inclination toward adopting smart home technologies. Complicated interactions have been shown to be one of the barriers preventing this group from embracing such technologies. An inability to visualize a role for the technology in their lives also affects acceptance negatively. The speed with which new technology is developed also functions as a deterrent for this group, making adjustments to the technology harder (Arthanat *et al.*, 2020; Song *et al.*, 2022; Lee, 2014; Abdelrahman *et al.*, 2021).

3. Theory

Based on previous research, the Theory of Consumption Values has been chosen for this chapter. Since the advantageous values of Smart Home Technologies (Aldossari & Sidorova, 2020; Marikyan *et al.*, 2021; Sequeiros *et al.*, 2021) fit so well with the consumption values of the Theory of Consumption Values, it is an appropriate theoretical framework for investigating acceptance and adoption of Smart Home Technologies. The theory has been used successfully to investigate intentions to adopt technology previously, showing that it is suitable to use when the intended interviewees do not own the product being investigated (Ali *et al.*, 2019).

3.1. *Theory of Consumption Values*

The Theory of Consumption Values was developed by Sheth *et al.* (1991). This theoretical framework aids researchers in framing consumption habits in different contexts (Talwar *et al.*, 2020; Turel *et al.*, 2010; Zailani *et al.*, 2019). There are three propositions that are self-evident to the theory: (1) Consumer choice is a function of multiple consumption values (Sheth *et al.*, 1991). There are five consumption values: functional, social, emotional, epistemic, and conditional. *Functional* is the value a consumer perceives from the utility of the product, based on its functional, utilitarian, and physical characteristics. *Social* value is the perceived utility from association with a social group or groups triggered by the consumption.

   Emotional value is the perceived utility from the feelings associated with a product or service. *Epistemic* value is the utility of a product or service ability to create a novel experience and arouse curiosity. *Conditional* value refers to the utility acquired by an alternative in a specific situation or set of circumstances (Sheth *et al.*, 1991; Papagiannidis & Davlembayeva, 2021). (2) Consumption values have a differential contribution in any situation where a choice is involved, meaning that consumption behavior can be triggered by all or any of the

Table 1.   Consumption values.

Consumption Value	Description	Example
Functional	The value from a product or service's functional characteristics.	Reliability, durability, price. A car may be purchased based on fuel economy and maintenance.
Social	The value from a product or service's association with social groups.	A car might be purchased for the social image or status it produces, rather than its functional performance.
Emotional	The value from a product or service's ability to arouse feelings.	The emotional response of romance in response to a candlelit dinner. Foods that arouse comfort (comfort foods). How individuals are sometimes said to have a love affair with their car.
Epistemic	The value from a product or service's ability to provide novelty and arouse curiosity.	Entirely new experiences (bungee jumping for the first time, or when the first iPhone was released). Alternatives that give a simple change of pace can also provide epistemic value, such as trying a new brand of coffee.
Conditional	The value offered from a product or service in a specific situation or set of circumstances.	Some products only have seasonal value (Easter eggs), or once in a lifetime situations (wedding gown for a wedding). There are also more subtle conditional associations, such as popcorn at the movie theater.

Source: Based on Sheth *et al.* (1991).

values. (3) The consumption values are independent, meaning that while it is optimal to maximize all five values, it is often not realistic, and consumers are often willing to accept less of one value to gain in another (Sheth *et al.*, 1991).

See Table 1 and Figure 1 for an easier overview of the theoretical framework.

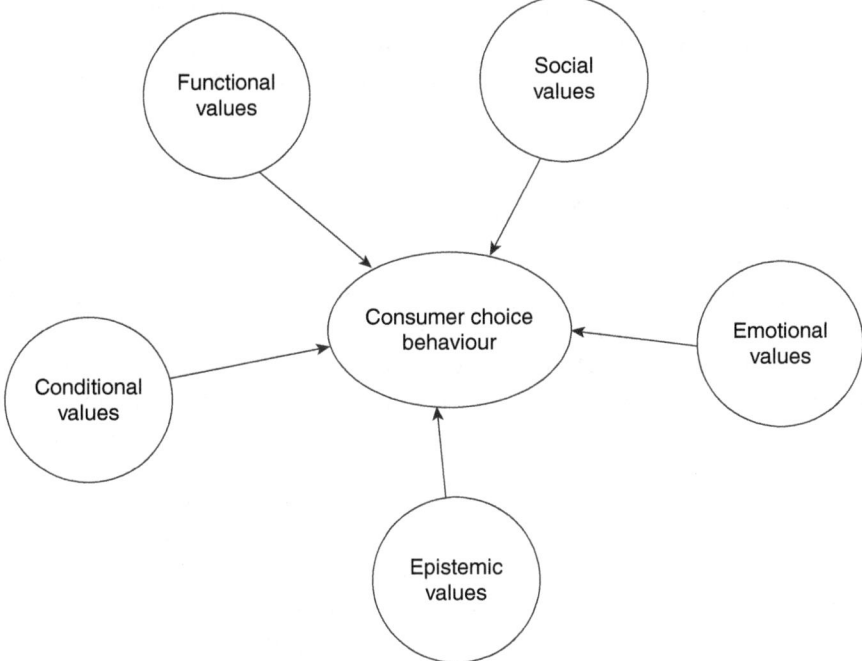

Figure 1. The five values influencing consumer choice.

Source: Based on Sheth *et al.* (1991).

4. Methodology

4.1. *Research Strategy*

This research is an interpretive qualitative study. Interpretive research in information systems (IS) and computing means to create understanding of the social context of an information system. These studies are not meant to prove a hypothesis but instead identify, explore, and explain how the elements in a certain social context are related. They investigate how individuals perceive their world and try to understand situations and occurrences through the values and meanings assigned to them by individuals. The goal of interpretive research is to develop an ample understanding of the context being investigated (Oates, 2006).

Since this research aims to provide a deeper understanding of how private consumers view the value of smart home appliances, and due to the interpretive nature of the research, a qualitative method is the most suitable option (Oates, 2006).

4.2. *Data Collection Strategy*

The most known methods for data collection in qualitative research are individual interviews, focus groups, and observations (Savin-Baden & Major, 2013; Oun & Bach, 2014). We have used semi-structured interviews as the data collection strategy since it allows for in-depth answers without leaving the boundaries of the area under research. Semi-structured interviews mean that questions have been prepared for the interview, but the person conducting the interview may need to change the order of questions or explore new questions that had not been prepared beforehand but might appear during the course of the interview. Semi-structured interviews combine specific questions that elicit anticipated information with open-ended questions to elicit unforeseen information. The interviewee has the possibility to speak freely and in detail about the questions and might also himself/herself introduce questions they find relevant (Oates, 2006; Hove & Anda, 2005).

Since the interviewees do not own a smart refrigerator or freezer, three scenarios were constructed to help them express their opinions and perceptions regarding the value of smart home appliances. Utilizing scenarios gives the interviewee a context that might be missing when discussing a product they do not own. When using qualitative methods, it is common practice to lift the topic of discussion from the abstract plane to something more concrete by utilizing scenarios or showing the interviewee pictures. Scenarios describe a certain course of events, followed by the interviewee answering questions to express their thoughts and ideas (Oates, 2006).

Scenario 1 — camera
"Imagine that you are in the grocery store when you realize that you don't know if you have any carrots at home. Instead of having to take a chance, you open the application for your smart fridge on the phone and take a picture of the inside of your fridge, showing that you are in fact missing carrots".

This scenario lets the interviewee put the camera capabilities of a smart refrigerator into a concrete context.

Scenario 2 — notifications
"Imagine that you have just taken the frozen salmon out from the freezer to thaw on the kitchen counter. You have left the kitchen and are now sitting down in the living room watching TV. The freezer is beeping because you accidentally left the door open, but you cannot hear it over the TV. Instead, you get a notification on your smartphone telling you that the freezer door is open. You walk into the kitchen and close the door before the freezer starts thawing and you end up with water all over the kitchen floor".

This scenario is meant to let interviewees imagine a concrete situation where the notifications from a smart freezer could be advantageous.

Scenario 3 — touch screen
"Imagine that you are going to cook dinner. You do not really know what to cook this evening. You take a look inside the refrigerator to see what ingredients you have available. Using the touch screen on the door with tablet-like capabilities, you search online for recipes matching the ingredients you have at hand. You find one that seems quick and easy to make and begin cooking, following the recipe on your smart refrigerator display".

The final scenario gives a concrete example of how one might use the touch-capable display, helping the interviewee see a concrete situation where they might use this functionality.

As stated earlier, none of the interviewees owned a smart refrigerator or freezer at the time of the interviews. Therefore, it was decided to show each interviewee a short video showcasing the abilities of a smart refrigerator and freezer. This is meant to better help lift the discussion from the abstract plane to something more concrete, as suggested by Oates (2006).

4.3. *Data Collection and Interview Process*

In this section, the execution of the data collection and how the participants were selected are described. The interview process is described, and the participants are presented.

4.3.1. Collection of Data

This study is based on six people interviewed in April 2022. There were four criteria for selection. The individual had to be between 20 and 30 years old, and they had to be a student in higher education or have graduated from higher education within the last 5 years. They could not own a smart refrigerator or freezer, and they had to be situated in Uppsala, Sweden.

4.3.2. Selection

Baudier *et al.* (2020) found that students in higher education were ready to embrace the concepts of smart home. This study therefore chose to extend this to students of higher education and recently graduated students. The limit was set to a maximum of 5 years since graduation. Since the author is situated in Uppsala and wished to conduct the interviews face-to-face, participants were recruited from Uppsala. Utilizing his network, the author found six interview subjects. The selection was based on gender, age, and occupation, in order to get an even mix of the age span, and gender and of students and non-students. The result was three women and three men, half of whom were students and half were working. The ages spanned from 23 to 28. None of the participants owned a smart refrigerator or freezer.

4.3.3. Interviewees

To maintain the anonymity of the students, their names have been changed, and they will only be presented with their fictive name, age, sex, and occupation as stated by themselves (please see Table 2).

Table 2.   Interviewees.

Name	Age	Sex	Occupation
Lisa	26	Female	Master's student
Jane	25	Female	Student
Peter	27	Male	Student
John	23	Male	Software developer
Adam	27	Male	Software engineer
Eve	28	Female	IT-Project manager

4.3.4. *The Interviews*

The interviews were conducted face-to-face at a place of the interviewees' choosing. All interviews were done in a quiet environment so as to not be disturbed or distracted. Each interview was recorded using a voice recording application on a smartphone and then transcribed. Prior to the interviews, the participants were informed of their rights. After each interview had been transcribed, the participant was asked to give their consent to the author using the transcribed interview for the study.

Once the interviewees had been informed about their rights, the interview started with quick background questions, after which they were given information about smart refrigerators and freezers. They were given information orally first, and after this, they watched a two-minute-long video showcasing the abilities of smart refrigerators and freezers.

When the participants had been informed both orally and visually, the questions regarding smart refrigerators and freezers began. After the first round of questions, the interviewees faced three short scenarios to give them concrete examples of how smart refrigerators and freezers might be used and were asked questions regarding the scenarios. Finally, two questions regarding the interview itself were posed.

After each interview, the voice file was transcribed as quickly as possible, in order for the author to maintain a fresh memory of the interview while working on the transcription. Doing it this way allowed for each interview to be transcribed before the next one began, minimizing the risk of the author confusing the interviews while transcribing.

4.3.5. *Data Analysis Process*

When all interviews had been transcribed, the thematic coding of the interviews began. The analysis of the transcripts was performed by reading them and highlighting certain words, phrases, and in some cases passages. Words and phrases that were common in the transcripts were coded in order to identify empirical themes. Inspired by Jovanovic *et al.* (2021), the empirical themes were further investigated to identify similarities between them. This resulted in the conceptual categories. Finally, the conceptual categories were grouped to aggregate dimensions, in this case, the five consumption values from the theoretical framework.

5. Findings

In this chapter, the five consumption values identified from data analysis are presented. The analysis is based on the theoretical framework of the Theory of Consumption Values and the themes and categories identified previously.

5.1. *Functional Values*

The interviewees have a surprisingly coherent view on the functional values of smart refrigerators and freezers, despite being split on how they value the product in general. Lisa and Eve have the most positive views as a whole, and they are the most positive to the functionality of a smart refrigerator and freezer. When the interviewees were asked how they felt about the capabilities of the product, Eve said, "*I feel that I must have one. I think they seem very smart*". While she acknowledged that some of the functions seemed a bit over the top and she probably wouldn't use them, she went on to say, "*Both to, as someone in the video saw the entire contents [of the refrigerator] from the grocery store, that would be super practical. But to, well, especially that you so easily, if you have like Alexa or Siri, can tell it like "We're out of milk" and it understands that it should put it on the shopping list. It would be amazing to not have to do that [manually]*". Lisa was in a similar manner very positive, stating, "*I just like this concept from the get go*". She was also very positive to the camera functionality, feeling that it is a great function, to be able to view the inside of your fridge/freezer from the grocery store. The rest of the interviewees were also at their most positive when speaking of the camera functionality. Such as Adam saying, "*Like being able to see in to the refrigerator from the mobile phone, that seems very useful*". This sentiment was shared by Jane and Peter. John was the only one to not bring up this functionality immediately. He instead expressed uncertainty about whether one would actually see everything inside when faced with Scenario 1. Jane, Peter, and Adam also added caveats for actually seeing everything inside their initial statements, but they remained positive to the functionality.

Another one of the remote functionalities that was received positively was the possibility for shopping lists. John felt that the syncing of shopping lists between the smartphone and refrigerator is a good function, specifically mentioning being able to create it on the refrigerator when you are looking at what you have at home and send to one smartphone and vice versa. *"Like the transfer of information"*. Other interviewees agreed, with Eve once again being positive to idea, and adding that anything that helped with food preparation and planning was useful.

Both Lisa and Eve liked being able to use the built-in touchscreen to search for recipes and follow them from the refrigerator screen. With Eve stating *"We have been thinking about buying some form of tablet specifically for the kitchen to use for such things [recipe searching]"*. Lisa felt that it was really smart to have this functionality and not having to use your phone. Especially the fact that you could follow the recipe from the screen on the door was a positive for them both, where they felt it would be easier to just look at the refrigerator and check off the parts that were completed there rather than having to use a tablet or smartphone that might get covered in grease and flour if you keep it on the countertop. This is where the rest of the interviewees have completely different views. They instead felt that it was a rather unnecessary function that they wouldn't use. Opinions included that it would be much more comfortable to sit on the couch and look up a recipe on your phone/tablet/computer instead of having to stand up and use the refrigerator screen and that the refrigerator screen would get just as dirty when you touch it with the same hands you are actively preparing a meal with. While most acknowledged that it might be a useful function for someone else, they felt that it would not be useful for them. Another aspect was that it might prove more bothersome to follow the recipe from the screen on the fridge, which you might have to turn around to view than to just have it on your phone or tablet next to you. *"I might as well take my iPad and place next to me on the countertop while I am chopping something"*, as Peter put it. This sentiment was shared by Jane, John, and Adam as well, with Adam summarizing it, *"They have just put an Ipad on the refrigerator door"*.

The price is one of the factors that the interviewees saw the most eye-to-eye on. Eve was the only real outlier in this case, feeling that you got a lot extra for the money and that she would definitely be prepared to pay the extra money for it. While Lisa was also generally positive to smart refrigerators and freezers, the price was a point of dithering. She felt it was a lot of money and was rather unsure if it would be worth it. She finally concluded that she probably would spend the extra money in the end, even if it felt like a lot. The rest of the interviewees were categorically negative to what they felt was an unjustifiably large extra cost. They all felt that they would be willing to pay a little extra for the camera functionality, but since all models that have the camera functionality currently lie at the higher end of the price range, it would not be worth it. If the camera functionality had been included in the lower price range of 2–3 thousand SEK more than a comparable non-smart refrigerator, the consensus was that it would be worth spending the extra money. They would however not be willing to spend that extra amount just for the notifications and remote controlling the temperature, as Adam said, "*I would personally go for the non-smart option. It does not feel like it is worth my money*".

Functional values as a whole had the strongest effect on the interviewees. If they felt that the utilitarian possibilities offered were really going to prove useful for them, it made them very positive to smart refrigerators. If they on the other hand felt like they would not really get much use out of the functions, the price was the deciding factor. If they could get the more advanced models, where they felt at least one of the functions would be something they used, for just an extra 1000–3000 SEK, they would probably purchase it. But at the current price (circa 10,000 SEK extra compared to a similar non-smart alternative), two-thirds of the interviewees would not consider buying a smart refrigerator or freezer.

5.2. *Social Values*

All interviewees agreed to some degree that someone they knew, like a friend or a family member, might positively influence their decision to purchase a smart refrigerator or freezer. The key theme lifted was that you got to hear the information from someone with first-hand experience and someone you trusted. Important to note was that the general consensus was that a friend owning a smart refrigerator and/or freezer and expressing that it was something worth buying, was something that would influence the interviewees positively. It was however not enough by itself to trigger any intentions toward purchasing; it would just increase the likelihood. And several interviewees expressed that a friend owning it would make it easier to decide whether to buy it or not since it would provide the interviewee not only with the opinions of an owner but also with the possibility of actually using it yourself, and seeing it being used in real life. Lisa expressed it as follows: "*You really get to see hands-on what it is, the things it can do in every day life. As well as how much that person uses it. It would really be a big factor for purchasing one*". While the other interviewees were also positive to the influence it would have, they were more cautiously so. They expressed a more general view that if you got to see and try it in real life, and someone you know speaks well of it, that increases the likelihood. *"I do not think a friend would get me to purchase it. But it would probably increase that small, small probability to a slightly, slightly, slightly bigger [probability]"*, as Jane stated. The other interviewees had similar thoughts, often expressing that while friends owning the product and liking it might influence positively, it was not that important. What really mattered was the functionality. And as an owner of a smart refrigerator/freezer, that friend could possibly enlighten the interviewee to possible functionalities or areas of use that they had not considered. John also brought up that it might subconsciously inspire you to purchase one when you see them using it. This sentiment was immediately followed up by saying that he still did not feel that it was something that would make him buy one but that it might increase the tendency that he would a little. Another thing brought up was how commonplace the product was would affect purchasing intention. If a lot of people you know own one, it would definitely increase the likelihood of oneself buying one.

When the interviewees were asked whether a celebrity or someone they followed on social media owning a smart refrigerator/freezer would increase the likelihood of themselves buying one, the answers were generally dismissive. Eve simply stated, *"No, I am not that kind of person"*. And Jane went as far as saying it might actually decrease the likelihood. Peter, John, and Adam simply felt that it wouldn't affect them at all, with Adam reasoning that it would not feel genuine. He did however leave a caveat for celebrities in the tech industry, such as famous tech YouTuber Linus Sebastian from Linus Tech Tips. If he, or someone like him, made a video speaking of how much they like the product, and it felt genuine, it would probably increase the likelihood of him purchasing it. But it could not feel like a sponsored video, he had to feel that it was an impartial, genuine review. The only one who felt that it actually would affect their intention to purchase and in a positive manner was Lisa: *"The ones who work as influencers, that you look up to. I mean they are called influencers for a reason... I am thinking like clothes, I want to purchase what they are wearing... If they were super advocates for a smart refrigerator, and I am redoing my kitchen, it might affect me"*.

Social values proved to be something that did not matter very much to the interviewees. While they all agreed that friends owning the products could increase the chance of themselves purchasing, not a single person saw it as a value that had a strong effect on them. They instead saw it as something that might increase the odds of them buying a smart refrigerator or freezer very slightly. So, while it had a positive impact on their intentions to purchase, that impact was very small.

5.3. *Emotional Values*

The emotional values were very mixed, both between the interviewees, where some only had negative feeling and some had mixed feelings with both positive and negative feelings toward smart refrigerators and freezers, and one person, Eve, expressed only positive emotions. Lisa was also among the most positive, expressing almost only positive feelings in regard to the products. She expressed feelings of joy and excitement, feeling that it was fun that you got so much (so many functions), saying that "*It has so many more qualities than I had expected, so it turns into sort of like a wow-effect*". She went on to talk about how lovely it all looked, to own a smart refrigerator and freezer. She speculated that her fondness for food and cooking might be why she feels so very good about the possibility of owning one and saying that she got so positively surprised by all the functions. The feeling of excitement was shared by Adam, although he was more excited about the technological possibilities, and what you can do with technology today.

Adam also expressed some negative feelings. While he could not find the exact word to describe how he felt, he expressed it as "*the feeling, well just like even more exaggerated gadgets for the home that they try to sell at an expensive price*". If one could consider it a feeling, unnecessary was a word that came to mind later on. This feeling of the product being unnecessary was shared by both Jane and Peter. To Peter, it felt like technology for technology's sake. He further expressed that the use cases felt so niched that what you actually ended up getting out of the product was bragging rights and owning a cool gadget. In his mind, it was more of a status symbol than anything else, and that was not something he was interested in. Especially in a refrigerator and freezer. Jane went even further stating that she felt irritated or annoyed. This feeling stemmed from two factors. She felt irritation over how unnecessary the product felt. But there was also a feeling of irritation over the product having so many functions that people would probably never use more than one or two of them.

She likened it to people owning Mac computers: *"A lot of people don't use all the functions, and end up purchasing a 25 000 SEK computer just to write emails and watch Netflix. And then I feel like you've lost your marbles"*. This feeling of irritation was for Jane something general. She felt herself getting annoyed at the idea of other people wasting their money to buy something that they will not utilize to its full potential.

On the other side of the spectrum, both Eve and John expressed positive emotions related to everyday life. The possibilities and simplicity where you could sync your calendar, for example, and make your daily life a little easier were lifted as an example by John, who also stated, *"It [the refrigerator] is smart to be able to improve, well, your everyday life"*. Eve was speaking of a similar feeling, stressing that everyday life might turn out easier and a bit calmer. One would not have to think too much about what groceries need to be purchased and what you have at home. Things would just be calmer, and one could forget about several everyday tasks that one otherwise would have to actively remember and perform.

The emotional values had a rather strong effect on the interviewees, in both a positive and negative manner. Those who had felt very positive about the utilitarian functions of a smart refrigerator and freezer, such as Lisa and Eve, also experienced stronger positive emotions, such as pure joy and a feeling of calm or serenity. If you had however had a more negative sentiment regarding the functional values, this also translated to a more negative view of emotional values, where pure irritation was one of the feelings expressed.

5.4 *Epistemic Values*

All of the interviewees expressed that the idea of a smart refrigerator and freezer had piqued their curiosity and interest in some way. It is one of the most consistent values among the participants, regardless of their general feelings toward the products. Lisa was surprised at her own curiosity since she does not feel that she usually is a *"gadget person"*, but in this case, she felt it truly affected her. Jane, who generally was rather negative, also expressed curiosity in the product, but for her, it was the remote capabilities that really piqued her interest: *"Being able to see what is inside the refrigerator, that I feel piques my interest. Specifically, on the mobile phone"*. John and Eve both felt interest and curiosity. Eve reiterated her desire to own a smart refrigerator and freezer in the future, perhaps when she had a larger home. John spoke of a general curiosity toward the entire industry surrounding the Internet of Things, and how much it is growing and innovating. He also thought it was interesting to see what one could do with these things: "*I mean, it is a refrigerator, but you get more functions. Can use for other things than just cooling groceries, like playing a video on the screen*". While it made him curious, he added that it also felt like there was too much going on functionality-wise.

Peter, who also was generally negative toward the products, felt that it had aroused his curiosity in regard to what one can do with such a product and how one could use it. Adams' technological excitement continued here, remarking that it definitely had aroused his curiosity for the technological possibilities. Pondering whether it was possible to develop your own programs and applications for it, "*Trying to create some sort of AI, that helps you at home with expiration dates and stuff like that*".

Like the social values, the epistemic values the interviewees saw were generally positive but not very strong. Since all the interviewees felt some interest and curiosity, but only two of them actually felt it was a product worth owning, one can rather safely say that it is not a value that has a strong influence on a consumer's intention to purchase a smart refrigerator or freezer.

5.5. *Conditional Values*

The conditional values expressed by the interviewees coincided to a great extent with the positive functional values. Lisa, who had already spoken of how much she liked the recipe functionality, spoke of the "circumstance" of cooking and how helpful being able to view a recipe on the refrigerator screen would be. This trend of expressing circumstances that fit the specific functionalities the interviewee had liked continued with the other interviewees. Jane who had been most interested in the camera functionality could see the specific circumstance in which she would really find that functionality useful, namely when she is in the grocery store and is not sure of what she has in her refrigerator. Peter had the same idea.

John, who had been most positive toward the syncing capabilities, spoke of the cases when someone could create a shopping list at the refrigerator and sync it to the inhabitants' phones, so one person could be at home and automatically send the list to the others' smartphone or their own.

While the things just described might not be categorized as truly conditional values, both Adam and Lisa could see a conditional value being when you have children. Lisa felt that some of the functionalities that had not interested her very much previously could be really nice to have when one has children. Such as using the screen to display photos, where the kids could get to pick a photo to display. Or perhaps the children have taken their own pictures showcasing their day and want to share them with the family. *"Perhaps you would become a little closer as a family if you use that function"*, as she said. Adam also saw the conditional value of a smart refrigerator and freezer when you have children, perhaps by using the refrigerator to send a picture of milk to show the kids what they are supposed to buy in the store. He also thought that it might generally make communications within the family easier if you use the refrigerator functions.

The conditional values expressed were often values that might generally be considered to actually be functional values. This could indicate that consumers have a hard time separating functional and conditional values when it comes to smart refrigerators and freezers. However, there was one truly conditional value, namely family. This was stated to be a circumstance during which it could be nice to have a smart refrigerator and freezer. It was the only condition brought up during the interviews that was not a reiteration of what an interviewee had said about the functions of the product. But, since none of the interviewees have children, it could not be specified to which degree starting or having a family would affect the intention to buy.

5.6. *Summary of Findings*

All five of the consumption values had some form of effect on the interviewees. However, two of them had a much stronger effect. The first one was functional values, which include utilitarian aspects, such as functions and price. It is clear from the interviews and subsequent analysis that this is what is most important to private consumers. The ones who felt that the functions were good and that they would use them were also the ones who felt like they wanted a smart refrigerator and freezer. If you only felt slightly positive to one or some of the functions, the price instead became the strongest functional value. In this case, it acted as a deterrent, with interviewees considering the price to be too high. The remote functionalities were the strongest positive functional value for all groups, with most considering them the functionalities that they would buy a smart refrigerator or freezer to obtain. The tablet functionality acted as both a deterrent and an incentive, depending on who you asked. The generally positive interviewees saw it as a smart feature that they wanted, while the rest saw it as superfluous, something they might as well use their phone, tablet, or computer for instead.

The emotional values also carried a strong influence. However, they appeared to be directly tied to the interviewee's thoughts on the functional values, suggesting that it is not an independent value when investigating smart home appliances. With that said, those who saw strong positive functional values experienced strong positive emotions regarding the products, such as joy, excitement, and serenity. These were tied to the possibilities the technology offered and feeling that it would improve their everyday lives. On the other side of the spectrum, the individuals who were not strongly positive to the functional values instead expressed negative emotional values, such as irritation and a feeling of the products being unnecessary. To them, a smart refrigerator and freezer constituted superfluous and over-the-top technology.

Social values were seen positively by all the interviewees. Although it did not affect them strongly. Mostly, it was tied to getting first-hand information. Either from the friend who owned a smart refrigerator and freezer telling you about it or by getting to try it out for yourself when visiting that friend. As well as seeing the social values positively, everyone agreed that it was not something that would have a strong effect on them.

The epistemic values also influenced the interviewees positively. All of them felt that their interest and curiosity in smart refrigerators and freezers had been piqued. Just like emotional values, positive attitudes toward epistemic values fell into the category of possibilities offered by technology. However, while they felt some interest, it did not have a strong influence on their intentions for the purchase. The ones who would not consider buying a smart refrigerator and freezer were still curious about the products but not enough to affect them at the time of the interviews.

Finally, the conditional values proved both different and similar to the social and epistemic values. The big difference was that the interviewees seemed to have a hard time separating conditional values from functional values. Interviewees mostly reiterated their thoughts on functional values when asked about any specific circumstance or condition under which they would consider a smart refrigerator and freezer nice to have. The only separate conditional value that eventually was brought up was family, with some interviewees believing a smart refrigerator and freezer might make daily life slightly easier if one had a family.

6. Discussion

This research aims to investigate private consumers' perceptions of value in smart home appliances. In doing so, a model of how the different consumption values affect the interviewees has been constructed (Figure 2).

The findings show that functional and emotional values have the strongest effect on private consumers' intentions to adopt smart home

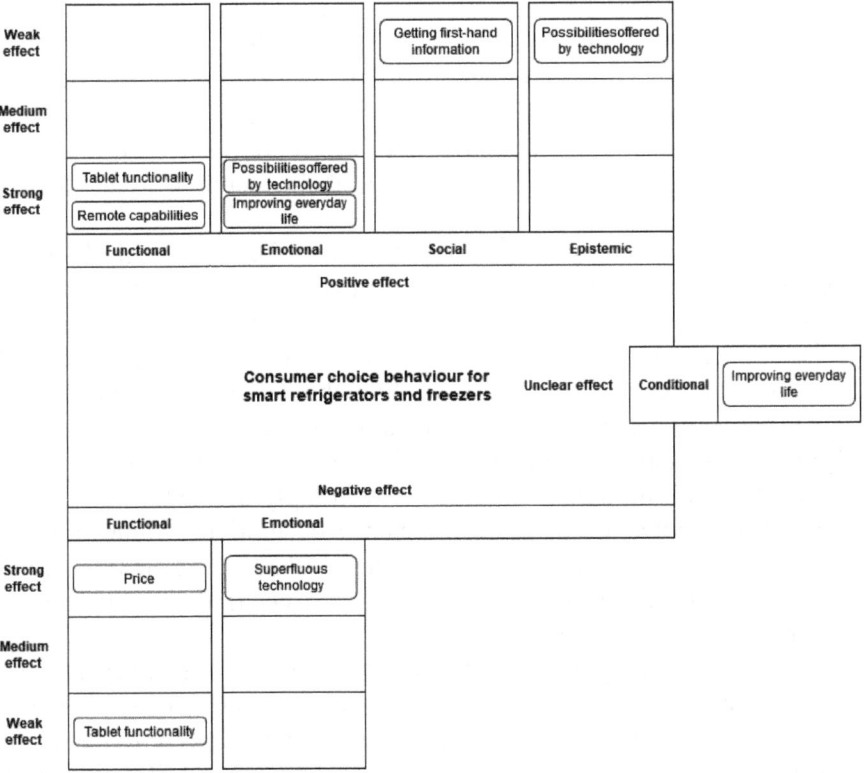

Figure 2. Values' effect on consumers' perception of smart refrigerators and freezers.

technology. This is in line with previous research which found that utilitarian and hedonic values act as drivers for intentions to adopt smart technology (Aldossari & Sidorova, 2020; Marikyan *et al.*, 2021; Sequeiros *et al.*, 2021).

The functional values that had the strongest positive effect proved the remote capabilities and tablet functionality. This aligns well with Yang *et al.*'s (2017) findings that saw monitoring and control, especially remote monitoring and control, as functions in smart home appliances that were of particular interest to consumers. The study could not confirm Baudier *et al.* (2020) findings regarding university students' readiness to adopt smart home technology.

The research further contributes to findings of deterrents for adoption of smart technologies. It shows that functional and emotional values not only have a positive influence but instead also can act as the strongest deterrents for intentions to adopt smart home technology. It also confirms previous research that cost acts as a strong deterrent for adoption of smart technology and technology in general (Hsu & Lin, 2018; Balta-Ozkan *et al.*, 2013; Park *et al.*, 2018; Nikou, 2019). The emotional deterrence is a new finding for this chapter, as it was not found in the related research. Together with cost, it was the strongest negative influence on the interviewee's acceptance of the technology and their intentions to adopt such technology.

Another new finding was the highlighting of a relationship between functional and emotional values. The consumers who were most positive about the functionality of a smart refrigerator and freezer, and not deterred by the cost, also showed strong hedonic values toward the products. But the individuals who were less positive about the functionality and deterred by the cost instead expressed negative emotional sentiment or even strong negative emotional sentiment regarding smart refrigerators and freezers. The fact that the emotional values were so strongly tied to the consumers' views on functional value could indicate that emotional values are not independent values when investigating smart technology. This finding has not been confirmed by previous research and needs to be investigated further before any conclusion can be drawn.

It was also found that social and epistemic values affect private consumers' intentions to adopt smart home appliances positively. However, the effect these values had was small, and they do not appear to be able to trigger any consumption behavior by themselves. Instead, it would seem like these values can only help trigger consumption in tandem with values that have a stronger effect on consumers, such as functional and/or emotional values. This inability to trigger purchasing intentions of smart home technologies could be further investigated and may yield interesting results that could further expand the model presented here.

Finally, this study has not found a clear influence of conditional values on consumers. It was often hard for the interviewees to separate their thoughts on conditional values from their thoughts on functional values. The only truly conditional value expressed was family. However, it did not show a strong effect, instead the interviewees speculated that it might be nice to have when you have a family. But since none of them currently have children, they could not specify to what degree they believed it would help them. New research could focus on bringing clarity to conditional values that affect consumers' intentions to adopt smart home technology.

6.1. *Limitations*

This research is not without limitations. Although there has been some research into the private context of smart home technology, it is still an underdeveloped area of inquiry (Marikyan *et al.*, 2021).

With six participants being interviewed, there is a need for larger studies as well. While a lot of data were gathered from these six individuals, a larger selection might yield different results. It is also possible that the findings related to the conditional values will not hold true if the questions are revised. One cannot exclude the possibility that they were unclear to the participants, although no interviewee expressed such concerns.

Another limitation is that the study was conducted on people who do not own smart refrigerators and freezers. While the interviewees had the artifacts described to them and viewed a short video showcasing the abilities of the artifact, it is possible that at least getting to interact with a smart refrigerator and freezer might have made the participants reach different conclusions. And if the participants had owned smart refrigerators and freezers, the products could most likely have been discussed in even greater detail, generating new insights.

The study was conducted with interview subjects from Uppsala, Sweden. While the findings largely appear in line with previous studies, one cannot say with certainty that the results would not have been different in a different country. One aspect that was not touched upon at all is the issue of wealth. The outcomes are likely to be different if a study like this was conducted in a developing country rather than in a wealthy nation.

7. Conclusion and Future Research

Private consumers' views on the values of smart home appliances are a field that still needs to be researched more. The private setting has been ignored in favor of the industrial and public setting.

This research has found that functional and emotional values are the values that most strongly affect private consumers' intentions to adopt smart refrigerators and freezers. This applies both to influencing consumers positively and negatively. A relationship between these two values was also discovered, suggesting emotional values might not be an independent value, although further research is necessary to confirm this.

Social and epistemic values showcased a weak but positive effect on consumers' intentions toward adoption of smart refrigerators and freezers, but neither were viewed as strong enough to trigger consumption without the help of functional and/or emotional values. The effects of conditional values were unclear and are in need of further research to draw any conclusions from.

Future research could include more appliances than what was possible for this chapter. As it stands now, it is not certain whether or not these findings can be generalized for other smart home appliances, or if they only hold true for smart refrigerators and freezers.

Another aspect that would be interesting in future research is that none of the participants in this study owned a smart refrigerator or freezer. When these products become more commonplace, a new study might yield different results. Similar studies to this one, where the participants get to physically interact with the artifact, would also be of interest, as it may yield different results.

As mentioned previously, a relationship between emotional and functional values was discovered in this chapter. This should be a focus for researchers using the theory of consumption values, as it could result in extensions and expansions of the framework when investigating smart technologies.

References

Abdelrahman, N. G., Haque, R., Polverento, M. E., Wendling, A., Goetz, C. M., & Arnetz, B. B. (2021). Brain-health: Attitudes towards technology adoption in older adults. *Healthcare, 9*(1). DOI: 10.3390/healthcare9010023.

Adapa, A., Nah, F. F.-H., Hall, R. H., Siau, K., & Smith, S. N. (2018). Factors influencing adoption of smart wearable devices. *International Journal of Human-Computer Interaction, 34*(5). DOI: 10.1080/10447318.2017. 1357902.

Alaiad, A. & Zhou, L. (2017). Patients' adoption WSN-based smart home healthcare systems: An integrated model of facilitators and barriers. *IEEE Transactions on Professional Communication, 60*(1). DOI: 10.1109/TPC. 2016.2632822.

Aldossari, M. Q. & Sidorova, A. (2020). Consumer acceptance of internet of things (IoT): Smart home context. *Journal of Computer Information Systems, 60*, 507–517.

Ali, S., Danish, M., Khuwaja, F. M., Sajjad, M. S., & Zahid, H. (2019). The intention to adopt green it products in Pakistan: Driven by the modified theory of consumption values. *Environments, 6*(5), 53. DOI: 10.3390/environments 6050053.

Arthanat, S., Chang, H., & Wilcox, J. (2020). Determinants of information communication and smart home automation technology adoption for aging-in-place. *Journal of Enabling Technologies, 14*(2). DOI: 10.1108/JET-11-2019-0050.

Ayla Networks (2020). What is a smart appliance — And how do you make one? (2020-03-19). https://www.aylanetworks.com/blog/what-is-a-smart-appliance-and-how-do-you-make-one. [2022-04-11].

Balakrishnan, S., Vasudavan, H., & Murugesan, R. K. (2018). Smart home technologies: A preliminary review. In *ICIT 2018: Proceedings of the 6th International Conference on Information Technology: IoT and Smart City* (pp. 120–127). DOI: 10.1145/3301551.3301575.

Balta-Ozkan, N., Amerighi, O., & Boteler, B. (2014). A comparison of consumer perceptions towards smart homes in the UK, Germany and Italy: Reflections for policy and future research. *Technology Analysis & Strategic Management, 26*, 1176–1195.

Balta-Ozkan, N., Davidson, R., Bicket, M., & Whitmarsh, L. (2013). Social barriers to the adoption of smart homes. *Energy Policy, 63*, 363–374.

Baudier, P., Ammi, C., & Deboeuf-Rouchon, M. (2020). Smart home: Highly-educated students' acceptance. *Technological Forecasting and Social Change, 153*. DOI: 10.1016/j.techfore.2018.06.043.

Bjelica, M. Z. (2018). How much smart is too much? *IEEE Consumer Electronics Magazine,* (November Issue), *7*(6), 23–28.

Brown, S. A. & Venkatesh, V. (2005). Model of adoption of technology in households: A baseline model test and extension incorporating household life cycle. *MIS Quarterly*, 399–426.

Bødker, M., Gimpel, G., & Hedman, J. (2009). The user experience of smart phones: A consumption values approach.

Chang, Y.-W. & Chen, J. (2021). What motivates customers to shop in smart shops? The impacts of smart technology and technology readiness. *Journal of Retailing and Consumer Services*, 58. DOI: 10.1016/j.jretconser.2020. 102325.

Chui, M., Colins, M., & Patel, M. (2021). The Internet of Things: Catching up to an accelerating opportunity. *McKinsey & Company*.

Citing Aldrich, F. K. (2003). Smart homes: Past, present and future. In Harper R. (ed.), *Inside the Smart Home*. London: Springer. DOI: 10.1007/1-85233-854-7_2.

Darby, S. J. (2017). Smart technology in the home: Time for more clarity. *Building Research and Information*, 46, 2018, 140–147. DOI: 10.1080/09613218. 2017.1301707.

Dragani, R. (2020). Definitions of smart appliances. (2020-03-25). *Hunker*. https://www.hunker.com/13409415/definition-of-smart-appliances.

Gao, L. & Bai, X. (2014). A unified perspective on the factors influencing consumer acceptance of internet of things technology. *Asia Pacific Journal of Marketing and Logistics*, 26(2), 211–231. DOI: 10.1108/APJML-06-2013-0061.

Hedman, J. & Gimpel, G. (2010). The adoption of hyped technologies: A qualitative study. *Information Technology and Management*, 11(4), 161–175. DOI: 10.1007/s10799-010-0075-0.

Hong, A., Nam, C., & Kim, S. (2020). What will be the possible barriers to consumers' adoption of smart home services? *Telecommunications Policy*, 44(2). DOI: 10.1016/j.telpol.2019.101867.

Hove, S. E. & Anda, B. (2005). Experiences from conducting semi-structured interviews in empirical software engineering research. In *11th IEEE International Software Metrics Symposium (METRICS)*. DOI: 10.1109/ METRICS.2005.24.

Hsu, C.-L. & Lin, J. C.-C. (2018). Exploring factors affecting the adoption of internet of things services. *Journal of Computer Information Systems*, 58(1), 49–57. DOI: 10.1080/08874417.2016.1186524.

IoT Analytics (2021). State of IoT 2021: Number of connected IoT devices growing 9% to 12.3 billion globally, cellular IoT now surpassing 2 billion. (2021-09-22). https://iot-analytics.com/number-connected-iot-devices. [2022-02-15].

Jovanovic, M., Sjödin, D., & Parida, V. (2021). Co-evolution of platform architecture, platform services and platform governance: Expanding the platform value of industrial digital platforms. *Technovation.* DOI: 10.1016/j.technovation.2020.102218.

Kang, L., Jiang, Q., Peng, C.-H., Sia, C. L., & Liang, T.-P. (2020). Managing Change with the support of smart technology: A field investigation of ride-hailing services. *Journal of the Association for Information Systems, 21*(6). DOI: 10.17705/1jais.00647.

Kang, W. M., Moon, S. Y., & Park, J. H. (2017). An enhanced security framework for home appliances in smart home. *Human-centric Computing and Information Sciences, 7*(6). DOI: 10.1186/s13673-017-0087-4.

Kim, S. & Baek, J. S. (2019). Definitions and attributes of smart home appliances. In *Proceedings of the 22nd International Conference on Engineering Design (ICED19)*, Delft, The Netherlands, 5–8 August. DOI: 10.1017/dsi.2019.213.

Lee, C. (2014). Adoption of smart technology among older adults: Challenges and issues. *Public Policy & Aging Report, 24*(1). DOI: 10.1093/ppar/prt005.

Mani, Z. & Chouk, I. (2017). Drivers of consumers' resistance to smart products. *Journal of Marketing Management, 33*(1–2), 76–97. DOI: 10.1080/0267257X.2016.1245212.

Marikyan, D., Papagiannidis, S., & Alamanos, E. (2019). The effect of behavioural beliefs on smart home technology adoption. In *UK Academy for Information Systems Conference Proceedings 2019.* No. 19. Available: https://aisel.aisnet.org/ukais2019/19. [2020-05-12].

Marikyan, D., Papagiannidis, S., & Alamanos, E. (2021). "Smart home sweet smart home": An examination of smart home acceptance. *International Journal of E-Business Research (IJEBR), 17*, 1–23.

Nikou, S. (2019). Factors driving the adoption of smart home technology: An empirical assessment. *Telematics and Informatics, 45.* DOI: 10.1016/j.tele.2019.101283.

Oates, B. J. (2006). *Researching Information Systems and Computing.* London; Thousand Oaks, California: SAGE Publications.

Osborne, H. (2020). Smart appliances may not be worth money in long run, warns which? *The Guardian,* June 8. Available: https://www.theguardian.com/technology/2020/jun/08/smart-appliances-may-not-be-worth-money-in-long-run-warns-which.

Oun, M. A. & Bach, C. (2014). Qualitative research method summary. *Journal of Multidisciplinary Engineering Science and Technology (JMEST), 1*(5), 252–258.

Papagiannidis, S. & Davlembayeva, D. (2021). Bringing smart home technology to peer-to- peer accommodation: Exploring the drivers of intention to stay in smart accommodation. *Information Systems Frontiers.* DOI: 10.1007/s10796-021-10227-4.

Park, E., Kim, S., Kim, Y., & Kwon, S. J. (2018). Smart home services as the next mainstream of the ICT industry: Determinants of the adoption of smart home services. *Universal Access in the Information Society, 17*, 175–190. DOI: 10.1007/s10209-017-0533-0.

PC Mag (n.d.). Internet-connected appliance. https://www.pcmag.com/encyclo-pedia/term/internet-connected-appliance. [2020-04-11].

Petrovčiková, K. & Sudzina, F. (2018). Smartphone adoption: Design of factors within the framework of theory of consumption values. In Bilgin, M. H., Danis, H., Demir, E., & Can, U. (eds.), *Consumer Behavior, Organizational Strategy and Financial Economics: Proceedings of the 21st Eurasia Business and Economics Society Conference* (pp. 53–62). Springer. DOI: 10.1007/978-3-319-76288-3_4.

Poushneh, A. & Vasquez-Parraga, A. Z. (2019). Emotional bonds with technology: The impact of customer readiness on upgrade intention, brand, loyalty, and affective commitment through mediation impact of customer value. *Journal of Theoretical and Applied Electronic Commerce Research, 14*(2). DOI: 10.4067/s0718-18762019000200108.

Prospero, M. (2019). What is a smart refrigerator, and is it worth it? *Tom's Guide.* (2019-03-26). https://www.tomsguide.com/us/what-is-a-smart-refrigerator, review-6307.html [2022-04-11].

Radanliev, P., De Roure, D. C., Maple, C., Nurse, J. R., Nicolescu, R., & Ani, U. (2019). Cyber risk in IoT systems. *Preprints.* March 1. DOI: 10.20944/preprints201903.0104.v1. https://www.preprints.org/manuscript/201903.0104/v1. [2022-02-22].

Savin-Baden, M. & Major, C. (2013). *Qualitative Research: The Essential Guide to Theory and Practice.* London: Routledge.

Sequeiros, H., Oliveira, T., & Thomas, M. A. (2021). The impact of IoT smart home services on psychological well-being. *Information Systems Frontiers,* 1–18. DOI: 10.1007/s10796-021-10118-8.

Serrenho, T. & Bertoldi, P. (2019). Smart home and appliances: State of the art. *Energy, Communications, Protocols, Standards.* EUR 29750 EN. Luxembourg: Publications Office of the European Union. DOI: 10.2670/453301.

Shea, S. (2020). Smart home or building (home automation or domotics). *Techtarget.* https://www.techtarget.com/iotagenda/definition/smart-home-or-building [2022-04-11].

Sheth, J. N., Newman, B. I., & Gross, B. L. (1991). Why we buy what we buy: A theory of consumption values. *Journal of Business Research, 22*(2), 159–170. DOI: 10.1016/0148-2963(91)90050-8.

Shuhaiber, A. & Mashal, I. (2019). Understanding users' acceptance of smart homes. *Technology in Society, 58.* DOI: 10.1016/j.techsoc.2019.01.003.

Song, Y., Yang, Y., & Cheng, P. (2022). The investigation of adoption of voice-user- interface (VUI) in smart home systems among Chinese older adults. *Sensors, 22*(4). DOI: 10.3390/s22041614.

Stojkoska, B. L. R. & Trivodaliev, K. V. (2017). A review of Internet of Things for smart home: Challenges and solutions. *Journal of Cleaner Production, 140*(3), 1454–1464. DOI: 10.1016/j.jclepro.2016.10.006.

Tsai, M. (2012). The trends and adoption behaviors of smart phones in Taiwan: A comparison between persons over 45 years of age and youth under 25. In *Proceedings of PICMET'12: Technology Management for Emerging Technologies* (pp. 1456–1462).

Turel, O., Serenko, A., & Bontis, N. (2010). User acceptance of hedonic digital artifacts: A theory of consumption values perspective. *Information & Management, 47*(1), 53–59. DOI: 10.1016/j.im.2009.10.002.

Venkatesh, V. & Brown, S. A. (2001). A longitudinal investigation of personal computers in homes: Adoption determinants and emerging challenges. *MIS Quarterly, 25*(1), 186–204.

Yang, H., Lee, H., & Zo, H. (2017). User acceptance of smart home services: An extension of the theory of planned behavior. *Industrial Management & Data Systems, 117*(1), 68–89. DOI: 10.1108/IMDS-01-2016-0017.

Yang, H., Lee, W., & Lee, H. (2018a). IoT smart home adoption: The importance of proper level automation. *Advanced Internet of Things and Big Data Technology for Smart Human-Care Services, 2018*. DOI: 10.1155/2018/6464036.

Zailani, S., Iranmanesh, M., Hyun, S. S., & Ali, M. H. (2019). Applying the theory of consumption values to explain drivers' willingness to pay for bio-fuels. *Sustainability, 11*(3), 668. DOI: 10.3390/su11030668.

Zhai, Y., Liu, Y., Yang, M., Long, F., & Virkki, J. (2014b). A survey study of the usefulness and concerns about smart home applications from the human perspective. *Open Journal of Social Sciences, 2*(11). DOI: 10.4236/jss.2014.211017.

Zion Market Research (2018). Global smart home market to exceed $53.45 billion by 2022. (2018-01-03). Available: https://globenewswire.com/news-release/2018/01/03/1281338/0/en/Global-Smart-Home-Market-to-Exceed-53-45-Billion-by-2022-Zion-Market-Research.html. [2022-02-13].

https://doi.org/10.1142/9789811295140_0009

Chapter 9

Digital Applications for Learning in the Space Domain

Andrew Herd

European Space Agency, Noordwijk, The Netherlands

andrew.herd@esa.int

1. Introduction

The fundamental need to learn through experience is most relevant in the organizational context, and none more so than in knowledge-rich or -centric organizations. Indeed, it could be argued that any operating entity only exists in a marketplace context because of some knowledge held by individuals, databases, or machines. In the world of space, where the concept of technology spin-out and spin-in (transferring from the space domain to other domains, and vice versa) is used for the greater good of society, the creation of new or highly enhanced capabilities to learn from experience is of relevance to both space and society. The European Space Agency (ESA), where knowledge is stated as being a prime asset of the Agency, undertook a user-needs-based technology development to advance its ability to learn from experience and in doing so created a transformational capability using digital transformation at its core which included utilizing artificial intelligence techniques. These techniques then opened up the possibility of socializing knowledge, allowing a knowledge-based discourse between (human) experts but also a discourse with machine-based experts.

2. Space Domain Learning from Experience

The European Space Agency (ESA) has been undertaking space missions for more than 50 years. During this time, it has gained a significant and unique collection of experience. This collection of experience, primarily held as knowledge by its experts, is one of the key assets of the Agency that will help address the current and future needs of space, as expressed for instance in Agenda 2025 (an ESA member state-endorsed vision of the Agency's near-term roadmap).

However, in the light of an ongoing retirement wave in ESA (50% retirement of its staff over a 10-year period) impacting this experience base, ESA has needed to introduce effective means of allowing this experience to be captured and shared.

One such means, introduced at the corporate level in the Agency in 2019, was Lessons Learned which sought to centralize dispersed efforts within the Agency (some of which had been active for more than 10 years at the time), creating a systematic process for the capturing and sharing of experience from ESA's space projects (the core of ESA "business").

Lessons Learned was then introduced as a central capability at the Agency primarily through the classic means of addressing people, process, and technology:

- People — assuring contribution and participation of the key stakeholders
- Process — defining a framework of policy and handbook covering the "why, who, and how"
- Technology — a corporate platform (Microsoft SharePoint) providing the central access point for capture and learning means.

During the initial activity of researching and setting up the corporate lessons learned process, it was identified from experiences of both space and non-space-related organizations introducing lessons learned that the capturing of experience was only one major transformational capability to instigate within an organization. The second and organizationally more important was the learning from the experience captured. Getting the right balance and emphasis between "capture" and "learning" was initially addressed by conceptually separating and naming both uniquely — with a two-part process: "lessons identified" and then "lessons learning" being proposed. In this way, it was intended to remove the term "lessons learned" from the organizational vocabulary, as it was believed that the use of the term lessons learned would imply that the learning was already embedded in the organization simply through identifying (and capturing) the needed learning.

The other initial consideration was the barriers to capture, as without the first step of gathering experience, there would be no learning. To achieve the needed level of simplicity, a detailed analysis was performed of all of the genres of experience capture types and the associated data (fields) for each of these. The Agency determined that there were three basic data fields:

1. Title
2. Background or situation
3. Proposed learning.

In addition to the core data fields, metadata fields were needed to be added to this to support processing, management, and maintenance (mostly attributed to each new entry automatically by the tool used). However, some five years later, this original simplistic approach still remains valid and found over this time to be sufficient to enable learning.

3. Digital Technology as Transformation Means for Space

In 2016, ESA presented Space 4.0, being analogous to, and intertwined with, Industry 4.0, considered the unfolding fourth industrial revolution of manufacturing and services. Through this vision, ESA continued to consolidate and carry out its plans in what the Agency saw as the next phase in Space business, as part of Space 4.0 being more than ever before linked to global challenges and societal issues, such as climate change, shortage of resources, conflicts, migration, and others. As such, ESA and Space 4.0 sought to contribute to policy and decision-making and inspire future generations and offer a tangible response to these issues. Beyond these elements, Space 4.0 relied on a new digital economy and a digital society.

The opportunities in Information and Communication Technology (ICT) have strongly enhanced the value of — digitally managed — data, information, and knowledge. Therefore, Space 4.0 was seen as being more information and knowledge driven than at any previous phase in the Space environment evolution. Space 4.0 in Europe then strongly depended on the appropriate management of this knowledge held and shared by ESA and its partners across member states with and between industry and with the science communities.

The European Digital Agenda for Space (EDAS) also released in 2016 by ESA provided a reference to existing rules and management practices and set out ESA's goals and rules to manage, preserve, and share data, information, and the derived knowledge managed by ESA.

In this regard, the application of digital technology means was important to the Agency as in addressing the EDAS aims and objectives, as it provided a single means to address significant parts of all three of the people-process-technology aspects.

In this way, for Lessons Learned, the new digital capability would meet the Agency needs for a common process, a common template, and a reference for retaining the experience of experts at the Agency through the course of the retirement wave — all this achieved through a consolidated and Agency-wide accessible activity of Lessons Learned. This then placed a significant burden of expectation on the lessons learned technology to meet the Agency's (and the Agency's workforce) needs, current and future.

This burden of expectation led to an almost constant examination and re-examination of the process leanness (effectiveness and efficiency); however, there appeared to be little improvement in this area as these aspects had already been fully considered and built in, such as the basis of simplicity (in terms of burden placed on a user to capture and retrieve learning).

The initial (Microsoft SharePoint-based) technical implementation of the lessons learned tool, the ESA Lessons Learned Portal, reflected some basic principles drawn both from users and stakeholders and also its governing principles (as stated in the lessons learned policy):

- Simplicity
- Openness and sharing
- Imparting learning.

4. Advancement of Digital Capabilities and User Needs

Even before the launch of the corporate Lesson Learned process (and tool) in 2019, along with the start of the systematic capture of lessons of its projects, it was realized that digital technologies were advancing rapidly in their ability to support data storage, manipulation, and representation. As an example of this, rapid and continuous SharePoint releases (each with new or improved capabilities) were applied as an advancing solution to lessons learned needs. Through the various stages of Directorate and Agency level development, the ESA Lessons Learned Portal was

- Initially developed in SharePoint 2007
- Updated capabilities with SharePoint 2013
- Adopted as part of a corporate service platform on SharePoint 2016
- Updated to SharePoint 2020
- Moving to SharePoint online planned for 2024.

Even with these advances of capability, user feedback was indicating that while the application and use of SharePoint for lessons learned had greatly advanced ESA's needs in this area, it did not (and seemingly could not) meet all user needs.

As a result, in 2019 — even while the corporate lesson learned process and tool were just being launched — a research activity and a development project were also defined acknowledging the need for an evolution of ESA lessons learned capabilities, to better and more directly meet initial user feedback. This user feedback was then further expanded in 2020 by involving a broader and more comprehensive range of stakeholders resulting in a set of 250 use cases being gathered. These use cases were then assessed and distilled down to identify key user needs with the following groups being identified:

- Communities of practice — connecting like-minded groups to specific and relevant learning
- Conversational Assistant — direct support in capturing and retrieving experience
- Data mining — drawing from unconfigured data
- Image-based search — using images where terminology is specific or unknown

- Justification for adoption — giving user rationale for adopting or adapting experience
- Keywords/Tags — assigning user-based tags
- Narrative — commenting on experience offered for learning
- Aspect-centric views
- Relational data — recognizing and showing links between entities through metadata
- Reports — ease of transferring or communicating search outcomes
- Supported searches — enabling user to target knowledge needed
- User roles — recognizing role of user and customizing access and capabilities
- Mobility/"Point of use" — proving access for capture or retrieval when and where it's needed.

5. Research into Technical Feasibility of AI Application to Learning

With the ongoing retirement wave limiting the availability of experts at the Agency (while being countered to some degree by a recruitment wave from a limited and niche marketplace), there was a real drive for the need to counteract the loss of valuable knowledge at the Agency. It was therefore determined that a more rapid and robust development of a knowledge capturing framework, and that for learning through improved knowledge representation, would be best enabled by utilizing novel means in the form of Knowledge Graphs (KGs). Knowledge graph capability was included in order to perform a back-end function of identifying relevant entities (as nodes) and establishing their inter-relationships. In addition, it was determined that the use of a conversational assistants (or chatbots) in the front end, using Natural Language Processing (NLP) and Named Entity Recognition (NER), represented a potential option to aid and improve the capturing of knowledge and transferring expertise in the space domain. However, this option needed to be further explored for viability, and a research activity was proposed to further explore this unique and complex arena of AI application to learning. The research activity was approved on the basis that it could reveal novel and enabling means to address the identified significant risk of knowledge loss within the organization, caused by an ongoing retirement wave (which could not be fully or directly addressed through recruitment). While this in part was

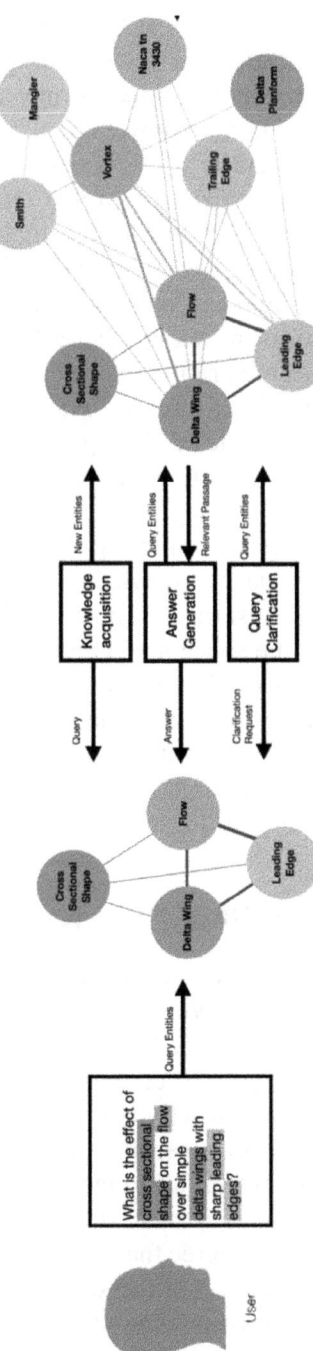

Figure 1. SCARLET concept of user questions prompting an expert response.

addressed by the existing capabilities at ESA in Lessons Learned, it was only considered a partial mitigation for encouraging experts to record experiential knowledge they have gained during their work on various projects, and for those seeking the knowledge, to use the portal to learn. In 2020, a 3-year research activity: *"Space Conversational Agent for Retrieving Lessons learned and Expert Training (SCARLET)"* was undertaken at the University of Strathclyde with the goal of creating an intelligent system capable of handling expert-level data input and questioning, allowing for the quality capture and retrieval knowledge (held as experiential information in the Lesson Learned Portal) in a conversational format. In the preliminary research prior to the creation of this conversational agent, it was discovered that little research exists in the domain of (quality) knowledge capture and retrieval through conversation and hence a new niche area of research exploration had been identified and created.

Now after 3 years of research by two PhD students, the conclusions are that the original hypothesis is valid, and these novel capabilities do well suit an application to quality knowledge capture and retrieval. The matching of capability to this use case is more valid when considering the limited (but niche) area of the space arena and also when applied within lessons learned, a highly process-based activity.

At its core, SCARLET was exploring the technical feasibility of creating the socialization of knowledge with a machine, and as a result of this conversation, the knowledge captured from or provided to the user would be of a higher quality (see Figure 1).

6. Realizing Theory within Deployed AI Capability

Unlike SCARLET research activity, the subsequent development activity of CLARK (*Captured Lessons Applied for the Reuse of Knowledge*) project, as the first major evolution of the Lessons Learned (LL) portal at the Agency, focused on the user, the user experience, and hence the user interface. The SCARLET research activity though has been a key forerunner to CLARK on an academic research level and through technical exchanges between the two teams informed the developers on the best approaches to system architecture and the discrete capabilities. This exchange contributed to such a degree that the initial design paradigm was changed — expanding the function of the knowledge graph. Initially, the CLARK designer had considered the knowledge graph as a visual means

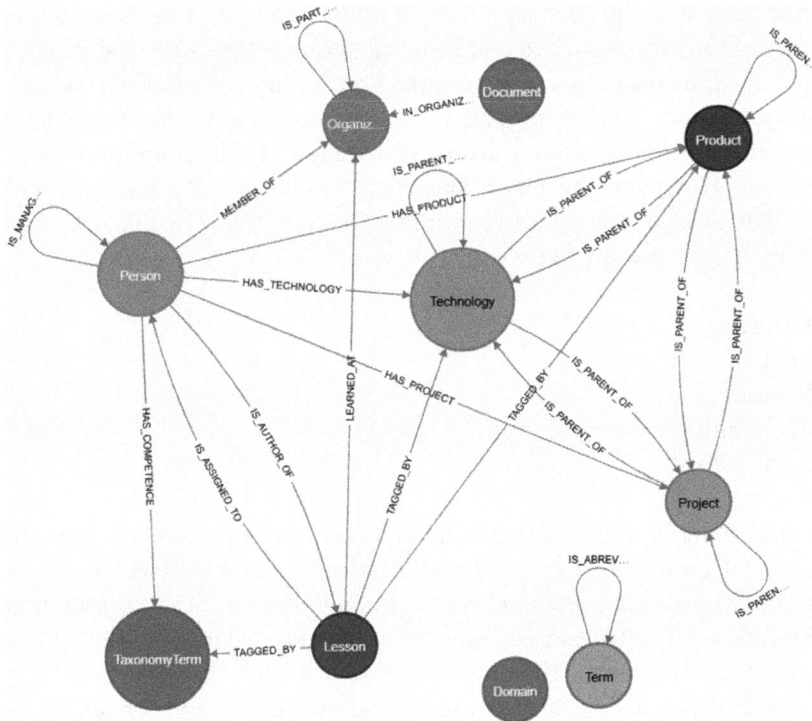

Figure 2. CLARK knowledge graph showing entity type and relationships (beta-version).

to display search results, so it was placed only at the user interface level. SCARLET showed that the knowledge graph also played a key role in the back-end functionality as well. As such SCARLET provided CLARK with important insights into the architecture of the system design, and, in doing so, created a means to more simply address user needs. With this change of the knowledge graph being placed as a core back-end and front-end capability, the CLARK knowledge graph (KG) was developed by combining data from multiple (previously unrelated) sources and through the identification of key nodes (entities) and their inter-relationships allowed for structuring of these data (see Figure 2).

The knowledge graph, while not providing the means to interact (converse or socialize) with the user, provided the user with an immediate sense of relevance and connectedness of the search term used to retrieve experience. This perspective presented to the user in a simple visual manner provides the user with a rapid understanding of the related terminology of the term searched and hence a greater means to socialize knowledge on the basis of a common vocabulary — the basis of all communication. This approach is by no means new, as, for example, visual thesauri exist already using knowledge graph techniques for presentation. However, the novel approach was to provide the user with a view that grouped together the similar term-type based results, i.e., results relating to and grouped by

- Project
- People
- Process
- Technology
- And so forth.

Additionally, an integrated chatbot was developed as a complementary novel capability being trained to provide an intelligent (and well-informed) conversational experience. As a result of these two integrated capabilities, CLARK enables the user to capture, search, and retrieve the captured knowledge of the employees across ESA through three simple interfaces ("classic" term-based search, knowledge graph for search, and, the chatbot for both capture and retrieval) connected to the core back-end system and data collection.

For CLARK, a three-tier data-driven architecture has been chosen, integrating data from nine different sources (of truth) in a single data collection and made available and structured to the knowledge graph and chatbot through a web service. The data collection has been structured specifically to work for KG and chatbot purposes. The KG enables users to search through keyword queries for related knowledge. The search result is then presented in both text and visual formats, with the latter knowledge graph representation being provided as summary nodes, reflecting the data content types of the different data sources (i.e., relating to a person, lesson, term, document, or a domain) and indicating the established relationships between these nodes.

The chatbot also uses data from both the central data collection, to assure consistency between the various integrated capabilities. The chatbot, implemented using RASA, enables users to interact in a conversational human-like way, with CLARK identifying the intent of the user, i.e., whether to capture and recycle the knowledge. The chatbot makes use of advanced natural language processing and querying capabilities and is trained specifically for LL space-related domains to improve its effectiveness.

During the first years of lessons learned at the Agency, the focus was mainly on capturing knowledge. From 2019, the emphasis was more on structuring this knowledge for future (re)use. The ESA Lessons Learned portal now contains high-value data made available ESA-wide, which covers not only the key project functions but also other non-technical disciplines on which the agency also relies. The LL portal has, as a result, proven to be particularly important enabler in the continuous collection of relevant knowledge within the organization. The next priority for the Agency is to implement knowledge sharing and distribution and this is greatly enabled through the novel capabilities that CLARK offers (Mihaylov *et al.*, 2022; Henriquez *et al.*, 2023).

7. Socialization of Experience Using AI Capabilities

The CLARK chatbot allows the user to capture the user's experience with an informed system in the form of a conversation. In doing so, the user is forming a trust with the capability, and this trust leads to a greater interaction between the user and the chatbot.

In the conversation based around capturing experience, the chatbot also guides the user in terms of capturing best practices. The chatbot highlights the use of keywords — matching those within a space glossary for relevance and providing the outcome of this comparison to the user. This approach is also followed with the use of abbreviations — the chatbot recognizing an abbreviation in a piece of text (in the lesson background or in the proposed learning) giving the user the understood expansion and adding to the system's knowledge where this match is not context relevant (the system registers this new abbreviation and expansion upon the user's confirmation of a match). As far as constructing a valid lesson, the chatbot recognizes terms or phrases that might invalidate the proposed learning (for example, using the phrase "as early as possible" in a lesson). The system can identify this as an excursion from the permitted phrases (as the data collection holds a list of non-permitted terms), highlight this to the user, and ask for a replacement with a more precise term or phrase. In this regard, there is a two-way exchange between two experts. The user has the expert experience to be captured and the chatbot has the drafting rules and glossaries for improved (quality) experience capture.

The discourse undertaken initially by the test community with an immature conversational agent required the tester's conversational language to be more biased toward the comprehension level of the chatbot (i.e., the machine). In this instance, the human was being asked to socialize using language better recognized by the CLARK, categorized as trigger terms, that prompted a better chatbot response than if a vaguer or more varied language (i.e., what the user would characterize as a more normal human conversation) was used. During this stage, it was quoted that "*at the present state of CLARK, we need our humans to think and talk like machines — however what we need is a machine that thinks and talks more like a human*".

This constrained conversation, the sharing of knowledge by the user but in a machine-understandable form, impacted the trust levels and ultimately the level of investment willing to be given by the tester. The user expressed that they needed to feel that the machine somehow understood the value of the knowledge or at least the time invested in committing it to the conversation (as all conversation is typed in the chatbot). Where the conversation broke down with a tester giving an instruction but the chatbot either didn't register or registered incorrectly, impacted any trust built up and the conversation dried up along with the knowledge exchange. Individual testers, however, showed a very varied level of tolerance and the feedback in a number of cases from the testers was still positive despite the acknowledgment of the limited conversation.

8. Analysis of the Impact of AI on Socialization of Knowledge

A model of communication was proposed by Cox and Tait (1991), which showed a transmitter and a receiver connected by a communication means (see Figure 3). At the time of writing in 1991, the idea that the transmitter could be anything other than a human was fairly inconceivable as a reality (and only as a science fiction). Since this time our means of social communication has not only increased but also become part of our way of life due to forced remote working in the COVID-19 times.

In our current work environment, we use the medium of face-to-face meetings, virtual meetings, and also hybrid ones (part virtual, part

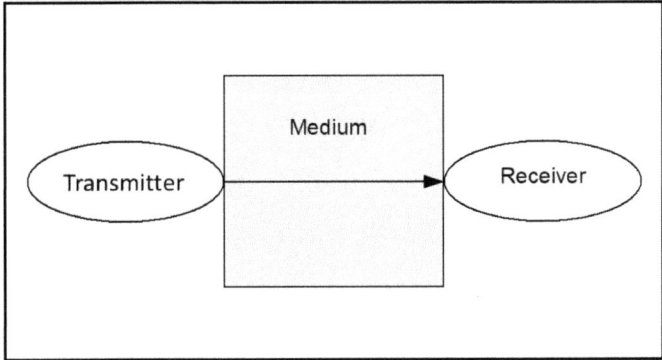

Figure 3. Communication from source to receiver via a medium.

face-to-face) to communicate (transmit and receive data). It is known that trust between transmitters and receivers plays an important part in the effectiveness of these meetings where these are held remotely. Trust also plays a key part in knowledge transmission and receipt. The optimal scenario is said to be holding face-to-face meetings first to establish a relationship between parties meeting for the first time and as trust is built up to move to virtual meetings (and gaining the environmental benefits of not traveling). Face-to-face meetings can then be re-established if situations dictate or communication, relationships, and understanding break down. It was recognized (Cox & Tait, 1991) that there were a number of influences on both the transmission and the receipt of the communication. These influences are based on the following:

(a) the interplay of perception of the transmitter on the receiver, and vice versa
(b) the interference of transmission and reception of the medium
(c) the perception of the information source of the data transmission and the information utilization of the data, by the receiver and transmitter, respectively.

So with this, if we re-consider the Cox and Tait (1991) model of communication, we must modify the communication medium, to include both a "real" medium and a "virtual" one (see Figure 4). The transfer can be a real (face-to-face) transmission (or exchange) between transmitter and

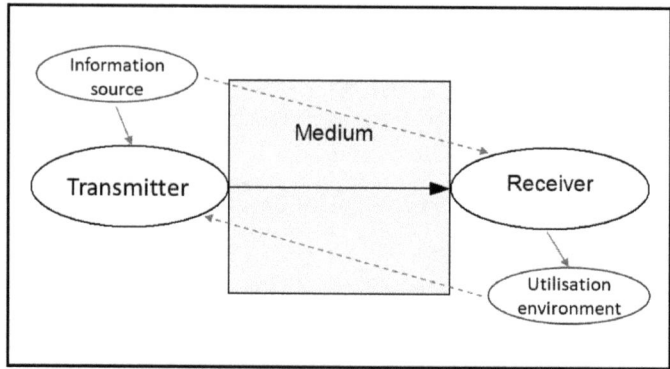

Figure 4. Influences on transmission and reception.

receiver, or it can be through a virtual means, with the virtual means providing only a (partial) representation of the two parties. For example, the resolution or content of the virtual representation may not be sufficient to provide the total communication between the involved parties. It is not a huge step to then consider the CLARK context where the chatbot, through a conversation with the user, is transmitting expertise or knowledge that was not only derived from an expert but also validated and evaluated prior to release to the CLARK data collection. The user would be provided with the data along with its source, providing and establishing trust of CLARK by the user. In the Cox and Tait (1991) model, CLARK would have no perception of the use of the data by the user, and there is no current means to make this part of the conversation. So to explore the "why do you want this data" or "what would this data be applied to or for", rather provide the best match of data to the search request of the user and complement this search outcome (through the knowledge graph) to provide all the related data (entities) that have a relationship to this search term and search result.

It is here that CLARK capability should be understood as only having the means to expand its own data collection based on user-approved knowledge increments. There are no capabilities in CLARK that create and present to the user unvalidated data, as there is always a human (expert) acknowledging either new data entries or the relationships between this and other data entries. These relationships are then available in the knowledge graph.

9. Socialization of Expert Knowledge versus Interaction with an Expert System

It is worth noting that at the Agency, we have derived a definition of an expert: someone who is authorized by their line manager to report or express an opinion on a topic. CLARK is a container of expert knowledge, however it is far from being an expert system (that could replace an expert, for example). Any knowledge that is garnered from the tool still has to be rationalized by the user.

Space development projects are very complex by their nature, not least due to the differing mission types and operational environments. In this, we consider that no knowledge is absolute. The knowledge and experience captured in the ESA LL Portal is always relevant to the context from which it was gained. The validation and evaluation process of lessons attempts to transform this specific experience into generic learning applicable across the activities of the Agency. However, each time the learning from a lesson is applied, this learning still needs to be assessed in the context of its application. The user then determines whether to

- apply the learning as is — "adopt" the lesson
- modify the learning to suit the application — "adapt" the lesson
- decide that the learning is not suitable in the instance — "reject" the learning.

We also have another definition of an expert; being that you know when you are talking to an expert, as in response to your question, they will ask more questions to understand the context and to best understand what you really need, as opposed to giving the answer to (only) what you asked for. For the Agency, this is the true concept of the socialization of knowledge: to be able to fully interact with an expert, to explore your data needs, and to arrive at the right answer to the right question.

Surely that is what we would hope for society as a preferred outcome of Digital Transformation.

10. Summary and Conclusion

The work at the European Space Agency to explore the tangibility of and to establish capability for using AI techniques in knowledge capture and retrieval has been shown to be ground-breaking.

From the early stages of CLARK development, testing, and deployment, we can see signs of the real organizational value in giving a user the capability to capture their experiences and knowledge through a user-centric interface. This same interface equally allows experts to retain (and retrieve) the knowledge of others in an effective and efficient manner.

However, it has been recognized that there not only needs to be more investigation into the use of these AI techniques, not least due to the rapid rate of technological advancement in this area, but also to further enhance what has been established as a baseline capability for the future of quality (effective and efficient) knowledge capture and retrieval (Diana *et al.*, 2023). As such this specific work of the Agency can be built on further as a spin-out technology application and is offered to other knowledge-centric organizations with similar needs or ambitions.

References

Cox, S. J. & Tait, N. R. S (1991). *Reliability, Safety and Risk Management*. London: Butterworth-Heinemann.

Diana, F., Juárez-Mora, O., Boekel, W., Hortensius, R., & Kret, M. (2023). How video calls affect mimicry and trust during interactions. *Philosophical Transactions of the Royal Society B: Biological Sciences B, 378*, 2021048.

Henriquez, M., Danènas, P., Dilijonas, D., Ontiveros, J., & Herd, A. (2023). CLARK: Building conversational intelligence for knowledge management in the space domain. In *24th European Conference on Knowledge Management*, Lisbon, Portugal (pp. 541–549).

Mihaylov, D., Broughton-Stuart, G., Vasile, M., & Herd, A. (2022). A space conversational agent for retrieving lessons-learned and expert training. In *73rd International Astronautical Congress*, Paris, France, pp. 18–22.

https://doi.org/10.1142/9789811295140_0010

Chapter 10

Navigating the Digital Frontier: The Art of Ambidextrous Leadership Definition of Digital Leadership

Kathryn Brohman

Queens's University, Kingston, ON, Canada

kathryn.brohman@queensu.ca

When it comes to leaders who have been recognized for successfully navigating their organizations through digital transformation, names such as Satya Nadella, Jeff Bezos, Bob Igor, and Ajay Banga come top of mind. Nadella, CEO of Microsoft, shifted the company's focus from traditional software to cloud services and embraced a culture of innovation to introduce products, such as Azure and Office 365. Bezos, founder and former CEO of Amazon, was relentless in sustaining focus on customer experience, data-driven decision-making, and investments in technologies like cloud computing and artificial intelligence. Igor, CEO of The Walt Disney Company, recognized the need to expand their digital footprint to remain competitive in the entertainment industry and launched the Disney+ streaming service. Finally, Banga, former CEO of Mastercard, played an important role in the digital transformation of the financial industry by re-imagining digital payment solutions to include contactless payments, mobile payments, and digital security innovations. From a strategy perspective, it is not surprising that each of these transformational success stories is unique in the way technology was leveraged to develop a competitive advantage. However, when it comes to leadership, there is much debate about whether notable changes in response to technological advancements have changed the qualities, styles, and approaches taken by today's CEOs and other organizational leaders.

To contextualize the debate, it is important to start by defining clear conceptual boundaries that describe *what digital leadership is* and *what it is not*. Inspired by a joint research project between Deloitte and MIT Sloan Management Review (Kane *et al.*, 2019), the first key point is that digital leadership IS NOT a new leadership style, inherent in digital leadership is a core set of general leadership skills that remain the same, as shown in Table 1.

In contrast, the second key point is that digital leadership IS unique in the management context that surrounds the digital leaders' mandate. For a digital leader, their playbook for success requires heightened levels of courage and tenacity as digital transformation requires the organization to explore new opportunities in ways that are often perceived to threaten the current status quo (Kirkland, 2014; Wimelius *et al.*, 2021). As such, to succeed in getting people to embrace change, digital leaders must also leverage existing capabilities to maintain the status quo when possible. Embedding the change within existing ways of doing business will reduce resistance and enhance progress.

Table 1.   Core leadership skills.

- Ability to clearly articulate the anticipated value the investment will generate for the organization where in the case of digital leadership, the investment is less about the technology and more about the business strategy or practice it will enable;
- Allocation of sufficient financial resources and support;
- Detailed planning beyond the technology department to a cross-functional approach that intertwines technology development and management of behavioral change;
- Secure buy-in from top management to signal to the rest of the organization that digital transformation efforts are high priority;
- Provide top management with information they need to provide effective oversight and design mechanisms (e.g., programs, incentives, and metrics) that enable cross-enterprise cooperation and ensure the initiative executes on desired business results;
- Recognize that top-down efforts are necessary but insufficient. Bottom-up change is also required to provide employees the time, motivation, and know-how to modify the way they work. Adequate training is a good start, but creative ways are also needed to give employees time and space to collaborate and adapt their day-to-day responsibilities to operationalize the change enabled by the technology.

As such, digital leaders must be capable of *exploring* new opportunities and *exploiting* existing competencies at the same time, a unique trait management scholars have defined as leadership "ambidexterity" (O'Reilly & Tushman, 2013) to highlight the paradoxical nature of this leadership challenge. In the context of digital leadership, all digital leaders must be ambidextrous; however, not all ambidextrous leaders are digital. Other organizational leaders may engage in the combination of exploitation and exploration activities, but this chapter focuses on digital leaders. As such, inherent in digital leadership, per Table 2, is a core set of technology-specific ambidextrous leadership skills that make it unique.

1. Evolution of IT Leadership

Informing the debate about whether notable changes in response to technological advancements have changed leadership qualities, styles, and approaches also includes the question of whether digital leaders are the same or different from other IT leaders. Again, these two types of leaders are closely related as both have responsibilities related to digital transformation; however, there are key differences in focus and scope. The distinct nature of these two types of leaders is best articulated by walking through how technology-based leadership has evolved in organizations.

Table 2.   Digital leadership skills.

- Ability to lead an organization through turbulent times by anticipating markets and trends, making bold and savvy business decisions and solving tough problems while at the same time being short-term focused, detailed, and tactical to ensure the approach to doing the complex work is thoughtfully planned, coordinated across departments, cost effective, and time efficient;
- Design new ways of doing things while at the same time anticipate and mitigate potential risks associated with the use of technology, fostering responsible and effective technology adoption and utilization;
- Embrace flexible methodologies that prioritize continuous delivery and customer feedback while maintaining a disciplined approach to managing projects and work;
- Focus on responding to market needs but also managing internal capabilities such as organizational learning, shared decision-making, collaborative and supportive interactions;
- Manage the tension between embracing digital innovation to stay competitive and ensuring robust architecture and security measures to protect sensitive data and systems.

In the early days of technology use in organizations (1960–1990s), IT leaders were mid-level managers with technical expertise (e.g., programming and system administration). They played a central role in building, managing technical infrastructure, ensuring data integrity, maintaining computer systems, and overseeing computer-based business operations. During this era, it was common for IT managers to report to the finance function of the organization due to the fact that many of the computer systems being implemented supported financial operations, IT initiatives created new risks (e.g., cybersecurity and data protection), and IT projects were often costly. Financial leadership was helpful in establishing cost control, risk mitigation, and ensuring investments in IT contributed effectively to the organization's financial objectives.

In the 1990s, the rise of the internet and e-business inspired ways for technology to become integral to a wider range of business operations. As technology became more strategic, it was during this era that IT leaders were invited to join the C-suite (e.g., CIO and CTO) to inform the development of technology strategy and align technology investments and objectives to achieve overall business goals. There was also a significant change to the roles and responsibilities of the IT manager that required them to acquire business expertise to translate business needs into technology solutions, manage IT budgets, and ensure that technology investments contributed to organizational success.

In the 2000s, the proliferation of the internet resulted in the globalization of business operations and the role of technology expanded once again to include the management of global teams, navigation of cultural differences, and oversight of outsourcing relationships including vendor management and contract negotiations. IT leaders took on the strategic responsibility for determining which IT functions should be outsourced and which should be retained in-house, managing adherence to relevant organizational and industry regulations and standards, as well as mitigating issues related to security and privacy. It was during this era (2003) that the *Harvard Business Review* published the infamous article by Nicholas Carr entitled "IT Doesn't Matter" that compared the evolution of IT in business to earlier technologies like railroads and electric power. Carr labeled IT as an "infrastructural technology" and argued that once an organization established its technology infrastructure, IT becomes a commodity input and no longer requires strategic leadership.

By the 2010s, senior leadership teams started to embrace the notion that IT infrastructure was indeed being commodified. As IT became more powerful, standardized, and affordable, companies such as Amazon, Facebook, and Google monetized the commoditization of infrastructure technology to develop products and services that allowed organizations to share information as well as rent and subscribe to infrastructure resources available "in the cloud". Coined as the era that democratized IT, it was during this decade when non-technical leaders became empowered to leverage technology for their own specific needs. User-friendly tools, social media, mobility, analytics, and cloud computing amplified by a growing recognition that technology is integral to various business functions resulted in greater autonomy of departments outside of IT to create their own technology-infused strategies and lead development initiatives. This trend became so pervasive that a new practice called "Shadow IT" emerged and was encouraged by departmental leaders when official IT systems were perceived to be too slow, restrictive, or unable to meet specific requirements. Within the IT department, the exact same practice took on a different name "Rogue IT" to signal that bypassing IT processes to enhance productivity created issues related to data security, compliance, and lack of integration for the IT department. As a result, this lack of alignment resulted in increased strain on the business–IT relationship in many organizations.

Now, before moving on to the next era, it is important to pause for a moment to reflect on the earlier discussion about digital leaders and their playbook for success. Recall that digital leaders require heightened levels of courage and tenacity to explore new opportunities in ways that are often perceived to threaten the current status quo. Using the leadership ambidexterity analogy, the emerging strain on the IT–business relationship can be explained by the issue that business leaders were focused on exploration (i.e., right handed) and IT leaders were focused on exploitation (i.e., left handed) and so the tension between shadow and rogue was left to fester, as opposed to being actively embraced and managed. This is one example of what inspired the ambidextrous digital leaders to emerge as a style of leadership in the 2020s.

2. Ambidexterity and the 4th Industrial Revolution

The ambidextrous digital leader is a concept rooted in organizational ambidexterity, emphasizing the need for organizations to manage both exploration and exploitation activities simultaneously to deliver on short-term priorities as well as ensure long-term success (Tushman & O'Reilly, 1996). In the digital realm, this framework has been extended to leadership giving rise to the ambidextrous digital leader who effectively manages both the optimization of current operations and the exploration of innovative digital initiatives. Exploratory activities involve experimentation, innovation, and the pursuit of new opportunities, while exploitative activities focus on refining existing processes and optimizing efficiency. The complicated nature of this dual paradoxical approach has been described as "fixing the plane while flying it" as digital leaders develop new ways to guide their teams to optimize existing processes and technologies while actively seeking out and integrating new solutions that can drive innovation. A study by researchers He and Wong in 2020 highlights the significance of digital ambidexterity in achieving competitive advantage as organizations that can simultaneously explore new digital technologies and exploit their existing digital capabilities are better positioned to navigate the complexities of the rapidly evolving digital landscape.

One way to explain the importance of digital ambidexterity in sustaining competitive advantage is the inherent need for organizations to navigate what experts are calling the 4th industrial revolution. Building on the foundation laid by the rise of computers and automation that created a connected society in the 3rd industrial revolution (late 20th century), technologies such as the Internet of Things (IoT), artificial intelligence (AI), blockchain, 3D printing, and biotechnology are amplifying connections to a hyper-connected state and having a transformative impact on the way people live and work. A good example of this is the fusion of physical and virtual workspaces that are not only altering how tasks are performed but also challenging traditional notions of time and space in the work context. This evolution underscores the need for organizations to rethink common artifacts such as the work day and work week as well as adapt their structures and policies to accommodate a more flexible and interconnected work landscape. Key features and implications of the 4th Industrial Revolution include the following:

- *Digital transformation*: The pervasive use of digital technologies across industries leads to increased connectivity, data-driven decision-making, and automation.
- *Disruption of industries*: Existing business models are disrupted as new technologies enable innovative approaches to production, distribution, and consumption.

- *New job roles*: The rise of automation and AI introduces new job roles and demands a shift in the skills required for the workforce.
- *Global connectivity*: The Fourth Industrial Revolution facilitates global connectivity, allowing businesses to operate on a more global scale and collaborate across borders.
- *Ethical and societal implications*: Issues such as data privacy, cybersecurity, and the ethical use of emerging technologies become critical considerations.

As the Fourth Industrial Revolution unfolds, organizations and societies are faced with both opportunities and challenges. Adapting to this era requires a proactive approach to embracing technological advancements, fostering innovation, and addressing the societal implications. Scholars have conceptualized this proactive approach as requiring increased levels of speed, scope, and scale (Lee *et al.*, 2018).

As highlighted by a report from McKinsey & Company (2019), companies that prioritize *speed* — swift decision-making, rapid implementation of digital initiatives, and agile responses to market dynamics — tend to outperform their competitors. The speed of information dissemination and processing is disrupting traditional business models at an unprecedented velocity by enabling businesses to make real-time decisions and respond swiftly to market changes. The automation of routine tasks and the emergence of smart technologies have streamlined processes, reducing time-to-market for products and services. Furthermore, the interconnectedness of global markets facilitated by digital platforms has amplified the pace of competition and collaboration. As outlined by a report from Davenport and Mittal (2023), organizations that harness the transformative power of the integration of advanced technologies such as AI, IoT, and big data analytics will gain a competitive edge by operating at a pace that aligns with the dynamic demands of the digital era. The changing speed of business underscores the need for companies to embrace organizational agility and digital innovation to thrive in this rapidly evolving landscape (Schwab, 2017).

In the digital age, the *scope* of business has witnessed a profound expansion, driven by technological advancements and the widespread adoption of digital platforms that have enabled organizations to transcend geographical boundaries and engage with a global audience. The new era of hyper-connectivity is blurring boundaries between traditional industries as well as physical and digital realms. Organizations are leveraging technology to increase the scope of their business by engaging in cross-industry collaborations and extending decision-making processes to enable businesses to better serve customer needs and anticipate market trends and customer preferences. One illustrative example of the changing scope of business is the evolution of the automotive industry. Traditionally focused on manufacturing and selling cars, the industry's scope has expanded significantly to extend beyond the business of producing and selling vehicles to providers of mobility services and digital solutions, such as car-sharing and in-car entertainment services. Another example is the shift in e-commerce, facilitated by platforms like Amazon and Alibaba, that has broadened the scope of retail to allow consumers the ability to browse and purchase products from virtually anywhere in the world. Moreover, the integration of artificial intelligence and data analytics has enhanced the scope of personalized customer experiences, enabling businesses to tailor their offerings to individual preferences (Nguyen *et al.*, 2022).

Finally, the widespread adoption of technologies such as cloud computing, big data analytics, and advanced communication networks has enabled businesses to operate on a larger *scale* by facilitating the storage and analysis of vast amounts of data, supporting global connectivity, and enhancing the efficiency of operations. A study by Bonnet and Westerman (2020) emphasizes the importance of scaling digital capabilities across the entire organization, ensuring that digital transformation efforts permeate various functions and business units. The ability to scale operations seamlessly has allowed businesses to expand their reach and penetrate new markets. Platforms have emerged as powerful tools for scaling business operations and fostering ecosystems of interconnected stakeholders as they provide digital infrastructures that enable companies to connect with customers, partners, and other businesses in a seamless and scalable manner (Parker *et al.*, 2016). Notable examples include platform-based companies like Amazon, which started as an online bookstore and scaled into a vast e-commerce platform hosting third-party sellers. Similarly, social media platforms like Facebook and Twitter/X have scaled globally, connecting billions of users and businesses worldwide. By leveraging platforms, businesses can efficiently reach wider audiences, tap into diverse markets, and create network effects that contribute to exponential growth.

Management scholars have identified ambidexterity as a crucial leadership capability in the face of the accelerating pace, broadening scope, and expanding scale of business (O'Reilly & Tushman, 2013). In the context of speed, organizations need the agility to swiftly adapt to rapidly changing technological landscapes and market dynamics. Ambidexterity allows them to balance the need for quick decision-making and implementation with a long-term focus on innovation. Moreover, in managing the expanding scope of business, ambidexterity enables organizations to navigate diverse markets and industries by both refining existing processes and exploring new opportunities. When it comes to scale, ambidexterity supports the expansion of operations by ensuring a delicate equilibrium between efficiency and flexibility. Leaders adept at ambidextrous approaches can strategically leverage existing capabilities while continuously innovating to meet the demands of a larger and more interconnected market.

3. The Rise of Digital Management

Leaders facing paradoxical situations must employ novel practices to navigate and leverage the inherent tensions effectively. In addition to ambidexterity, leaders can adopt a sense-making approach when managing paradoxes. According to Lewis and Smith (2014), sense-making involves actively interpreting and understanding the complexities of a paradoxical situation. Leaders who engage in sense-making collaborate with their teams to explore the underlying tensions, encourage open dialog, and foster a shared understanding of the paradox. Leaders can also employ a transformational leadership style to manage paradoxes by promoting adaptability and inspiring organizational change. Bass and Riggio (2006) argue that transformational leaders motivate and empower their teams to embrace change, emphasizing a collective vision that transcends apparent contradictions. By fostering a culture of continuous learning and adaptation, transformational leaders enable organizations to navigate paradoxes by viewing them as opportunities for growth and evolution rather than as insurmountable challenges. This approach encourages agility and resilience, allowing organizations to thrive in dynamic and complex environments.

Digital transformation scholars have explored these different practices for managing paradoxes and positioned their insights within a contemporary business competency defined as *digital management*. Digital management is closely linked to digital strategy where organizations align their business objectives with digital capabilities to create value; however,

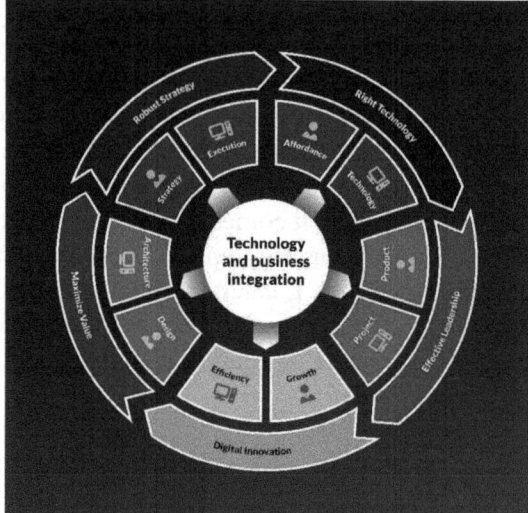

As such, the role of digital management extends to various aspects of traditional organizational functioning, including strategy, technology, leadership, innovation, and value generation. By combining the concept of digital management with the paradoxical demands of speed, scope, and scale, a framework was developed to further define the core set of digital leadership skills introduced at the beginning of this chapter.

Figure 1.   Framework for digital management.

digital management also embraces the more tactical activities that ensure digital technologies are effectively used to enhance organizational performance, innovation, and competitiveness. When organizations develop a digital management competency, they not only aspire to enhanced customer experiences and streamlined operations but they also actualize opportunities to deliver results that help the organization gain a competitive edge in the ever-evolving digital landscape. As such, digital management requires both transactional and transformational leadership styles. Westerman *et al.* (2014) define successful digital management as leading transactional behaviors to design and implement digital solution as well as transformational leadership to foster a digital mindset throughout the organization to cultivate a culture of innovation, agility, and continuous learning.

Figure 1 depicts a framework for digital management, with various key components as highlighted in the following:

Robust strategy — Strategy-execution paradox: There are competing demands between top-down, senior leaders who provide the forward-looking vision and foresight for what is possible and bottom-up insights from mid-level managers who are closer to the existing capabilities and legacy technologies that already exist. The debate between top-down and bottom-up approaches in digital leadership revolves around the question of how decisions and innovations are initiated and implemented within an organization. Organizations that exclusively adopt a top-down approach risk becoming rigid and slow to adapt in the rapidly changing digital landscape. On the other hand, a purely bottom-up approach may result in fragmented initiatives without a coherent overarching strategy. Within this paradox is also the need to balance centralized control and decentralized autonomy. In the digital age, companies leverage various technologies such as cloud computing and collaborative platforms, enabling decentralized decision-making and fostering agility. However, this decentralization must be balanced with a certain level of central control to maintain coherence in organizational strategies and ensure compliance with regulatory frameworks. As noted by Bughin *et al.* (2018), finding the right equilibrium between decentralization and centralization is crucial for increasing speed, scope, and scale. A study by Raisch and Birkinshaw (2008) highlights the importance of integrating top-down and bottom-up elements to foster a culture of innovation within organizations, particularly in digital contexts. This integration allows organizations to benefit from the strategic vision provided by top management while tapping into the creativity and expertise of employees on the ground.

Right technology — Technology-affordance paradox: The technology affordance paradox refers to the situation where a technology designed to deliver on a set of pre-defined intentions yields unexpected outcomes or unintended consequences when put into use. It arises from the inherent dual nature of technology affordances — both enabling and constraining (Leonardi, 2011). The affordances of a technology influence how it is adopted, adapted, and integrated into daily practices and the paradox becomes apparent when users, despite having access to certain functionalities or capabilities, experience unexpected challenges, negative consequences, or misuse of the technology. Take social media as an example, while platforms such as Facebook and Instagram are designed to connect people and facilitate communication, they have been associated with issues, such as misinformation, cyberbullying, and the amplification of echo chambers. Understanding and managing the technology affordance paradox is crucial for designers, developers, and organizations to anticipate and mitigate potential risks associated with the use of technology, fostering responsible and effective technology adoption and utilization.

Effective leadership — Project-product paradox: The project-product paradox is a concept that underscores the tension between managing projects in the short-term and realizing business value from high-quality products in the long-term. Projects are temporary endeavors with specific goals, timelines, and resources, while products are the outcomes of those projects, intended for long-term use and value creation. The paradox arises as organizations must balance the focus on completing projects on time and within budget with the imperative of delivering products that meet or exceed customer expectations in terms of functionality, quality, and adaptability. Striking the right equilibrium between project management and product development is essential for ensuring sustained success in the dynamic business landscape. The resolution of the project-product paradox involves integrating project management practices with product-oriented thinking. Effective project managers recognize the need to go beyond project completion metrics and focus on the long-term value derived from the delivered product. Similarly, product managers and developers need to understand the project constraints and collaborate closely with project teams to ensure that product development aligns with project goals (Highsmith, 2009). Successfully navigating this paradox requires organizations to embrace flexible methodologies that prioritize continuous delivery and customer feedback while maintaining a disciplined approach to project management principles. By doing so, organizations can foster an environment that maximizes both project efficiency and product excellence.

Digital innovation — Growth-efficiency paradox: There are competing demands between adapting to changing market and environmental conditions to promote growth and stabilizing the internal organization to drive efficiency. Creating an internal environment that values learning and efficiency can aid an organization in building "capacity for adaption in a dynamic environment by building a workforce with broad collective knowledge" (Miller & Martignoni, 2016, p. 69). In digital management, demands from the outside-in can be driven by senior leaders who are highlighting changes in market trends as well as digital innovation teams that apply user-centric, design thinking practices to empathize with customer needs. As such, outside-in can shape organizational strategies as well as digital initiatives (Day, 2011). In contrast, inside-out management traditionally involves an internal focus, where organizations prioritize their existing capabilities, processes, and technologies when making strategic decisions (Prahalad & Hamel, 1990). Similarly, inside-out demands span across levels of leadership. Senior leaders focused on efficiency and cost reduction will place priority on ensuring the optimization of internal processes and capabilities, and employees in the IT department are incented to amplify existing capabilities and mitigate risk. Research supports the idea that combining both inside-out and outside-in perspectives is crucial for effective digital management. Teece (2014) argues that a dynamic capability approach, which involves a blend of internal and external orientations, is necessary for organizations to succeed in the rapidly changing digital environment.

Maximizing value — Design-architecture paradox: The design-architecture paradox highlights the need to balance stability and innovation in the digital landscape. Design is often characterized by "ill-structured" problems, where there is no single correct solution. In contrast, architecture provides a structured framework to guide decision-making. Resolving this tension involves aligning the detailed design decisions with the broader architectural vision, ensuring that user experience considerations do not compromise the integrity of the overall system architecture. The tension also underscores the need for iterative feedback loops between architects and designers, allowing for continuous refinement and adaptation as digital projects progress. The tension arises as organizations seek to harmonize the constraints of architectural guidelines with the desire for innovative, aesthetically pleasing, and user-centered digital designs. As highlighted by Chui *et al.* (2016), the rapid adoption of digital technologies brings about new opportunities for innovation but also introduces unprecedented cybersecurity challenges. Organizations must manage the tension between embracing digital innovation to stay competitive and ensuring robust security measures to protect sensitive data and systems. While design-driven practices may lead to rapid innovation and responsiveness to user needs, it introduces concerns related to security, compliance, and overall IT governance within the organization (Kruse, 2014). Research suggests that this paradox is prevalent in the digital era because employees have easy access to a variety of no-code, low-code tools that are being used outside the IT department's purview (Cisco, 2016). However, despite potential security and governance risks, design-driven practices are improving the agility and innovativeness within organizations. It highlights the need for IT departments to strike a balance between enabling innovation and maintaining control over the technology environment.

At the core of managing these paradoxical tensions is the multifaceted challenge of technology-business integration. To achieve this, a key requirement of digital management is to overcome organizational silos and foster collaboration between IT and non-IT departments. Bridging this gap necessitates cultural shifts, emphasizing the importance of cross-functional teams, shared goals, and mutual understanding between IT professionals and business leaders. Additionally, the rapid pace of technological change poses a considerable challenge for organizations seeking to integrate technology effectively into their business strategies. Leaders must contend with the challenge of managing technology portfolios, selecting the right innovations, and ensuring that these align with evolving business needs. The dynamic nature of technology necessitates a flexible and agile approach to business integration that is achieved by managing the aforementioned paradoxes.

4. IT Leadership versus Digital Leadership

In 2010, Kaplan and Haenlein (2010) claimed digital management pushes beyond traditional IT management practices by leveraging digital technologies, data-driven insights, automation, and advanced analytics to make informed decisions and optimize operations. However, the notion of digital leadership is relatively new and evolving to describe the critical role of top leaders of an organization in creating an environment that enables stability while nurturing and encouraging the ability to change and adapt. To date, there is no universal theory that informs the topic. That being said there are several frameworks that offer insights into the principles and practices of digital leadership. Let's explore a few notable ones, as shown in the following:

- Gartner's Digital Leadership Model outlines the competencies required for effective digital leadership. The model includes aspects, such as digital business acumen, stakeholder alignment, organizational culture, and technology governance. It provides a roadmap for leaders seeking to navigate digital transformation successfully by defining five leadership styles digital leaders can adopt depending on their situation and desired outcomes: commanders, catalysts, coaches, collaborators, and consultants.
- Deloitte's Digital Leadership Model positions digital leadership as an application of traditional leadership fundamentals tailored to deal with

the volatility, uncertainty, change, and ambiguity that is pervasive in the digital age. As such, their model identifies a set of eight (8) traditional leadership capabilities that need to be deployed in a digital context and four (4) unique skills or "potentials" that have become more critical due to the complexity and pace of the digital revolution: change potential, intellectual potential, people potential, and motivational potential.

- The European Commission developed the Digital Leadership Framework (DLF) to provide a comprehensive model for digital leadership in the public sector. It focuses on seven key areas: vision, engagement, culture, capacity, governance, infrastructure, and services. The framework aims to help public sector organizations harness the potential of digital technologies to deliver better services and achieve strategic objectives.
- The 4Ps of Digital Leadership framework were inspired by Holonomics in 2015 to encourage business leaders to embrace a more systemic perspective when thinking about marketing and scaling new products and services. The traditional 4Ps (product, price, place, and promotion) need to be supported by the new 4Ps (purpose, people, platforms, and planet) in order to deliver elevated forms of value to customers in a manner that will scale and create value financially as well as benefit people and planet.

Now that we have explored ambidexterity and a variety of paradoxes related to digital management, it seems plausible that digital leaders are unique in their pursuit of paradoxical situations. By leveraging practices such as agile, digital capabilities, sense-making, and transformational leadership, they can help effectively lead their organizations in recognizing the value of innovation while implementing strategies to manage associated risks effectively (Weber *et al.*, 2022). As such, the final question we need to address before wrapping up this chapter is whether digital leaders are indeed unique from IT leaders.

To answer this question, we draw a parallel between three types of organizational leaders — traditional, innovation, and IT:

- A traditional leader is an organizational leader (e.g., CFO and COO) who establishes the strategy, structures, processes, incentives, etc. within the business environment. This type of leader often values stability, order, and predictability, seeking to maintain a sense of control over the organizational operations.

- An innovation leader plays a pivotal role in driving organizational success by fostering a culture of creativity, continuous improvement, and forward-thinking strategies. As highlighted by Dyer *et al.* (2019), an effective innovation leader is not only adept at generating novel ideas but also skilled at creating an environment where employees are encouraged to experiment, take risks, and challenge the *status quo*.
- An IT leader is characterized by a combination of technical expertise, strategic vision, and effective management skills. Such leaders play a critical role in aligning information technology with overall business objectives.

Table 3 compares these types of leaders across three perspectives (macro, technical, and micro) to draw out the similarities and differences and inform whether digital leadership is in fact unique from the traditional IT leader. Each perspective is described in detail and insights are drawn to highlight some interesting results.

At the macro level, leadership involves a comprehensive and strategic approach that goes beyond individual or team-focused initiatives to focus on navigating and shaping the overarching goals, structures, and culture of an entire enterprise. Macro leaders are responsible for setting the overall direction of an organization, aligning its mission with larger

Table 3.   Traditional versus digital leadership.

| | | Digital Leadership | |
	Traditional Leadership	Digital Innovation Leadership	IT Leadership
Macro	Playing Not to Lose	Playing to Win	Playing Not to Lose
	Strategically Rigid	Strategically Fluid	Strategically Rigid
	Alliances and Partnerships	Ecosystems	Alliances & Partnerships
Technology	Technology as a Function	Technology at the Core	Technology as a Function
	Technology Informed	Technology Literate	Technology Literate
	Technology as a Tool	Technology as a Capability	Technology as a Tool
Micro	Strategy Delegation	Strategy Execution	Strategy Delegation
	Hierarchical (Vertical)	Networks (Horizontal)	Hierarchical (Vertical)
	Consultants	Researchers	Consultants

industry trends and societal changes. From this perspective, traditional leadership in mid-to-large size organizations have a "play not to lose" mindset that focuses on risk aversion and maintaining the *status quo* rather compared to innovation leaders that "play to win" by embracing risk and pursuing innovation and growth. Traditional leaders follow a rigid, systematic, and comprehensive strategic planning process compared to innovation leaders who approach strategy in a more "fluid" way to be adaptable, flexible, and responsive to changes in the external environment. Finally, traditional leaders enable collaboration and resource sharing through formal alliances and partnerships compared to innovation leaders who participate in ecosystems as a more dynamic form of collaboration. Now, while some may have anticipated the difference between traditional leaders and innovation leaders at the macro-level, few IT professionals would agree that IT leaders are inherently risk-averse and rigid. While it's true that the nature of IT leadership involves managing and mitigating risks, particularly in areas like cybersecurity and data integrity, generalizations about the risk aversion or rigidity of IT leaders oversimplify the diversity within this professional domain. In contemporary business environments, IT leaders increasingly recognize the importance of embracing innovation and agility to stay competitive and many IT leaders are actively involved in driving digital transformation initiatives, where they collaborate with other business units to leverage technology for strategic advantages. As such, we argue when an IT leader embraces innovation and agility on top of their traditional IT leadership responsibilities, they will need to manage a number of paradoxical tensions in their pursuit. As such, they will need to mature beyond IT leadership to digital leadership.

The micro-level perspective is similar in that traditional leaders delegate the strategy down their hierarchical department whereas innovation leaders tend to be more hands-on in executing the tactical requirements of the strategy and collaborate with individuals across a broader, horizontal network. Traditional leaders tend to be more consultants or experts compared to innovation leaders who are driven by curiosity, inquiry, and research. While it is also true that IT leadership tends to be more expert-driven, delegation of responsibility down the IT department, many IT leaders also recognize the need to be more tactical and research-oriented as well as work beyond the boundaries of the IT organization. As such, when IT leaders embrace tactics, networks, and research, they mature beyond IT leadership to digital leadership.

Finally, the technology perspective calls attention to the integration of IT and business as a strategic imperative. As illustrated, technology literacy differentiates digital innovation and technology leaders from traditional leaders. However, digital innovation leaders are unique in that they place technology at the core of organizational strategy to drive innovation, competitiveness, and operational excellence (Westerman *et al.*, 2014) compared to traditional leaders who define IT as a support function. Similarly, traditional leaders tend to think about technology as a tool that is used to perform particular functions or tasks compared to digital innovation leaders who think about technology as a capability that builds competencies and enhances organizational processes. As IT is indeed a set of tools managed by a business function, when technology leaders embrace paradoxical situations to become more innovative, they evolve toward digital leadership.

5. Digital Leadership in Practice

The intent of this chapter was to inform the debate about whether notable changes in response to technological advancements have changed leadership styles and approaches. By highlighting the role of ambidexterity, unique aspects of digital leadership emerged. However, it is also important to note maturing to the point of leadership ambidexterity is difficult due to the need to reconcile contradictory demands, shift organizational culture, balance resource allocations, design effective structures, and foster a continuous learning environment. As successfully navigating the challenges is complex, the best place to start is to work toward mastering the following five digital leadership practices:

1. **Situational leadership:** Assess the unique needs of teams and the dynamic nature of the technological environment and shift your leadership styles based on the situational demands — whether emphasizing innovation and adaptability during phases of exploration or focusing on efficiency and optimization during periods of exploitation. This dynamic approach acknowledges that a one-size-fits-all leadership strategy is inadequate in the fast-paced and ever-changing digital realm.
2. **Squads:** Manage teams as a self-contained squad of individuals with diverse skills and expertise who have autonomy to make independent

decisions and take ownership of tasks but work together toward common objectives. This dynamic and flexible approach not only enhances efficiency but also cultivates a culture of continuous improvement, ensuring teams are equipped to navigate the complexities of the ever-evolving digital landscape.

3. **Proof beyond promise:** This practice challenges leaders to push beyond goal setting and aspiration to demand tangible proof of measurable achievements and results. By adhering to this ethos, businesses not only build trust with stakeholders but also establish a reputation for reliability and accountability, ensuring that their commitments are backed by tangible evidence of success. Experimentation is an example of proof beyond promise and when effective, leaders encourage employees to take calculated risks, learn from failures, and discover innovative solutions.

4. **Orchestration:** A micro-level practice that optimizes the interplay between expert-driven vertical delegation and inquiry-driven, horizontal tactical execution to leverage existing strengths and core competencies and foster innovation and change at the same time (Brohman *et al.*, 2019). Orchestration involves a skillful arrangement static capabilities to provide stability and reliability and dynamic capabilities that inject adaptability and agility. Static capabilities leverage traditional structure (e.g., decision rights and policies) and dynamic capabilities are agile and responsive to immediate demands and embrace change. Awareness is a modern capability that is essential for managing the interplay and is enabled by systematic analysis of data that allows leaders to cultivate a deeper understanding of what is really going.

5. **Agile management:** Characterized by iterative and flexible approaches to project execution, agile management emphasizes collaboration, customer feedback, and a willingness to adapt plans as circumstances evolve. Agile methodologies provide a structured framework for managing innovation and operational efficiency concurrently.

To summarize, it is important to highlight one final paradox that truly differentiates digital leadership practice from traditional IT leadership. The *humility-expert paradox* encapsulates the challenge of balancing leadership qualities associated with humility, such as openness to feedback and a collaborative mindset, with the need for expertise and authoritative decision-making in the rapidly evolving digital landscape.

Leaders who exhibit humility are more likely to foster a collaborative environment, empower their team members, and promote a culture of experimentation, critical elements in digital transformation initiatives. However, as many organizations lack technology literacy, it is also important that digital leaders showcase domain expertise, provide a clear vision, make informed decisions, and guide their teams through the intricacies of digital challenges. In conclusion, the interplay between humility and expertise is a delicate dance that, when harmonized, fosters environments where knowledge is shared, collaboration thrives, and the collective strengths of the individuals are maximized.

References

Bonnet, D. & Westerman, G. (2020). The new elements of digital transformation. *MIT Sloan Management Review*, *62*(2), 82–89.

Brohman, M. K., Brown, E., & McSheffrey, J. (2019). *Shift: A New Mindset for Sustainable Execution*. University of Toronto Press, Toronto, ON, Canada.

Bughin, J., Catlin, T., Hirt, M., & Willmott, P. (2018). Why digital strategies fail. *McKinsey Quarterly*, *1*, 61–75.

Carr, N. (2003). IT doesn't matter. *Harvard Business Review*, *81*(5), 41–49.

Chui, M., Manyika, J., & Miremadi, M. (2016). Where machines could replace humans-and where they can't (yet). *McKinsey Quarterly*.

Davenport, T. H. & Mittal, N. (2023). How companies can prepare for the coming "AI-first" world. *Strategy & Leadership*, *51*(1), 26–30.

Day, G. S. (2011). Closing the marketing capabilities gap. *Journal of Marketing*, *75*(4), 183–195.

Dyer, J., Gregersen, H., & Christensen, C. M. (2019). *The Innovator's DNA, Updated, with a New Preface: Mastering the Five Skills of Disruptive Innovators*. Harvard Business Press.

Highsmith, J. (2009). *Agile Project Management: Creating Innovative Products*. Pearson Education.

Kane, G. C., Phillips, A. N., Copulsky, J., & Andrus, G. (2019). How digital leadership is (n't) different. *MIT Sloan Management Review*, *60*(3), 34–39.

Kaplan, A. M. & Haenlein, M. (2010). Users of the world, unite! The challenges and opportunities of social media. *Business Horizons*, *53*(1), 59–68.

Kirkland, R. (2014). Artificial intelligence meets the C-suite. *McKinsey Quarterly*. Available: http://www.mckinsey.com/insights/strategy/artificial_intelligence_meets_the_c-suite.

Lee, M., Yun, J. H. J., Pyka, A., Won, D. K., Kodama, F., Schiuma, G., Park, H. S. *et al.* (2018). How to respond to the fourth industrial revolution, or the second information technology revolution? Dynamic new combinations between technology, market, and society through open innovation. *Journal of Open Innovation: Technology, Market, and Complexity*, *4*(3), 21.

Leonardi, P. M. (2011). When flexible routines meet flexible technologies: Affordance, constraint, and the imbrication of human and material agencies. *MIS Quarterly*, *35*(1), 147–167.

Miller, K. D. & Martignoni, D. (2016). Organizational learning with forgetting: Reconsidering the exploration–exploitation tradeoff. *Strategic Organization*, *14*(1), 53–72.

Nguyen, T. M., Quach, S., & Thaichon, P. (2022). The effect of AI quality on customer experience and brand relationship. *Journal of Consumer Behaviour*, *21*(3), 481–493.

O'Reilly III, C. A. & Tushman, M. L. (2013). Organizational ambidexterity: Past, present, and future. *Academy of Management Perspectives*, *27*(4), 324–338.

Parker, G. G., Van Alstyne, M. W., & Choudary, S. P. (2016). *Platform Revolution: How Networked Markets Are Transforming the Economy and How to Make Them Work for You*. WW Norton & Company.

Raisch, S. & Birkinshaw, J. (2008). Organizational ambidexterity: Antecedents, outcomes, and moderators. *Journal of Management*, *34*(3), 375–409.

Schwab, K. (2017). *The Fourth Industrial Revolution*. Currency.

Teece, D. J. (2014). The foundations of enterprise performance: Dynamic and ordinary capabilities in an (economic) theory of firms. *Academy of Management Perspectives*, *28*(4), 328–352.

Tushman, M. L. & O'Reilly III, C. A. (1996). Ambidextrous organizations: Managing evolutionary and revolutionary change. *California Management Review*, *38*(4), 8–29.

Weber, E., Krehl, E. H., & Büttgen, M. (2022). The digital transformation leadership framework: Conceptual and empirical insights into leadership roles in technology-driven business environments. *Journal of Leadership Studies*, *16*(1), 6–22.

Westerman, G., Bonnet, D., & McAfee, A. (2014). *Leading Digital: Turning Technology into Business Transformation*. Harvard Business Press.

Wimelius, H., Mathiassen, L., Holmström, J., & Keil, M. (2021). A paradoxical perspective on technology renewal in digital transformation. *Information Systems Journal*, *31*(1), 198–225.

Chapter 11

Driving Digital Transformation Through Entrepreneurial Resilience

Arman Sadreddin[†] and Suchit Ahuja[*,‡]

John Molson School of Business, Concordia University
Montreal, Quebec, Canada

[†]*arman.sadreddin@concordia.ca*

[‡]*suchit.ahuja@concordia.ca*

1. Introduction

Digital transformation of business and society has gained prominence since the COVID-19 crisis. "The COVID-19 crisis is rapidly reshaping the "what" and "how" of digital transformation agendas — for the better" (Swift, 2020).[1] Building a sustainable and inclusive world involves building resilient businesses and communities, especially for post-pandemic recovery (Schwab & Sternfels, 2022). Entrepreneurship has traditionally been a driver for innovation and growth. Entrepreneurship initiatives suffered a slowdown during the pandemic, just like most other things. The pandemic has highlighted the need for resilience in entrepreneurship and the importance of developing resilience capabilities for businesses. Resilience can foster sustainable growth initiatives, and entrepreneurs

---

[*]Corresponding author.
[1]https://enterprisersproject.com/article/2020/5/digital-transformation-positive-changes.

may be able to navigate future adverse events (Darkow, 2019). Resilience is "the ability to absorb disturbances, to be changed, and then to re-organize and still have the same identity" (Walker *et al.*, 2004). Resilience includes the ability to learn from a crisis or an adverse situation, build appropriate response mechanisms, and adapt to external shocks (Cumming *et al.*, 2005). In other words, this view defines resilience as an ability to absorb and adapt to challenges. In another research stream, resilience has been described as "the return or recovery time of a social–ecological system determined by (1) that system's capacity for renewal in a dynamic environment and (2) people's ability to learn and change (which, in turn, is partially determined by the institutional context for knowledge sharing, learning, and management, and partially by the social capital among people)" (Aldunce *et al.*, 2014). In other words, this view defines resilience as an ability to absorb and transform. The entrepreneurship literature has also explored resilience from the perspective of "resilient mindset of entrepreneurs" (Duchek, 2018) and how individual resilience leads to survival and success of firms (Branicki *et al.*, 2018). This study looks into different conceptualizations of resilience in entrepreneurial firms.

Resilience research that explores organizational, intra-organizational, and extra-organizational factors focuses on two broad categories of crises that require resilience: (1) sudden or catastrophic adversity and (2) ongoing adversity (Williams *et al.*, 2017). While past research on resilience in entrepreneurship is focused heavily on sudden or ongoing adversity approaches, there is limited investigation of resilience approaches that stem from ongoing and sudden adversity (Spector, 2019). Furthermore, there is a lack of empirical studies on how adversity allows entrepreneurs to reimagine their businesses and pivot toward newer business models, learning from past experiences in dealing with ongoing adversity (Faik *et al.*, 2020).

Recent research points to new theoretical and practice-based advances in resilience due to its intersections with entrepreneurship research (Korber & McNaughton, 2017; Williams *et al.*, 2017). It also shifts focus to higher levels of analysis than the individual entrepreneur, such as organizations, communities, and governments (Korber & McNaughton, 2017; Nambisan *et al.*, 2019). Resilience research calls for integrating perspectives from different disciplines and exploring how entrepreneurs, SMEs, and communities leverage digital tools, platforms, and business models (Korber & McNaughton, 2017; Williams *et al.*, 2017). This is particularly important as entrepreneurs, businesses, governments, and communities seek to emerge from a global pandemic by relying on digital technologies (Ahuja *et al.*, 2021; Rai, 2020; Watson & Chandra Kruse, 2020). While large organizations have the resources to invest in digital tools and technologies, micro-enterprises and SMEs have not fully leveraged digital innovation to build their entrepreneurial resilience capabilities (Munoz, 2010; Qureshi, 2020). However, the pandemic has allowed them to digitalize their business and operations. Nonetheless, there is a lack of empirical evidence that provides an in-depth explanation of how firms build entrepreneurial resilience when faced with sudden adversity, such as a pandemic, while leveraging different resources and capabilities gained due to ongoing adversity in their day-to-day activities.

This chapter answers the following research question: *How do small firms build entrepreneurial resilience for digital transformation when encountering ongoing and sudden adversity?* We present two case studies with small firms that were facing ongoing challenges but encountered severe challenges during the pandemic. These firms built entrepreneurial resilience capabilities through adaptation and transformation by leveraging digital technologies, benefiting from accumulated environmental resources, and tapping into their existing knowledge and resources, improving their value propositions.

Using a grounded theory approach, we extend the theoretical understanding of entrepreneurial resilience by developing resilience capabilities during ongoing and sudden adversity. With this, we lay a foundation for future research in this area. Next, we present the relevant literature, research design, findings, and discussions around these findings.

2. Literature Review

2.1. *Ongoing and Sudden Adversity*

The stream of resilience research that explores organizational, intra-organizational, and extra-organizational factors focuses on two broad categories of crises that require resilience: (1) sudden adversity and (2) ongoing adversity (Williams *et al.*, 2017). Literature on the "sudden adversity" category takes an event-oriented approach and perceives crises as random events that disrupt the normal lifecycle of the organization or community. This can include studies exploring sudden adverse events, such as oil spills (Colten *et al.*, 2015), floods (Kuang & Liao, 2020), earthquakes (Sakurai *et al.*, 2014), and wars/conflicts (Imperiale & Vanclay, 2016).

These are different from everyday challenges and are typically non-routine contingent events, isolated in space and time, have a discernable source or cause, and have a high impact (Williams *et al.*, 2017). On the other hand, the literature on "ongoing adversity" takes a process-oriented view of crises, which is supported by much of the foundational literature in crisis management. For example, cities with a long history of poverty, inappropriate land use patterns, and environmental problems experience a slow, ongoing crisis (Ultramari & Rezende, 2007). This approach focuses on adversity as a temporal event that unfolds in different stages and enables the organization to develop responses and adapt to changing environmental stimuli. While past research on resilience in entrepreneurship is focused heavily on either sudden or ongoing adversity approaches, there is limited investigation of approaches that integrate both (Spector, 2019) to examine how adversity provides the opportunity for entrepreneurs to reimagine their business and pivot toward newer business models.

2.2. *Entrepreneurial Resilience*

The entrepreneur is the central force driving the critical decisions regarding mechanisms of building resilience, especially in the context of SMEs. Past research shows that the individual leader contributes to organizational resilience, yielding higher payoffs in resource-constrained contexts and times of crisis (Korber & McNaughton, 2018). Therefore, it is important to consider the entrepreneurial mindset, entrepreneurial abilities, and entrepreneurial behavior of firm founders and employees (Baker & Nelson, 2005; Maritz *et al.*, 2020). The characteristics of the environment are also important considerations because these characteristics fuel the "entrepreneurial spirit" (Acs *et al.*, 2017). Firms facing ongoing adversity often operate in environments that are resource-constrained and develop creative and innovative ways to address these resource constraints, such as bricolage, jugaad, and improvisation (Baker & Nelson, 2005; George *et al.*, 2019; Prabhu, 2017). There are several examples of how firms creatively respond to constraints involving business functions, technology availability, social challenges, or poor infrastructure (George *et al.*, 2016; Maritz *et al.*, 2020).

Both positive and negative outcomes result from resilience (Korber & McNaughton, 2018; Williams *et al.*, 2017). Although resilience likely enhances perseverance, adaptability, and durability during challenging events, it may also result in resistance to change, failure to learn and adapt, and an inability to pivot or transform (Williams *et al.*, 2017). Depending on the context of the organization, negative outcomes may be unavoidable if absorbing the effects of adverse events is short term rather than long term. Although well-developed organizational structures, resources, technologies, business models, and governance mechanisms may assist during immediate disruption, they make a firm less flexible and innovative in the face of a changing environment that sometimes demands "a new normal" (McKinsey, 2020). It is essential to scan the environment for such long-term trends regularly.

2.3. *The Role of Digital Technology*

During the current era in the aftermath of a global pandemic, there is a renewed focus on how small and medium-sized enterprises (SMEs) that operate in environments where ongoing adversity is an "everyday challenge" are coping with this sudden event (Shepherd & Williams, 2020; Spector, 2019). SMEs may need to leverage their routinized resilience activities to address ongoing adversity while developing new resilience capabilities to address the sudden adversity for "survival and adaptation" (Korber & McNaughton, 2018; Spector, 2019). The opportunity exists to investigate the role of digital technologies in developing these capabilities (Watson & Chandra Kruse, 2020). Digital technologies play an important role in the age of the pandemic (Rai, 2020) due to their unique characteristics (Kallinikos *et al.*, 2013) and the importance of social and institutional contexts in the digitalization process (Chan *et al.*, 2019; Tilson *et al.*, 2010). Similarly, recent research has shown how firms can leverage digital technologies, innovations, and business models to survive in adverse operating conditions (Ahuja *et al.*, 2022; Chan *et al.*, 2020). According to the World Economic Forum (2020), entrepreneurs with the ability to leverage digital tools are more likely to survive ongoing crises as the pandemic has accelerated the process of digital transformation across almost all sectors. Digital tools provide entrepreneurs the potential to boost social mobility and facilitate shared value creation, expediting the post-pandemic recovery (Wong, 2020). In information systems, crisis management, as well as entrepreneurship literature, there has been a vibrant discussion on how digital technologies that are affordable, decentralized, and democratized can be used to provide information and critical services during times of adversity (Ahuja *et al.*, 2021; Chan *et al.*, 2019; Leidner *et al.*, 2009; Nambisan *et al.*, 2019). This study also highlights the role of emerging digital technologies as well as other affordable and accessible "readily available" technologies (Sadreddin & Chan, 2023).

Although the extant literature provides these theoretical perspectives, we lack a comprehensive framework to capture the development of entrepreneurial resilience capabilities by leveraging digital technologies considering both ongoing and sudden adversity. This paper attempts to build such a framework using case studies and a grounded theory approach, resulting in a research framework that can serve as a foundation for future studies. Next, we discuss our research design.

3. Research Design

We used the qualitative multiple case study method to research how small businesses facing ongoing and sudden adversity over time build resilience capabilities. This method provided us with in-depth insights into the behavioral and contextual factors that enable the process of resilience capability development in entrepreneurial firms. Furthermore, as the social and cultural context is essential to answer the research question of this study, the qualitative method is recommended (Myers, 2019). Also, one reason to choose qualitative research is to understand different viewpoints on the same phenomenon and analyze people's behavior within a particular context to find out what is happening and why it is happening (Patton, 2014). Therefore, since each entrepreneur has a different perspective on the pandemic and may react differently, qualitative research can provide the best tools to investigate small firms' resilience capability development process.

3.1. *Data Collection*

The data presented here is part of a more extensive study where new small business ventures were interviewed to understand how they leverage digital technologies for innovation and survival. In this study, we followed four criteria for selecting our two cases: (1) We chose the firms that required physical interactions with their clients and end users to operate their business. We believe these firms were impacted the most, and insights from their experiences can help other firms when faced with a crisis.

(2) We selected cases that were leveraging digital technologies extensively in their product or service (i.e., market offerings) or were utilizing them as an external enabler to facilitate their daily business operations (von Briel, Davidsson, *et al.*, 2018; von Briel, Recker, *et al.*, 2018). (3) We selected new ventures since they operate under extreme uncertainty, face many ongoing challenges and opportunities in their business operations, and have limited resources to respond to their opportunities and challenges (Packard *et al.*, 2017; Seidel *et al.*, 2016). (4) We identified firms operating in different environments with different levels of support provided by local agencies (e.g., government) to capture contextual factors that may facilitate or inhibit firms' capabilities when facing a crisis such as a pandemic.

In this study, we present two illustrative cases using multiple data sources, such as semi-structured interviews with founders/co-founders who had an in-depth understanding of the technical and managerial challenges the firms faced during their lifetime and publicly available data on the web. The interview guideline required informants to provide background information on their business (e.g., core product or service, motivation to start the business, employment and financial structure of the firm), use of digital technologies in their business process, challenges and opportunities that the firm faced before and during the pandemic, organizational and technological capabilities that helped the firm address the opportunities and challenges before and during the pandemic, the role of supporting agencies, such as governments in their ecosystem to help them go through the pandemic, and measures of performance before and during the pandemic. We guaranteed the confidentiality of all collected data and allowed participants to withdraw their data at any time before publication of the findings to enhance the accuracy of our informants' statements. The interviews were conducted and recorded over Zoom and later transcribed. We developed a case study database to include all the collected data from different sources in a shared space (Yin, 2013). We also reviewed the publicly available data related to firms on YouTube, monitored their website, their social media accounts, and how the firms are portrayed in the media and news networks.

3.2. *Data Analysis*

Since we are interested in exploring the process by which small businesses built resilience before and during the pandemic, we followed a mixed approach to qualitative analysis that allows analyzing data

(Langley, 1999) and captures the idiosyncrasies and context-specific patterns through interpretive and inductive analysis (Gioia *et al.*, 2013). The first stage of our data analysis involved detailed reading of interview transcripts to track a record of entrepreneurs' critical events, activities, and decisions, which helped them build resilience over time. Based on our interpretation of key events and activities, we developed a narrative for each case, which helped us understand the antecedents of entrepreneurial resilience development. In the second stage, we followed Gioia *et al.*'s (2013) inductive approach to data analysis by doing first-order coding using NVivo 11.0 software. This approach allowed us to stay close to data by identifying first-order codes. We then looked for similarities and differences between first-order open codes to aggregate them into emerging themes using the axial coding technique (Straus & Corbin, 1990). In the final step, we returned to the case transcripts, selectively coding them and establishing links to aggregated dimensions for each case. Based on this analytical process, we found inter-relationships among existing resources of the firm and their interaction with the environment to develop resilience capabilities. Following this coding process, we found that one of the firms developed resilience through its ability to transform, while the other built resilience based on its ability to adapt. Next, we present our key findings.

4. Findings

4.1. *e3D*

e3D started as an implant production firm using 3D printers in early 2019. The first sign of building resilience to ongoing adversity can be seen in the case of e3D. This involves making observable changes in the firm's value proposition. This pattern requires the firm to transform its business model, organizational architecture, and internal activities. For example, going through different ongoing challenges such as finding the right product-market fit (i.e., the extent to which the product can satisfy market demand) and raising funds. According to the e3D co-founder: *"Before the pandemic, the challenges were mainly, at least in our stage, focused on raising our next round of funding and going forward with our process of product-market fit"*.

As a response to ongoing adversity, e3D's first pivot occurred four months after it was founded, as the co-founder detected an existing mismatch between the market and the products supplied to hospitals. e3D pivoted from an implant production firm using 3D printers to a software as a service (SaaS) company; they instead provided guidelines and protocols for hospitals dealing with legal issues of making medical implants and provided guidelines, protocols, work forms, pre-filled documents about 3D printing of implants for hospitals in the Netherlands. In other words, e3D gives hospitals a step-by-step guide to designing patient-specific implants at hospitals equipped with 3D printers. This shift in the value proposition (i.e., pivoting), which is part of the ongoing challenges of new ventures, was enabled by the ability of the firm to leverage digital technologies, such as Blockchain and 3D printing. Leveraging digital technology at this stage enabled the firm to transform its value proposition to a new one that increased the auditability and transparency of processes and activities taken for making 3D-printed medical implants, thus facilitating the regulatory barriers in the industry.

Next, in the initial months of the global pandemic, a sudden adversity, all their clients (i.e., hospitals) closed their doors to e3D. e3D also lost support from potential investors as they would not invest until the uncertainty associated with the pandemic subsided. According to the co-founder: "*[before COVID, the question was] can we raise it in the valuation that we want. But then suddenly, all of the investors that we were talking to, they were like, we are sorry, we are not going to invest until further notice. We will let you know. Goodbye ... And the same thing happened with hospitals. We had a lot of hospitals in line to start working with us, to start testing, trial the product ... And then they were like, Sorry, we do not have the budget, we do not have the human resources anymore, We do not even do surgeries anymore, So why do we need 3D printed products? ... at first it was actually very confusing for us, what are we going to do now?*"

During the early days of the pandemic, e3D also faced difficulty in receiving support from third parties such as government agencies. According to the co-founder: "*It is very hard to support a startup that does not have a full-fledged product because even in a normal situation, there is a question of if this company is going to survive after this phase. And during the crisis, of course, the government would prefer to funnel those funds to companies working for 5 to 10 years and needing money to survive*".

In addition to the financial crisis due to losing clients and other funding agencies, e3D faced an internal human resource challenge as the technical co-founder left the company. This made the other co-founder doubt if e3D could continue in this challenging time, and he felt extreme uncertainty. In the following months, a new co-founder joined the firm, and e3D successfully pivoted again, given the co-founder's previous successful pivoting experience, which gave him the ability to learn and experiment with new business models and his resilient mindset. Moreover, the transformation at this stage was made possible since the firm could successfully manage its slack financial resources. This time, the firm developed a digital platform for transacting and communications, contacted experts in the field of 3D printing all around the world, interviewed them, and started publications with them to come up with educational content that was disseminated from their platform. In this way, e3D could adapt to the uncertainty in the new environment. Also, e3D started various collaborations with universities to teach its methods in online classes during the pandemic (e.g., biomedical engineering courses). According to the co-founder: *"We funneled most of the money and activities towards the [name of the digital platform] during that time, so we used that time to build [name of the digital platform]. It is now a one-year-old website; I would say it is a media website. And what we did was that we actually tried to use that time to reach out to experts in the field that were scattered around the world"*.

As a result of constantly dealing with ongoing adversity stemming from deep uncertainties of entering a new market, challenges of funding and scaling up as a technology-based startup, and issues with human resources, e3D learned how to leverage its resources and capabilities in a way that enabled the firm to successfully absorb the challenges and transform its business model when facing an adverse event, such as the COVID-19 pandemic.

4.2. *eTeach*

eTeach is a non-profit enterprise helping children between the ages of 3 and 10 in rural parts of India by designing educational programs. eTeach provides an educational app, SMS, phone-based, and FM radio programs for delivering home-based learning opportunities to children. They curate and specialize the educational programs' contents to meet local communities' needs and present the activities in English and vernacular regional languages.

The eTeach's value proposition has been to provide high-quality education to children in rural India. However, given the venture's constant need to deal with persistent resource constraints in its environment (which is conceptualized in this paper as ongoing adversity), eTeach built resilience through constant learning and business model adaptation.

eTeach's founder established the firm because he realized there was a lack of proper education for children in the rural areas of India. He realized that children did not get the skills needed to prosper in the community. He and his co-founders initially started creating physical learning centers, but then they realized they could not reach all the students in this way. Therefore, they decided to leverage digital technologies such as smartphones to reach a greater audience.

During the initial stages of developing a digital business model, the founders considered delivering online education content directly to the parent's smartphones. However, given the low access of rural families to the internet and smartphones, the founders soon realized that they needed to adapt their business model by changing how they deliver their value proposition. Therefore, they started mobilizing local community educators to help deliver their learning material to the students. This shift in the value delivery mechanism was enabled by combining local resources with digital resources. In fact, instead of using the technology to deliver educational content to students directly, they used the technology as an enabler to provide community educators with curated and locally specified teaching and evaluation material. The use of technology enabled the firm to easily track the performance of the educators and provide them with feedback to improve the quality of their programs. Before the pandemic, eTeach delivered education programs to children online and offline. This shows the adaptability and flexibility of eTeach. After years of constantly dealing with resource constraints, such as limited financial resources, as mentioned by the founder, eTeach was able to build and integrate local resources and digital capabilities to overcome those challenges.

During the pandemic, eTeach faced a significant challenge since they could no longer rely on the physical component of their operations and lost a significant portion of their revenues. As mentioned by the founder: *"With the COVID, the first challenge was generating revenues because we lost out on major projects, implementation projects during COVID, which we had finalized pre-COVID. So that obviously was one aspect in terms of loss of revenue ... all our programs had a physical component to it. So when the lockdown happened, and all education centers closed, we were in a spot as to how to reach out to children. How do we reach out to educators? Basically, the challenge was to make sure that the children are continuing their learning".*

Once they realized the need to shift how they delivered their educational program after the pandemic, eTeach started delivering home-based learning programs in April 2020. The idea was to deliver the educational content directly to the parents' featured phones using interactive voice response (IVR) solutions, local radio stations, and SMS. The educators, in turn, get back to children and their parents weekly by phone calls to track their progress. According to the founder: *"So from April 2020, eTeach has been implementing a new product, the home-based learning program, to ensure that the children are continuously learning. So from the past, it has been more than eight months, and we have already reached out to many children with activity-based content using remote instructions by phones, simple text messages, automated voice calls, and IVRs ... We are using web-based technology, a simple web-based solution which community educators are using to track children. So, you have technology wherein they have all the assigned children, students that they are on their platform, they simply see which week activities they need to call and check and fill up that data".*

Based on our interpretation of the data, we argue that three main factors contributed to the successful evolution of the value proposition at eTeach during the pandemic: (1) eTeach was successful at adopting a new approach to deliver its educational program. It had already developed social capital by establishing deep connections with the local community. The social resources accumulated by eTeach before the pandemic allowed it to maintain its reputation and build new partnerships with government and non-government organizations to help them expand their services across different geographical areas. (2) eTeach's core team has not changed significantly since the beginning of 2016. Even after the pandemic, one of the main priorities of eTeach was to keep its employees despite facing financial issues. This established a high degree of trust and mutual understanding across team members. Moreover, the team members at eTeach had enough time to make better sense of all key activities required for this social venture's survival and growth. For instance, the Founder mentioned: *"I think the first, I might not say that as a unique thing, but I think the team bonding, and even though I had mentioned before that communication was a challenge, I felt that the team was always in sync with the very mission that we are working. So, I think that one of our advantages is that everyone was aligned".*

eTeach was able to leverage affordable and accessible technologies such as SMS, IVR, and Radio to reach a significant number of audiences efficiently. Instead of relying on high-end and expensive technologies that require huge investments and may take lots of time to develop, they searched for the most efficient and accessible ways of delivering value to their customers.

As a result of constantly dealing with ongoing adversity stemming from interacting with persistent resource constraints in its environment and facing challenges during the pandemic, eTeach learned how to leverage its resources and capabilities in a way that enabled the firm to successfully absorb the challenges and progressively adapt to the new environment when facing an adverse event.

5. Discussion

After analyzing the key events and actions taken by e3D and eTeach before and during the pandemic, we found that eTeach followed a different path toward resilience than e3D, unlike the case of e3D, which shows the resilience dimension of absorbing shock and transforming. Contrastingly, eTeach built resilience by absorbing the shock and progressively adapting to the new environment. eTeach did not experience any transformation in its initial value proposition when dealing with ongoing resource constraints in the environment and during the sudden adversity (i.e., the pandemic).

Our findings reveal that although both cases experienced ongoing and sudden adversity, each faced different levels of uncertainty, had access to different resources, leveraged them accordingly, and relied on social support. These factors and other contextual, behavioral, and organizational differences led to different patterns through which they built resilience that ultimately helped these small businesses evolve or transform their business models in the face of sudden and ongoing diversity.

As discussed earlier, digital technology helps entrepreneurs innovate and find new ways to survive through adversities (Chan *et al.*, 2020). When facing ongoing adversity, entrepreneurs in both cases used digital technology to plan for their firm's growth. However, digital technologies have different degrees of complexity and functionality in each case. The case of eTeach shows that small businesses operating in resource-constrained environments can rely on readily available technologies (Chan *et al.*, 2020) to adapt their business model. For example, in addition to in-person programs, eTeach used simple and affordable technologies such as Radio, SMS, and Interactive Voice Response to reach rural communities in remote areas of India. These technologies can be leveraged efficiently and with little investment in technology infrastructure.

Another critical factor contributing to the resilience in the case of eTeach is receiving social support. eTeach prioritized scaling deep rather than scaling up (Kim & Kim, 2021), which means it sought to establish deep connections within its customer communities. They built trust among the community educators and leveraged it to create and deliver value to the community. This aligns with Kim and Kim's (2021) notion of "growing like an Oak Tree", which reflects the real social and environmental impact of businesses deeply embedded in their locality. Thus, we argue that by establishing deep connections with the local actors, eTeach built resilience at the organizational level and contributed to community resilience.

This research enriches the literature on entrepreneurial resilience while remaining grounded in the RBV and dynamic capabilities literature. It also extends the theoretical scope of entrepreneurial resilience research by investigating resilience as a response to ongoing and sudden adversity. Moreover, it is among the few studies empirically demonstrating the underpinnings of entrepreneurial resilience in more than a single context, thus providing fertile ground for future theory development. The research provides rich insights into the strategies and tools that entrepreneurial ventures develop and deploy to survive crises where they already conduct their business in resource-constrained, adverse contexts.

Given the importance of digital transformation and digital technologies in the age of pandemics (e.g., SARS-2003) (Leidner *et al.*, 2009; Pan *et al.*, 2005; Vial, 2019), we also highlight the role of affordable and accessible digital technologies to help entrepreneurs build resilience to both ongoing and sudden adversities. Furthermore, this research will interest entrepreneurs and policymakers as we emerge from the pandemic. Policymakers can utilize the research to refine and update policies for supporting entrepreneurial ventures during crises and providing them with appropriate support mechanisms during the current pandemic. Figure 1 presents the research model developed based on the findings of this study.

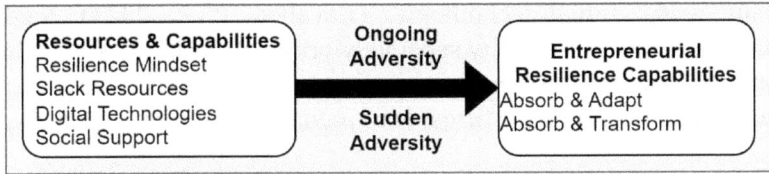

Figure 1.   Research model.

6. Conclusion

This study also has some limitations that identify future research opportunities. First, this study does not claim causality between organizational resources and capabilities and entrepreneurial resilience capabilities; instead, evidence of possible impacts is provided. Future studies can investigate this relationship further. Second, this study only presented two cases. We invite future studies to examine more cases as this can increase the generalizability of our findings. Finally, we acknowledge that other factors, such as product architecture (e.g., Sadreddin *et al.*, 2023), may contribute to developing resilience capabilities for the two cases.

This study contributes to the entrepreneurship and information systems literature by highlighting the role of different resources and capabilities, including digital technologies, in developing entrepreneurial resilience instead of only focusing on organizational and environmental factors contributing to such capabilities' developments (Sussan & Acs, 2017). In particular, this article responds to calls for research on entrepreneurial resilience (Sakurai & Chughtai, 2020) and the role of digital technologies in enabling resilience capabilities (Parker & Ameen, 2018). Digital technologies such as mobility, cloud computing, social media, and analytics, which were not the focus of this study, were found to be important driving factors for digital transformation that ultimately contribute significantly toward building resilience capabilities. Although there has been much research on the adaptation of organizations given changes in their environment (such as turbulence and uncertainty), our research highlights the importance of building resilience by absorbing sudden shocks while continuously absorbing lessons from ongoing shocks. This enables organizations to adapt or transform and enables the development of resilience capabilities to counter future adversities. Previous studies have highlighted how small firms that face ongoing challenges, such as financial and regulatory constraints, leverage their contextual knowledge to innovate using digital technologies (Levallet *et al.*, 2023). Studying ongoing and sudden adversity separately provides limited insights, but an empirical investigation of the combination has allowed us to provide more powerful insights for small firms, entrepreneurs, and policymakers alike.

Acknowledgments

Sincere thanks to Reza Khoee, Alireza Jahandideh, and Mohammad Qorbani Hesari for their contributions to the development of this paper. We recognize the funding by the Social Sciences and Humanities Research Council of Canada (SSHRC) institutional explore grant and the National Bank Initiative for Entrepreneurship and Family Business at John Molson School of Business, Concordia University, Canada.

References

Acs, Z., Stam, E., Audretsch, D., & O'Connor, A. (2017). The lineages of the entrepreneurial ecosystem approach. *Small Business Economics*, *49*(1), 1–10. https://doi.org/10.1007/s11187-017-9864-8.

Ahuja, S., Chan, Y. E., & Krishnamurthy, R. (2023). Responsible innovation with digital platforms: Cases in India and Canada. *Information Systems Journal*, *33*(1), 76–129.

Ahuja, S., Sadreddin, A., & Chan, Y. E. (2021). Readily available technologies for building community resilience: Lessons from India during the Covid-19 pandemic. *The Journal of Community Informatics*, *17*, 3–25.

Aldunce, P., Beilin, R., Handmer, J., & Howden, M. (2014). Framing disaster resilience: the implications of the diverse conceptualisations of "bouncing back". *Disaster Prevention and Management*, *23*(3), 252–270.

Baker, T. & Nelson, R. E. (2005). Creating something from nothing: Resource construction through entrepreneurial bricolage. *Administrative Science Quarterly*, *50*(3), 329–366. https://doi.org/10.2189/asqu.2005.50.3.329.

Branicki, L. J., Sullivan-Taylor, B., & Livschitz, S. R. (2017). How entrepreneurial resilience generates resilient SMEs. *International Journal of Entrepreneurial Behavior & Research*, *24*(7), 1244–1263.

Chan, Y. E., Ahuja, S., Boroomand, F., & Sadreddin, A. (2019). Technology affordances in digital innovation research: Quo Vadis? *Twenty-Fifth Americas Conference on Information Systems (AMCIS)*.

Chan, Y. E., Krishnamurthy, R., & Desjardins, C. (2020). Technology-driven innovation in small firms. *MIS Quarterly Executive*, *19*(1), 39–55.

Colten, C. E., Grismore, A. A., & Simms, J. R. (2015). Oil spills and community resilience: Uneven impacts and protection in historical perspective. *Geographical Review, 105*(4), 391–407.

Cumming, G. S., Barnes, G., Perz, S., Schmink, M., Sieving, K. E., Southworth, J., Binford, M., Holt, R. D., Stickler, C., & Van Holt, T. (2005). An exploratory framework for the empirical measurement of resilience. *Ecosystems, 8*(8), 975–987.

Darkow, P. M. (2019). Beyond "bouncing back": Towards an integral, capability-based understanding of organizational resilience. *Journal of Contingencies and Crisis Management, 27*(2), 145–156. https://doi.org/10.1111/1468-5973.12246.

Duchek, S. (2018). Entrepreneurial resilience: A biographical analysis of successful entrepreneurs. *International Entrepreneurship and Management Journal, 14*(2), 429–455.

Faik, I., Barrett, M., & Oborn, E. (2020). How information technology matters in societal change: An affordance-based institutional logics perspective. *Management Information Systems Quarterly, 44*(3), 1359–1390.

George, G., Baker, T., Tracey, P., & Joshi, H. (2019). Inclusion and innovation: A call to action. In *Handbook of inclusive innovation* (pp. 2–22). Edward Elgar Publishing.

George, G., Howard-Grenville, J., Joshi, A., & Tihanyi, L. (2016). Understanding and tackling societal grand challenges through management research. *Academy of Management Journal, 59*(6), 1880–1895.

Gioia, D. A., Corley, K. G., & Hamilton, A. L. (2013). Seeking qualitative rigor in inductive research: Notes on the Gioia methodology. *Organizational Research Methods, 16*(1), 15–31.

Imperiale, A. J. & Vanclay, F. (2016). Experiencing local community resilience in action: Learning from post-disaster communities. *Journal of Rural Studies, 47*, 204–219. https://doi.org/10.1016/j.jrurstud.2016.08.002.

Kallinikos, J., Aaltonen, A., & Marton, A. (2013). The ambivalent ontology of digital artifacts. *MIS Quarterly, 37*(2), 357–370.

Kim, S. & Kim, A. (2022). Going viral or growing like an oak tree? Towards sustainable local development through entrepreneurship. *Academy of Management Journal, 65*(5), 1709–1746.

Korber, S. & McNaughton, R. B. (2018). Resilience and entrepreneurship: A systematic literature review. *International Journal of Entrepreneurial Behavior & Research, 24*(7), 1129–1154.

Kuang, D. & Liao, K.-H. (2020). Learning from floods: Linking flood experience and flood resilience. *Journal of Environmental Management, 271*, 111025.

Langley, A. (1999). Strategies for theorizing from process data. *Academy of Management Review, 24*(4), 691–710.

Leidner, D. E., Pan, G., & Pan, S. L. (2009). The role of IT in crisis response: Lessons from the SARS and Asian Tsunami disasters. *The Journal of Strategic Information Systems, 18*(2), 80–99.

Levallet, N., Ahuja, S., & Wood, C. (2023). Agility and improvisation in Ontario's craft breweries: Capabilities for constraints-based innovation. *Journal of Small Business Management*, 1–42. https://doi.org/10.1080/00472778.2023.2182442.

Maritz, A., Perenyi, A., De Waal, G., & Buck, C. (2020). Entrepreneurship as the unsung hero during the current COVID-19 economic crisis: Australian perspectives. *Sustainability, 12*(11), 4612.

McKinsey. (2020). Which small businesses are most vulnerable to COVID-19 — And when. https://www.mckinsey.com/featured-insights/americas/which-small-businesses-are-most-vulnerable-to-covid-19-and-when.

Munoz, J. M. S. (2010). *Contemporary Microenterprise: Concepts and Cases.* Edward Elgar Publishing, UK.

Myers, M. D. (2019). *Qualitative Research in Business and Management.* Sage Publications, Thousand Oaks, CA.

Nambisan, S., Zahra, S. A., & Luo, Y. (2019). Global platforms and ecosystems: Implications for international business theories. *Journal of International Business Studies, 50*(9), 1464–1486.

Packard, M. D., Clark, B. B., & Klein, P. G. (2017). Uncertainty types and transitions in the entrepreneurial process. *Organization Science, 28*(5), 840–856.

Pan, S. L., Pan, G., & Devadoss, P. R. (2005). E-government capabilities and crisis management: Lessons from combating SARS in Singapore. *MIS Quarterly Executive, 4*(4), 385.

Parker, H. & Ameen, K. (2018). The role of resilience capabilities in shaping how firms respond to disruptions. *Journal of Business Research, 88*, 535–541.

Patton, M. Q. (2014). *Qualitative Research & Evaluation Methods: Integrating Theory and Practice.* Sage Publications, Thousand Oaks, CA.

Prabhu, J. (2017). Frugal innovation: Doing more with less for more. *Philosophical Transactions of the Royal Society A: Mathematical, Physical and Engineering Sciences, 375*(2095), 20160372.

Qureshi, S. (2020). *Why Data Matters for Development? Exploring Data Justice, Micro-Entrepreneurship, Mobile Money and Financial Inclusion.* Taylor & Francis.

Rai, A. (2020). Editor's comments: The COVID-19 pandemic: Building resilience with IS research. *Management Information Systems Quarterly, 44*(2), iii–vii.

Sadreddin, A. & Chan, Y. E. (2023). Pathways to developing information technology-enabled capabilities in born-digital new ventures. *International Journal of Information Management, 68*, 102572.

Sakurai, M. & Chughtai, H. (2020). Resilience against crises: COVID-19 and lessons from natural disasters. *European Journal of Information Systems*, *29*(5), 585–594. https://doi.org/10.1080/0960085X.2020.1814171.

Sakurai, M., Watson, R., Abraham, C., & Kokuryo, J. (2014). Sustaining life during the early stages of disaster relief with a frugal information system: Learning from the great east Japan earthquake. *IEEE Communications Magazine*, *52*(1), 176–185. https://doi.org/10.1109/MCOM.2014.6710081.

Schwab, K. & Sternfels, B. (2022). Three keys to a resilient postpandemic recovery. https://www.mckinsey.com/capabilities/risk-and-resilience/our-insights/three-keys-to-a-resilient-postpandemic-recovery.

Seidel, V. P., Packalen, K. A., & O'Mahony, S. (2016). Help me do it on my own: How entrepreneurs manage autonomy and constraint within incubator organizations. In L. E. Cohen, M. D. Burton, & M. Lounsbury (eds.), *Research in the Sociology of Organizations* (Vol. 47, pp. 275–307). Emerald Group Publishing Limited, UK.

Shepherd, D. A. & Williams, T. (2020). Entrepreneurship responding to adversity: Equilibrating adverse events and disequilibrating persistent adversity. *Organization Theory*, *1*(4). https://doi.org/10.1177/2631787720967678.

Spector, B. (2019). There is no such thing as a crisis: A critique of and alternative to the dominant crisis management model. *Journal of Contingencies and Crisis Management*, *27*(3), 274–279.

Straus, A. & Corbin, J. (1990). *Basics of Qualitative Research: Grounded Theory Procedures and Techniques*. Newbury Park, CA: Sage. SAGE Publications, Inc., California.

Sussan, F. & Acs, Z. (2017). The digital entrepreneurial ecosystem. *Small Business Economics*, *49*(1), 55–73. https://doi.org/10.1007/s11187-017-9867-5.

Tilson, D., Lyytinen, K., & Sørensen, C. (2010). Research commentary — Digital infrastructures: The missing IS research agenda. *Information Systems Research*, *21*(4), 748–759.

Ultramari, C. & Rezende, D. (2007). Urban resilience and slow motion disasters. *City & Time*, *2*(3), 47–64.

Vial, G. (2019). Understanding digital transformation: A review and a research agenda. *The Journal of Strategic Information Systems*, *28*(2), 118–144.

von Briel, F., Davidsson, P., & Recker, J. (2018). Digital technologies as external enablers of new venture creation in the IT hardware sector. *Entrepreneurship Theory and Practice*, *42*(1), 47–69.

von Briel, F., Recker, J., & Davidsson, P. (2018). Not all digital venture ideas are created equal: Implications for venture creation processes. *The Journal of Strategic Information Systems*, *27*(4), 278–295.

Walker, B., Holling, C. S., Carpenter, S. R., & Kinzig, A. (2004). Resilience, adaptability and transformability in social–ecological systems. *Ecology and Society*, *9*(2), 5.

Watson, R. T. & Chandra Kruse, L. (2020). *Digital Resilience – Liechtenstein Consortium for Digital Capital Creation.* http://digitalcapital.li/?p=582.

Williams, T. A., Gruber, D. A., Sutcliffe, K. M., Shepherd, D. A., & Zhao, E. Y. (2017). Organizational response to adversity: Fusing crisis management and resilience research streams. *Academy of Management Annals, 11*(2), 733–769.

Wong, B. A. (2020). How digital entrepreneurs will help shape the world after the COVID-19 pandemic. World Economic Forum. https://www.weforum.org/agenda/2020/06/entrepreneurs-must-embrace-digital-during-pandemic-for-society/.

Yin, R. K. (2013). *Case Study Research: Design and Methods.* Sage Publications, Thousand Oaks, CA.

Chapter 12

The Future of Work in a Digital World

David Eisenberg

New Jersey Institute of Technology, Newark, USA

Feliciano School of Business, Montclair State University, Montclair, New Jersey, USA

esenbergd@montclair.edu

1. Introduction

Schwab (2017), the chair of the World Economic Forum, has stated, "A paradigm shift is underway in how we work and communicate", foreshadowing a societal change led by changing technology. Artificial intelligence (AI), the Internet of Things (IoT), robotics, 3D printing, autonomous vehicles, nanotechnology, materials science, biotechnology, quantum computing, and energy storage are among those technologies that Schwab describes as leading the way. Many of these same technologies that drive Industry 4.0 and the burgeoning Industry 5.0 will bring about a digital workplace revolution as well, one that is arguably already underway.

Elon Musk said in an interview with British Prime Minister Rishi Sumac, "I think we are seeing the most disruptive force in history" and then explained his belief that there will be "a point where no job is needed ... [when] the AI will be able to do everything". AI holds enormous potential for the future of work and has made its way into popular understanding, with its applications for military, human resources, industry, healthcare, marketing, and management. However, AI is not an independent actor in the technological changes that are coming together to create dramatic societal and workplace transformations. It is only perhaps the most obvious one. Behind the scenes, various technologies are either working to support the expanding power of AI applications or quietly incorporating the powers of AI into other technologies that will eventually become as much a part of everyday life and discourse as AI has suddenly become. It is therefore through the integrated applications of numerous emerging digital technologies that a bold new digital world comes into existence.

This review aims to confront those digital technologies that will drive the workplace of the future, whether that is a physical or virtual one, or even an asynchronous workplace that only exists online. As these technologies evolve, integration between them often occurs in the background, until suddenly something emerges from their synergy that, when unleashed, changes the way we work and live. Such technologies, like artificial intelligence, may seem to have arrived suddenly and take society by surprise, yet, those who are in the know may have seen their evolution and anticipated their arrival for a long time. It is through emerging integration of these developing technologies that the true potential for revolutionizing the workplace and the perhaps prophesized Industry 4.0 and Industry 5.0 industrial revolutions can more gradually be seen to take shape. Hence, while AI holds the promise of much of these technologies to learn, grow, and even collaborate autonomously, understanding how a multitude of technologies are integrating and synergizing truly captures its real potential.

Nevertheless, as the new digital workplace unfolds, it brings with it a flood of ethical concerns about job loss, privacy, copyright protections, network security, and many other issues. In the first industrial revolution, unprecedented inequalities and a massive, albeit temporary, degradation of worker rights came about. Through forward-looking public policies, one can hope that such hardship could be averted, and the enormous benefits of the emerging digital world will hold promise and benefits for everyone.

2. A Digital World

In the 18th century, the steam engine brought about dramatic changes in how people worked during the first industrial revolution. The rise of mass manufacturing and electricity during the mid-19th century has been referred to as the second industrial revolution, while the proliferation of the microchip has been called a third industrial revolution. Industry 4.0, or what is being called the fourth industrial revolution, is the current fundamental change to the manner in which work is done, one that is defined by the digital technologies discussed in this chapter, and their integration into the warehouses, factories, offices, and anywhere work environments of the 21st century.

Propelled into workplace prominence during the COVID-19 pandemic, recent advances in communications technologies enabled workers to perform their job responsibilities from anywhere, a phenomenon that has lingered in many industries even after the pandemic ceased to drive public policy. The Internet of Things (IoT) further enables remote work to utilize sensors, drones, and various devices to allow connectivity, bringing about the potential for both robot and people to work together in unforeseen ways. Soft robotics aims to make robots and machinery and, importantly, AI-enabled machinery to work side-by-side with people safely and comfortably (Abhari & Eisenberg, 2023; Abhari *et al.*, 2023).

Virtual and augmented reality aims to both provide a more interactive and holistic remote work environment, while also enhancing the ability for IoT devices to be ever more precisely controlled remotely and with greater added value for the future of work. Moreover, the metaverse has the potential to truly become a norm in future workplaces, if and when the metaverse can be seen as a more useful and comfortable remote work environment than telecommuting through more traditional video conferencing tools.

When described separately from Industry 4.0, Industry 5.0 is not directly described as the burgeoning of new technologies but, instead, is a phenomenologically different manner of human–computer interaction, one that integrates AI and technologies into people's everyday lives and workplaces. These terms are introduced as a helpful framework for understanding the evolution of the future of work, providing a heuristic for understanding how the synergy of technologies can take shape. Also, putting the digital workplace evolution in the context of previous industrial revolutions lays the groundwork for understanding the enormous societal changes and potential ethical challenges that lie ahead.

3. Virtual and Remote Work

The surge of the COVID-19 pandemic has accelerated the already rapid growth of the independent contractor and gig economy, boosting the adoption of remote work and transforming it into a lasting alternative for the bulk of the workforce. This trend has increased geographical and temporal flexibility and autonomy for workers. Virtual collaboration and video conferencing technologies have empowered companies and people to engage more meaningfully than traditional telecommuting previously allowed, a trend that may advance further with the advent of virtual reality or metaverse telecommuting. Moreover, the emergence of online freelance work platforms has offered access to such flexible work opportunities; in fact, almost every Fortune 500 company makes use of one or more of these specialized online talent pools. According to Fuller *et al.* (2020), 90% of corporate frontline and C-suite officials surveyed in 2020 found these highly skilled talent platforms were critical to their perceived competitive advantage. In fact, half of the corporate executives who they polled predicted that the proportion of full-time workers on payroll would drop dramatically in the next few years, and two-thirds predicted that their organization would become more dependent on specialized gig talent, as well as incorporating practices such as talent sharing, borrowing, or renting.

Hence, these platforms have proven very beneficial for employers, providing access to an ever-expanding international pool of on-demand talent.

Among workers, a shift in perception toward anywhere work has resulted in a nearly equal number of workers considering freelancing as a long-term career option, compared to those viewing freelancing as only a temporary arrangement. As the conventional notion of being a true employee diminishes, the term "digital nomad" or "anywhere worker" has changed from analogous to being underemployed, to perhaps even becoming an aspirational term for many employees seeking greater autonomy and work–life balance. These terms refer to individuals who are allowed to meet their work obligations without temporal, physical, or geographic constraints, opting instead to work from anywhere and often at the time of day of their choice. Before the outbreak of the pandemic, the prevalence of remote work in the United States was minimal, with less than 5% of Americans estimated to be working remotely, according to Yang *et al.* (2021). However, by April 2020, their study showed that a significant shift had occurred, with over 37% of the workforce transitioning to remote work. An increasing prevalence of remote work among younger age groups, particularly millennials, has suggested a trajectory toward a more pronounced preference for independence at work. This trend is likely to grow significantly over time as millennials age, such as

Gen Z, and subsequent generations may continue this trend. Technologies that support virtual work environments, such as IoT, sensors, surveillance, and extended reality, may advance in response to these preferences of both workers and employers alike.

Nevertheless, the move to remote work presents businesses and workers with not only benefits but also challenges. For workers, while temporal and geographic flexibility offers enormous quality of life benefits, some have felt isolated, increased stress of managing an overlap between their home and professional life, difficulty in forming social connections with other workers, lost time from technology failures, and challenges in finding adequate space at home for uninterrupted work.

Employers and managers, on the other hand, have struggled to ensure that work is truly being done while employees are at home. In an effort to cope with employer concerns, technologies for monitoring, managing, and surveilling remote workplaces have seen a rapid rise as remote working becomes more common. These tools include a broad spectrum of hardware and software solutions, ranging from keystroke logs, monitoring of application and website usage, and detailed tracking of file usage to capturing desktop screenshots. Advanced technologies such as AI, machine learning, talent analytics, automation, IoT, and gamification are increasingly being integrated into suites of digital tools used to oversee remote employees, increase efficiency, and reduce costs.

4. The Rise of Surveillance Technologies

Workplace surveillance technologies monitor behavior, performance, and physical aspects of an employee's life. In their study of 645 workers in the United States, Vitak and Zimmer (2023) found that close to 40% of employees noted an introduction of new surveillance tools by their employers during the pandemic. Phone call content and metadata, social media posts, screenshots from their work computer, email tracking, keystrokes, web browser tracking, attendance, workplace network logins, and sensor data from wearable technologies are just some of the potentially intrusive methods of surveillance that have been introduced to monitor workers both remotely and in an office. Some employee monitoring technologies include IoT-enabled equipment that is "always on", tracking employee behavior throughout the workday in order to facilitate remote monitoring and the formation of collective intelligence.

Many employees are also uncertain about what surveillance or employee tracking systems are in use, leading to concerns about transparency on the part of companies deploying these methods. Given that workers may dislike knowing they are being surveilled, and since there are no public policies requiring disclosure, withholding specifics about employee tracking systems from the workforce could even be intentional by some companies. Lack of transparency could be a means to avoid potential damage to employee morale, or even curtailing efforts by some workers to trick the tracking system, or perhaps even to hack into it and undermine it altogether.

The effects on mental health and well-being associated with remote work must also be considered, a problem that could be exacerbated should the needs of employees for personal privacy and autonomy be disregarded. Moreover, being surveilled is no substitute for actual human contact, and the possibility of loneliness in remote work environments has become a concern as well, while more frequent virtual meetings have also been a source of added stress among workers. The introduction of the metaverse into the workplace, allowing remote workers to interact with others in a virtual or augmented reality work environment, has actually shown promise to solve these problems, leading the way toward greater development and use of virtual environments and the sensing and IoT technologies that support them, for the future of work in an increasingly digital world.

5. The Role of Sensors in the Future of Work

A rapid proliferation of sensor systems is quietly but exponentially increasing real-time data that can be derived from workers, consumers, and their environments. Sensors can observe the physical world and quantify that observation into data — data that can then be analyzed by AI and subsequently utilized by a connected IoT device. Such sensors already operate in the background of people's smartphones, smartwatches, and smart home devices, collecting information that allows their apps and services to function as expected (Hasan *et al.*, 2020; Pias *et al.*, 2019a, 2019b; 2022). Sensors also lie inside red-light cameras, automated toll booths, facial recognition systems, many worn or implanted personal medical devices, and many more aspects of society, quietly and often inconspicuously.

Next-generation placeable, wearable, and implantable sensor technologies may generate new jobs based on the interpretation and response to real-time sensor-derived tracking data from customers and consumers as well. Enhanced human–robot interaction that sensor systems can bring about a rise to data that can be used to enhance services and advertising for customers but may also use that data to better enable robots to work with humans. Thus, the advent of new capabilities and applications of sensors will fuel a rise of robotics in the workplace, enabling vastly expanded Human–Robot and Human–IOT interactions. While new jobs may also be created to continue to program and maintain software, it is equally possible that the automation of computer programming and the rise of no-code/low-code platforms could eliminate at least as many jobs in specialized software development.

In the workplace, occupational sensors have already been incorporated into confined spaces, warehouses, and factory settings to ensure worker safety. These include embedded sensors in vests, safety helmets, eyeglasses or goggles, footwear, watches or wristbands, and contact lenses, enabling the real-time monitoring of hazardous or dangerous conditions. Conditions including respiration, social distancing, temperature and heat stress, fall detection, body water loss, heart rate, worker location, and other physiological and environmental data help those who work in potentially dangerous environments safe. Many of these sensors were originally developed for workplaces based on American companies meeting requirements to comply with Occupational Safety and Health Administration (OSHA) or Mine Safety and Health Administration (MSHA), though now may be used for purposes outside of their original mandate.

Surgical and health-related IoT solutions have been developed such as remote IoT sensor systems to allow surgeons to operate robotic assistants in impossibly small bodily areas (Howard *et al.*, 2021). In these cases, sensor technologies work hand-in-hand with soft robotics, and virtual or augmented reality, to allow surgeons to explore, understand, practice, or even perform actual surgical procedures inside a patient's body. These IoT technology integrations have been later adapted to allow engineers, military personnel, or factory managers to engage remotely with specialized equipment and even manipulate enormously either large or incredibly small environments.

Bodily wearable devices, along with devices attached or implanted in one's body, have also increasingly been developed and approved for medical purposes, before having the potential for an increased rollout for consumer or company use. This includes cutting-edge options like e-textiles, head-worn sensors, and smart patches. The medical field has worked with such sensors for remote mood or behavior monitoring (Akter *et al.*, 2022); nutritional, drug, or food intake tracking; the monitoring of blood pressure, pulse, body temperature, or oxygen level; sleep tracking; posture maintenance; blood glucose level; and many more benefits to doctor–patient monitoring. With each such medical use, the potential for these data-rich technologies to be repurposed commercially or in the workplace exists. Even Brain–Computer Interfaces (BCI), which have enormous medical benefits for people with neurological or motility issues, having been approved for medical uses, are at the same time being considered for commercial and workplace use in the near future.

Contemporary neural and physiological tracking systems designed to instantly communicate via the IoT and integrated data networks can potentially monitor and influence real-time emotions, health, feelings, physiology, and behavior of both current and potential customers. If sensor-driven real-time consumer analytics is potentially more predictive than any previous data mining of individuals, then does the hiring organization hold any social responsibility for their own employee's autonomy, data privacy, and personal agency? Eisenberg *et al.* (2024) asked the following question: "Can companies know people better than they know themselves?" This work explores the real-time AI-driven sensor systems that could generate customer behavior analytics to predict purchasing behavior at the precise moment in time and place when the customer is most likely to buy. While the paper focused on the strategic marketing potential of neural sensors being able to understand the behavior of consumers better than themselves, the work exposes an equally interesting and concerning ethical and strategic management quandary about employee tracking. If neural or physiological sensors can understand employee behavior better than employees understand their own motivations, then does that allow an unprecedented and perhaps disproportionate amount of influence over employee behavior?

While employers may wish to use sensors in the interest of increasing employee accountability, their deployment also increases the potential for workers to perceive them as unnecessary and invasive. Privacy concerns intended for managers to monitor productivity may be counterproductive if their use leads to worker anxiety, dissatisfaction, or mistakes on the job (Chang *et al.*, 2015; Langenderfer *et al.*, 2009). Such sensor surveillance may eventually be seen as commonplace, or as a necessary and trivial sacrifice when offered the enhanced work–life balance of working remotely. Alternatively, it may be a grudgingly accepted element of simply having a job in an increasingly digital world. If this were the case, however, the detriment to employee morale and job satisfaction may remain, even as it is not a deterrent for employee retention.

Alternatives may emerge as a consequence of technological advancement of integrated digital technologies. Few workers will complain about the tracking of occupational health conditions in dangerous environments to ensure worker safety, as mentioned earlier in this section. For example, if extended reality (XR) work requires the use of sensor and data collection to operate headsets, gloves, or goggles, similar to how one's mobile phone or smartwatch does, then employee tracking would be seen as a consequence, rather than an intention, of the devices necessary for performing one's job. This may alter the perception of workers from seeing such data collection as intrusive, to simply seeing it as needed for operation of devices. Collaborative robots (or "cobots") may offer a similar unintended benefit. That is, when soft robots work alongside people, the need for those robots to obtain constant sensor data about the workers around them can be necessary for worker safety, allowing the collection of that data without it appearing intentionally invasive or for solely tracking worker performance.

6. Soft Robotics

Soft robotics enables the ability of robots, or in such cases of human–robot collaboration, called cobots, to work safely alongside people. Inspired by biological systems, soft robotics provides special features, such as safe contact with fragile items and adaptability to intricate environments (Majidi, 2014). Using soft materials, control algorithms, and sensor systems to immediately observe and respond to their environment, soft robotics allow for the better integration of robots into workplaces. Common attributes or development aims of soft robotics include joint elasticity or physical compliance, often to enhance their mobility and energy efficiency.

Prior to the advent of soft robotics, and still in many workplaces, robots might need to be isolated from people, to prevent the likelihood of robots eventually causing people unintentional harm. Much like the early machines of the industrial revolution, where many injuries occurred to factory workers, those working alongside traditional rigid robots could be injured by the robot that was designed to assist them. Consequentially, soft robotics were developed to curtail these concerns, making it possible for people to work literally hand-in-hand with robots, without fear of injury.

The interdisciplinary discipline, drawing from materials science, bio-mechanics, and artificial intelligence, however, is increasingly integrated with sensors. In addition to being soft and flexible, soft robotics is greatly dependent on sensor systems to anticipate the robot's environment, as well as to adjust its motion to either avoid contact or collision, and upon making contact with a person or object in its vicinity. This ability to sense and respond to the environment makes the robot immensely more adaptable to working alongside people and in some ways similar to how people would adapt to their environment.

Such robots use data derived from the robot's own sensors, as well as data from sensors in their environment and the people working within that environment, thus incorporating robust AI systems to interpret, analyze, and immediately respond to vast amounts of real-time data. Sensors thus extend the soft robot's softness, elevating that robot so that it's not just a machine that won't hurt if it hits you. Instead, the cobot can anticipate the behaviors, actions, and needs of the people or objects around them. Research has even explored the idea of affective touch for soft robots or the ability for robots to actually connect better with people by touching affectionately or in a friendly way when appropriate.

This ability to use AI to anticipate potentially extends the cobot far beyond just safety, although it does promise to dramatically improve the safety of working alongside robots. Instead, this turns a cobot into a potentially ideal coworker, one that knows what it needs to do to support its human coworker, even before the human next to it knows. With sensors surveilling every aspect of the human environment in a warehouse or factory, as well as continually analyzing mood, health, fatigue, and other data from their human coworker's smartwatch or smartphone, the cobot can protect the worker, ensure the worker is meeting their productive potential, and even know when its colleague is overstressed or overtired.

Ultimately, the ability for robots to not just be safe and tolerated in the workplace, but to thrive working alongside people, may depend on their ability to make people not only feel comfortable working with a robot but actually like their robot. Many of the same sensors being embedded in soft robots are also being experimented for use in prosthetics, allowing prosthetic hands or limbs to "behave" or understand their environment in as close to the same way that a person's original hand may have reacted to stimuli.

Perhaps eventually, that robot may appear preferable to the average worker from how their work would get done with a human collaborator.

7. Metaverse and the Future of Work

Sensors play an important role in virtual reality (VR), allowing people's motions, and potential emotions to be incorporated into interactions in a metaverse. The metaverse is an immersive virtual shared environment aimed at digitally mimicking while also enhancing every element of the actual world (Wang *et al.*, 2023; Eisenberg *et al.*, 2022). In the metaverse, people could socialize, work, and play. Virtual and Augmented Reality (AR) or cumulatively labeled Extended Reality (XR) has developed tremendously in its educational and video gaming use for students and children, with research demonstrating benefits for struggling learners. As XR increasingly gains acceptance and popularity among younger generations, its technology may in turn cultivate a burgeoning generational workforce prepared to incorporate the metaverse into their daily work and personal lives. Moreover, that same younger generation, showing increasing interest in remote work environments, may enter into a workplace designed for the integration of XR for anywhere workers.

The promise of an XR workplace is a promise of truly integrated technology. There is no meaningful XR or metaverse experience without my metaverse self being able to see, hear, feel, touch, and even potentially smell the same things, without realizing a difference between my physical and virtual selves (Biocca, 1997; Ancis, 2020). This technology requires vast advancement in optical, haptic, and other neurophysiological sensors. Moreover, if XR work is not only to exist in a virtual world but directly impact the physical world, then cobots, potentially working alongside the human in a physical work environment, would also come to pass. That is, if the virtual workplace mimicked an actual workplace, then a cobot could be performing work in a physical world while its collaborating human is somewhere else operating virtual or augmented reality equipment. In this coming to fruition of the digital workplace, actual on-site operations could largely be performed by cobots, but humans would be working alongside their cobots in a metaverse that largely mimicked the real storefront, warehouse, factory, hospital, chemical plant, mine, or any other work environment. Other workspaces that do not exist in the real world may be available for humans operating virtually, to have meetings, water-cooler talks, or brainstorming sessions, when not directly working with or overseeing their cobot.

Such a vision for the future of work brings to life all the potential of a metaverse for the future workplace. However, such an actualization of the concept would certainly require advancements and synergies of AI, IoT, XR, sensors, and soft robotics in addition to potential energy, Internet connection, and quantum computing technologies that go beyond the scope of this chapter.

8. Artificial Intelligence and Ethical Considerations for the Future of Work

Stephen Hawking stated, "The rise of powerful AI will either be the best or the worst thing ever to happen to humanity. We do not yet know which". AI is the capacity of machines to execute tasks that normally demand human intelligence, including learning, solving problems, generating novel ideas, and making decisions.

There has been heated debate in both academic research and media concerning whether AI in the workplace would augment human labor or automate away jobs (Kudyba *et al.*, 2020; Miller & Davenport, 2021). Automation involves utilizing technology to carry out tasks with little or no human intervention, whereas augmentation entails using technology to improve human physical or cognitive capabilities beyond what people could do without assistance. According to Frey and Osborne (2017), an estimated 35% of workers in the United Kingdom and 47% of those in the United States may be replaced by technology in the next two decades. Academics and practitioners have expressed apprehension on the potential consequences of automation and artificial general intelligence, citing the possibility of substantial job losses or even a sizable expansion of income and wealth inequality.

However, automation and augmentation might very well be two sides to the same coin. That is, the same technology that could otherwise have been used to automate away people's jobs could alternatively be deployed by management in such a way that augments employee's work. Thus, the decision becomes managerial rather than technological — whether to use AI to free up time for workers to be creative and engage meaningfully with customers, or to reap greater profits by cutting the workforce as much as can be replaced by AI.

One increasingly common use of AI in the workplace is for human resources and employee screening. Job applicants may submit their resumes online through a job application website, which are then first screened by an AI-based system prior to any person reviewing each candidate. In this instance, only candidates that meet the criteria given to the AI and succeed in its algorithmic screening process will advance to being reviewed by a human. In this scenario, each candidate must be able to (1) fully access and navigate the website to successfully submit their digital resume online and (2) provide a digital resume that passes a series of algorithmic criteria that are likely not known by the candidate and may not even be understandable to the human resources executives of the company itself.

While AI, IoT, and new, cutting-edge communication technologies hold vast potential for bringing people together, it has also proven to exacerbate any prejudice and discrimination already prevalent in society. The algorithms and datasets used to build the future of work are only as ethical and reliable as the individuals who select and/or create them. For these reasons, workplaces have been faced with typically unintended bias in their utilization of artificial intelligence systems for such purposes as performance reviews and job candidate screening. For these reasons, employers should inform their workers about how they are being surveilled, evaluated, or screened, and through which devices or algorithms their tracked information might be used.

Explainable AI (XAI) has gained popularity as one option for increasing transparency, explainability, and interoperability. AI algorithms are often discussed as a "black box", due to the difficulty in understanding how the programming of AI is often clouded in hidden layers of artificial neural networks. XAI aims to address this inherent problem of AI systems by putting forth industry best practices of creating code that is intuitive and understandable for other programmers to understand why that AI system makes the decisions and operations it does in practice. Technology design standards are another way of addressing the issue of the future of work ethics. Algorithmic and dataset concerns, in addition to societal consequences and accessibility, could all be significantly improved by a thorough consideration of responsible design during the engineering of a digital or digitally connected technology. Such design protocols have included such worthy standards as increased transparency, accessibility, control, and interpretability and have gained some traction in policy discussions as AI has entered further into public discourse.

Finally, no discussion of the future of digital technology would be complete without addressing cybersecurity. With so many cutting-edge digital technologies interfacing to create the future of work, each of their vulnerabilities offers the potential for hacking and threats to be exploited. Any such exploits could not just undermine the benefits availed by the utilization of these technologies but also cost inestimable monetary, intellectual property, and reputational harms to any organization that implements such advancements without necessary protections in place. Threats to the security of integrated systems including multiple devices and technologies may include monetary theft of online payment or virtual currency, dissemination of misinformation or disinformation, the infiltration of cloud storage, or hacking IoT devices, among many other potential concerns.

Numerous potential solutions are proposed for increasing security along digital networks and within AI systems, and the field of cybersecurity is vast and constantly growing. Some potential solutions have included the incorporation of decentralized blockchain technologies, smart contracts, enhanced encryption, and multifactor authentication. However, the security of such integrated and new technologies has great potential for vulnerability and threats. While cybersecurity evolves incredibly fast, threats to corporate and personal information security can be an impediment to the rollout of these technologies in the workplace.

In order for a future of work to truly succeed in a digital world, companies as well as their employees and customers will all need to feel confident that their online data, finances, intellectual property, and personal privacy are secured, problems that may become exponentially more difficult to resolve in light of increasing complexity of the systems needed to protect.

9. Conclusion

In conclusion, the future of work in the digital world offers unprecedented opportunities to increase productivity, drive innovation, and increase worker satisfaction on the job. This chapter suggests an architecture for the future digital workplace that includes several technologies interfacing with one another to form an integrated digital workplace, one that would be more impactful and add more value to a present workplace than any individual discussed technology would on its own.

However, the discussion of the future of work in the digital world is concluded with a brief overview of the ethical and security considerations that must be addressed for such a workplace to benefit everyone and be sustainable for all stakeholders. To that end, forward-looking public policy should be put in place to confront and prevent the significant ethical, social, and security concerns that could threaten the implementation of a truly inclusive, humane, and productive work environment. If such policies are not implemented, the risk of undermining gains in intellectual capital and production in the long term is great.

References

Abhari, K. & Eisenberg, D. (2023). Shaping the future of work: Responsible design and public policy for generative AI. *AMCIS 2023 TREOs* (Vol. 123).

Abhari, K., Xiao, B., & Eisenberg, D. (2023). Responsible digital innovation in dark: Toward access-control-transparency theory. *AMCIS 2023 Proceedings* (Vol. 25). https://aisel.aisnet.org/amcis2023/sig_adit/sig_adit/25.

Akter, S., Prodhan, R. A., Pias, T. S., Eisenberg, D., & Fresneda Fernandez, J. (2022). M1M2: Deep-learning-based real-time emotion recognition from neural activity. *Sensors*, *22*(21), 8467. https://doi.org/10.3390/s22218467.

Allen, T. D., Golden, T. D., & Shockley, K. M. (2015). How effective is telecommuting? Assessing the status of our scientific findings. *Psychological Science in the Public Interest*, *16*(2), 40–68. DOI: 10.1177/1529100615593273.

Ancis, J. R. (2020). The age of cyberpsychology: An overview. *Technology, Mind, and Behavior*, *1*(1). https://doi.org/10.1037/tmb0000009.

Biocca, F. (1997). The cyborg's dilemma: Progressive embodiment in virtual environments. *Journal of Computer-Mediated Communication*, *3*(2), 1. JCMC324. https://doi.org/10.1111/j.1083-6101.1997.tb00070.x.

Calisti, M., Picardi, G., & Laschi, C. (2017). Fundamentals of soft robot locomotion. *Journal of The Royal Society Interface*, *14*(130), 20170101. https://doi.org/10.1098/rsif.2017.0101.

Chang, S. E., Liu, A. Y., & Lin, S. (2015). Exploring privacy and trust for employee monitoring. *Industrial Management & Data Systems*, *115*(1), 88–106. https://doi.org/10.1108/imds-07-2014-0197.

Davenport, T., Guha, A., Grewal, D., & Bressgott, T. (2019). How artificial intelligence will change the future of marketing. *Journal of the Academy of Marketing Science*, *48*(1), 24–42. https://doi.org/10.1007/s11747-019-00696-0.

Daza, M. T. & Ilozumba, U. J. (2022). A survey of AI ethics in business literature: Maps and trends between 2000 and 2021. *Frontiers in Psychology*, *13*, 1042661.

Eisenberg, D., Pias, T. S., & Lee, M. J. (2022). Improving virtual classroom engagement with augmented reality filters. *ACM Journal of Computing Science in Colleges*, 38(3). https://dl.acm.org/doi/abs/10.5555/3580523.3580527.

Eisenberg, D., Pias, T. S., Fjermestad, J., & Fresneda, J. (2024). Neuromarketing techniques to enhance consumer preference prediction. *Proceedings of the 57th Hawaii International Conference on System Sciences*. https://hdl.handle.net/10125/107396.

Eisenberg, D. & Fjermestad, J. (2023). Knowledge sharing challenges for the anywhere distributed workforce. *AMCIS 2023 TREOs*, Vol. 123.

Fuller, J., Raman, M., Bailey, A., & Vaduganathan, N. (2020). Rethinking the on-demand workforce: Digital talent platforms have matured, and many companies are using them to hire skilled gig workers. Now they need to get strategic about it. *Harvard Business Review*, *2020* (November–December), 1–9.

Franken, E., Bentley, T., Shafaei, A., Farr-Wharton, B., Onnis, L., & Omari, M. (2021). Forced flexibility and remote working: Opportunities and challenges in the new normal. *Journal of Management & Organization*, *27*(6), 1131–1149. https://doi.org/10.1017/jmo.2021.40.

Hassan, R., Hasan, S., Hasan, J., Jamader, R., Eisenberg, D., & Pias, T. S. (2020). Human attention recognition with machine learning from brain-EEG signals. *2020 IEEE 2nd Eurasia Conference on Biomedical Engineering, Healthcare and Sustainability (ECBIOS)*, Tainan, Taiwan (pp. 16–19). https://doi.org/10.1109/ECBIOS50299.2020.9203672.

Howard, J., Murashov, V., Cauda, E., & Snawder, J. (2021). Advanced sensor technologies and the future of work. *American Journal of Industrial Medicine*, *65*(1), 3–11. https://doi.org/10.1002/ajim.23300.

Kudyba, S., Fjermestad, J., & Davenport, T. (2020). A research model for identifying factors that drive effective decision-making and the future of work. *Journal of Intellectual Capital*, *21*(6), 835–851. https://doi.org/10.1108/JIC-05-2019-0130.

Langenderfer, J. & Miyazaki, A. D. (2009). Privacy in the information economy. *Journal of Consumer Affairs*, *43*(3), 380–388.

Majidi, C. (2014). Soft robotics: A perspective — Current trends and prospects for the future. *Soft Robotics*, *1*(1), 5–11. https://doi.org/10.1089/soro.2013.0001.

Merola, R. (2022). Inclusive growth in the era of automation and AI: How can taxation help? *Frontiers in Artificial Intelligence*, *5*. https://doi.org/10.3389/frai.2022.867832.

Micklem, L., Weymouth, G. D., & Thornton, B. (2022). Energy-efficient tunable-stiffness soft robots using second moment of area actuation. *2022 IEEE/RSJ International Conference on Intelligent Robots and Systems (IROS)*. https://doi.org/10.1109/iros47612.2022.9981704.

Miller, S. & Davenport, T. (2021). AI and the future of work: What we know today. *The Gradient*.

Modaresnezhad, M. & Nemati, H. (2020). Participatory sensing or sensing of participation: Awareness and privacy concerns with smart device applications. *International Journal of Technology and Human Interaction (IJTHI)*, *16*(3), 124–143.

Pias, T. S., Eisenberg, D., & Islam, M. A. (2019a). Vehicle recognition via sensor data from smart devices. In *2019 IEEE Eurasia Conference on IOT, Communication and Engineering (ECICE)* (pp. 96–99). https://doi.org/10.1109/ECICE47484.2019.8942799.

Pias, T. S., Eisenberg, D., & Fresneda Fernandez, J. (2022). Accuracy improvement of vehicle recognition by using smart device sensors. *Sensors*, *22*(12), 4397. https://doi.org/10.3390/s22124397.

Pias, T. S., Kabir, R., Eisenberg, D., Ahmed, N., & Islam, M. R. (2019b). Gender recognition by monitoring walking patterns via smartwatch sensors. In *2019 IEEE Eurasia Conference on IOT, Communication and Engineering (ECICE)* (pp. 220–223). https://doi.org/10.1109/ECICE47484.2019.8942670.

Poon, T. S.-C. (2018). Independent workers: Growth trends, categories, and employee relations implications in the emerging gig economy. *Employee Responsibilities and Rights Journal*, *31*(1), 63–69. DOI: 10.1007/s10672-018-9318-8.

Pullokaran, L. J. & Joseph, P. K. (2023). Working remotely: Employees benefits and challenges. *International Journal of Engineering Technology and Management Sciences*, *7*(1), 34–37. https://doi.org/10.46647/ijetms.2023.v07i01.007.

Schwab, K. (2017). *The Fourth Industrial Revolution* (1st U.S. edn.). New York: Crown Business.

Sison, A. J. G., Daza, M. T., Gozalo-Brizuela, R., & Garrido-Merchán, E. C. (2023). ChatGPT: More than a "weapon of mass deception" ethical challenges and responses from the human-centered artificial intelligence (HCAI) perspective. *International Journal of Human–Computer Interaction*. DOI: 10.1080/10447318.2023.2225931.

Subhan, F., Mirza, A., Su'ud, M. B., Alam, M. M., Nisar, S., Habib, U., & Iqbal, M. Z. (2023). AI-enabled wearable medical internet of things in healthcare system: A survey. *Applied Sciences*, *13*(3), 1394. https://doi.org/10.3390/app13031394.

Trinidad, M., Calderon, A., & Ruiz, M. (2021). Gorace: A multi-context and narrative-based gamification suite to overcome gamification technological challenges. *IEEE Access*, *9*, 65882–65905. https://doi.org/10.1109/access.2021.3076291.

Vitak, J. & Zimmer, M. (2023). Power, stress, and uncertainty: Experiences with and attitudes toward workplace surveillance during a pandemic. *Surveillance & Society*, *21*(1), 29–44. https://doi.org/10.24908/ss.v21i1.15571.

Wang, Y., Su, Z., Zhang, N., Xing, R., Liu, D., Luan, T. H., & Shen, X. (2023). A survey on Metaverse: Fundamentals, security, and privacy. *IEEE Communications Surveys & Tutorials*, *25*(1), 319–352. https://doi.org/10.1109/comst.2022.3202047.

Youssef Abdelmajied, F. (2022). Industry 4.0 and its implications: Concept, opportunities, and future directions. *Supply Chain — Recent Advances and New Perspectives in the Industry 4.0 Era*. https://doi.org/10.5772/intechopen.102520.

Zweig, D. & Webster, J. (2002). Where is the line between benign and invasive? An examination of psychological barriers to the acceptance of awareness monitoring systems. *Journal of Organizational Behavior*, *23*(5), 605–633. https://doi.org/10.1002/job.157.

Index